BIOGRAPHICAL PREFACE

VIRGINIA WOOLF was born Adeline Virginia Stephen on 25 January 1882 at 22 Hyde Park Gate, Kensington. Her father, Leslie Stephen, himself a widower, had married in 1878 Julia Jackson, widow of Herbert Duckworth. Between them they already had four children; a fifth, Vanessa, was born in 1879, a sixth, Thoby, in 1880. There followed Virginia and, in 1883, Adrian.

Both of the parents had strong family associations with literature. Leslie Stephen was the son of Sir James Stephen, a noted historian, and brother of Sir James Fitzjames Stephen, a distinguished lawyer and writer on law. His first wife was a daughter of Thackeray, his second had been an admired associate of the Pre-Raphaelites, and also, like her first husband, had aristocratic connections. Stephen himself is best remembered as the founding editor of the *Dictionary of National Biography*, and as an alpinist, but he was also a remarkable journalist, biographer, and historian of ideas; his *History of English Thought in the Eighteenth Century* (1876) is still of great value. No doubt our strongest idea of him derives from the character of Mr Ramsay in *To the Lighthouse*; for a less impressionistic portrait, which conveys a strong sense of his centrality in the intellectual life of the time, one can consult Noël Annan's *Leslie Stephen* (revised edition, 1984).

Virginia had the free run of her father's library, a better substitute for the public school and university education she was denied than most women of the time could aspire to; her brothers, of course, were sent to Clifton and Westminster. Her mother died in 1895, and in that year she had her first breakdown, possibly related in some way to the sexual molestation of which her half-brother George Duckworth is accused. By 1897 she was able to read again, and did so voraciously: 'Gracious, child, how you gobble', remarked her father, who, with a liberality and good sense at odds with the age in which they lived, allowed her to choose her reading freely. In other respects her relationship with her father was difficult; his deafness and melancholy, his excessive emotionalism, not helped by successive bereavements, all increased her nervousness.

Stephen fell ill in 1902 and died in 1904. Virginia suffered another breakdown, during which she heard the birds singing in Greek, a language in which she had acquired some competence. On her recovery she moved, with her brothers and sister, to a house in Gordon Square, Bloomsbury; there, and subsequently at several other nearby addresses, what eventually became famous as the Bloomsbury Group took shape.

Virginia had long considered herself a writer. It was in 1905 that she began to write for publication in the *Times Literary Supplement*. In her circle (more loosely drawn than is sometimes supposed) were many whose names are now half-forgotten, but some were or became famous: J. M. Keynes and E. M. Forster and Roger Fry; also Clive Bell, who married Vanessa, Lytton Strachey, who once proposed marriage to her, and Leonard Woolf. Despite much ill health in these years, she travelled a good deal, and had an interesting social life in London. She did a little adult-education teaching, worked for female suffrage, and shared the excitement of Roger Fry's Post-Impressionist Exhibition in 1910. In 1912, after another bout of nervous illness, she married Leonard Woolf.

She was thirty, and had not yet published a book, though *The Voyage Out* was in preparation. It was accepted for publication by her half-brother Gerald Duckworth in 1913 (it appeared in 1915). She was often ill with depression and anorexia, and in 1913 attempted suicide. But after a bout of violent madness her health seemed to settle down, and in 1917 a printing press was installed at Hogarth House, Richmond, where she and her husband were living. The Hogarth Press, later an illustrious institution, but at first meant in part as therapy for Virginia, was now inaugurated. She began *Night and Day*, and finished it in 1918. It was published by Duckworth in 1919, the year in which the Woolfs bought Monk's House, Rodmell, for £700. There, in 1920, she began *Jacob's Room*, finished, and published by the Woolfs' own Hogarth Press, in 1922. In the following year she began *Mrs Dalloway* (finished in 1924, published 1925), when she was already working on *To the Lighthouse* (finished and published, after intervals of illness, in 1927). *Orlando*, a fantastic 'biography' of a man–woman, and a tribute to Virginia's close friendship with Vita Sackville-West, was written quite rapidly over the winter of 1927–8, and published, with considerable success, in October. *The Waves* was written and rewritten in 1930 and 1931 (published in October of that year). She had already started on *Flush*,

ORLANDO

MICHAEL H. WHITWORTH is a University Lecturer in English at the University of Oxford and Tutorial Fellow at Merton College, Oxford. He is the author of *Einstein's Wake: Relativity, Metaphor, and Modernist Literature* (Oxford, 2001), *Virginia Woolf* (Oxford, 2005) in the Oxford World's Classics Authors in Context series, and *Reading Modernist Poetry* (Wiley-Blackwell, 2010). He is the editor of *Modernism* (Blackwell, 2007), and has contributed a chapter on literary and popular scientific texts in *The Oxford Critical and Cultural History of Modernist Magazines* (Oxford, 2009), ed. Peter Brooker and Andrew Thacker. He is the editor of *Night and Day* for the Cambridge Edition of the Works of Virginia Woolf.

OXFORD WORLD'S CLASSICS

For over 100 years Oxford World's Classics have brought readers closer to the world's great literature. Now with over 700 titles—from the 4,000-year-old myths of Mesopotamia to the twentieth century's greatest novels—the series makes available lesser-known as well as celebrated writing.

The pocket-sized hardbacks of the early years contained introductions by Virginia Woolf, T. S. Eliot, Graham Greene, and other literary figures which enriched the experience of reading. Today the series is recognized for its fine scholarship and reliability in texts that span world literature, drama and poetry, religion, philosophy, and politics. Each edition includes perceptive commentary and essential background information to meet the changing needs of readers.

OXFORD WORLD'S CLASSICS

VIRGINIA WOOLF

Orlando
A Biography

Edited with an Introduction and Notes by
MICHAEL H. WHITWORTH

OXFORD
UNIVERSITY PRESS

OXFORD
UNIVERSITY PRESS

Great Clarendon Street, Oxford, OX2 6DP,
United Kingdom

Oxford University Press is a department of the University of Oxford.
It furthers the University's objective of excellence in research, scholarship,
and education by publishing worldwide. Oxford is a registered trade mark of
Oxford University Press in the UK and in certain other countries

Biographical Preface © Frank Kermode 1992
Chronology © David Bradshaw 2000
Introduction, Select Bibliography, Explanatory Notes © Michael H. Whitworth 2015

The moral rights of the author have been asserted

First published as a World's Classics paperback 1992

Reissued as an Oxford World's Classics paperback 1998, 2008
New edition 2015

Impression: 1

Published in the United States of America by Oxford University Press
198 Madison Avenue, New York, NY 10016, United States of America

British Library Cataloguing in Publication Data

Data available

Library of Congress Control Number: 2014941326

ISBN 978–0–19–965073–6

Printed in Great Britain by
Clays Ltd, St Ives plc

CONTENTS

ORLANDO

the story of Elizabeth Barrett Browning's pet dog—another success
with the public—and in 1932 began work on what became *The Years*.

This brief account of her work during the first twenty years of her
marriage is of course incomplete; she had also written and published
many shorter works, as well as both series of *The Common Reader*, and
A Room of One's Own. There have been accounts of the marriage very
hostile to Leonard Woolf, but he can hardly be accused of cramping
her talent or hindering the development of her career.

The Years proved an agonizingly difficult book to finish, and was
completely rewritten at least twice. Her friend Roger Fry having
died in 1934, she planned to write a biography, but illnesses in 1936
delayed the project; towards the end of that year she began instead
the polemical *Three Guineas*, published in 1938. *The Years* had meanwhile appeared in 1937, by which time she was again at work on the
Fry biography, and already sketching in her head the book that was
to be *Between the Acts*. *Roger Fry* was published in the terrifying
summer of 1940. By the autumn of that year many of the familiar
Bloomsbury houses had been destroyed or badly damaged by bombs.
Back at Monk's House, she worked on *Between the Acts*, and finished
it in February 1941. Thereafter her mental condition deteriorated
alarmingly, and on 28 March, unable to face another bout of insanity,
she drowned herself in the River Ouse.

Her career as a writer of fiction covers the years 1912–41, thirty
years distracted by intermittent serious illness as well as by the
demands, which she regarded as very important, of family and
friends, and by the need or desire to write literary criticism and social
comment. Her industry was extraordinary—nine highly-wrought
novels, two or three of them among the great masterpieces of the
form in this century, along with all the other writings, including the
copious journals and letters that have been edited and published
in recent years. Firmly set though her life was in the 'Bloomsbury'
context—the agnostic ethic transformed from that of her forebears,
the influence of G. E. Moore and the Cambridge Apostles, the individual brilliance of J. M. Keynes, Strachey, Forster, and the others—
we have come more and more to value the distinctiveness of her
talent, so that she seems more and more to stand free of any context
that might be thought to limit her. None of that company—except,
perhaps, T. S. Eliot, who was on the fringe of it—did more to estab-
lish the possibilities of literary innovation, or to demonstrate that

such innovation must be brought about by minds familiar with the innovations of the past. This is true originality. It was Eliot who said of _Jacob's Room_ that in that book she had freed herself from any compromise between the traditional novel and her original gift; it was the freedom he himself sought in _The Waste Land_, published in the same year, a freedom that was dependent upon one's knowing with intimacy that with which compromise must be avoided, so that the knowledge became part of the originality. In fact she had 'gobbled' her father's books to a higher purpose than he could have understood.

Frank Kermode

INTRODUCTION

SHOULD one read *Orlando* for its plot? Virginia Woolf's previous novel, *To the Lighthouse* (1927), notoriously lacks a 'plot' in any conventional sense: 'the issue is simply whether or not a family on holiday in the Hebrides will be able to row out to the lighthouse';[1] its focus is internal; its really significant events are changes in the minds of its characters. *Orlando*, by contrast, is external in its focus, and if plot requires things to happen to a character, there are plenty of happenings: in the reign of Queen Elizabeth I, its protagonist, a young nobleman and aspiring poet, falls in love with a string of young women and, in the reign of King James I and VI, during the Great Frost of 1608, has his heart broken by a Russian princess; he retreats to his country estate, tries to take advice from the poet Nick Greene (friend to Shakespeare and Marlowe), but finds his trust betrayed; he is appointed ambassador by King Charles II. (If at this point the prospective reader wonders how many years have elapsed, then she—or he—has noticed something significant.) While serving as ambassador, Orlando falls into a trance that lasts seven days, and wakes to find himself a woman. (The reader's doubts about the probability of the story may here be confirmed.) She lives for some time with Turkish gipsies, though there are many difficulties of mutual understanding, before returning to England in the early eighteenth century; there she struggles to adjust to her new social and legal status as a woman, and on one occasion ventures out into London at night dressed as a man. The coming of the nineteenth century deepens the limitations on her movement, though she finds love in the form of a young romantic traveller, Marmaduke Bonthrop Shelmerdine. As the nineteenth century turns to the twentieth and to Woolf's present moment of 1928, Orlando finds a kind of freedom in writing and another kind of freedom in her car; she publishes the poem she has been writing since the sixteenth century, and encounters once again Nick Greene, who has transformed himself into a respectable man of letters.

[1] Walter Allen, *The English Novel: A Critical History* (London: Phoenix House, 1954), 334.

It might reasonably be asked whether this constitutes a plot. True, Orlando's hopes are raised and dashed, his (and her) trust engaged and abused by individuals and by society, but such setbacks do not in themselves constitute a plot. It would be hard to shape *Orlando* into a Hollywood-style narrative: beginners' guides to writing screenplays and novels tell us that the protagonist should desire to accomplish a goal, should encounter successive conflicts, should find on overcoming one conflict that the stakes have been raised and another obstacle created, and should eventually reach some form of resolution. (Sally Potter's 1992 film adaptation was firmly in a European art-house tradition in which such ideas of plot are secondary.) Though Orlando desires to be a poet, that desire is not crucial to the narrative. The reader is drawn into *Orlando* not only by an interest in Orlando's stumbling encounters with the world, but by the question of the improbability of his longevity and then his change of sex. And therein lie other, subtler plots. *Orlando: A Biography*, to give the work its full title, has a narrator, a biographer who would like to make sense of Orlando's life within the confines of a conventional biography of a great man, but who at times struggles to understand his material: historical records go missing, opinions vary, and above all, the protagonist's love of writing and of the life of the imagination defies the requirement that the biography of a great man (or woman) deal in observable and documentable events. The question of whether the narrator will ever fully understand his subject is one of the subtler plots. Moreover, the narrator fails to remark upon the chronological outrage that Orlando's lifespan represents. The question of whether he will ever acknowledge the peculiarities of Orlando's narrative is a further tantalizing dynamic.

How Woolf came to devise an improbable fiction that defies expectations about longevity and gender is explained by the first words that the reader encounters after its title page: its dedication, to Vita Sackville-West. The dedication is a clue to a personal side to the novel, and a clue to some of its sources. Knowing the story of Vita and Virginia illuminates otherwise obscure references and private jokes. But it is not the whole picture: far from wanting to write for an audience of one, Woolf had other readers in mind, and indeed wished to reach as wide an audience as possible. *Orlando* tells private jokes, but it also asks public questions.

'The longest and most charming love-letter in literature'[2]

'Yesterday morning I was in despair', wrote Woolf to Sackville-West on 9 October 1927:

I couldn't screw a word from me; and at last dropped my head in my hands: dipped my pen in the ink, and wrote these words, as if automatically, on a clean sheet: Orlando: A Biography. No sooner had I done this than my body was flooded with rapture and my brain with ideas. I wrote rapidly till 12.[3]

The two writers had first met in December 1922 at a dinner hosted by Woolf's brother-in-law Clive Bell, who knew Vita and her husband, the diplomat Harold Nicolson. Vita was 30, Virginia 40. Woolf's first impressions were mixed. In her diary she described Vita as 'lovely' and 'aristocratic', but recorded that she was 'not much to my severer taste': 'florid, moustached, parakeet coloured, with all the supple ease of the aristocracy, but not the wit of the artist'.[4]

Woolf's designation 'aristocrat' was not used lightly: Vita's family could trace its origins to Herbrand de Sackville, who had come to England in 1066 with William the Conqueror.[5] Though they were slow to build on this auspicious start, the family's place in English society rose significantly with Sir Richard Sackville (d. 1566), who built the family fortune, and who became Queen Elizabeth's under-treasurer of the Exchequer. Richard's son Thomas Sackville (1536–1608) attained high office under both Elizabeth and her successor King James I and VI. It was Queen Elizabeth who in 1566 granted the Sackville family a country house and land at Knole, outside Sevenoaks in Kent. Due to the terms of an existing lease they did not gain access to the house until 1603; when they did, they remodelled it at great expense into the house that survives to the present day. At the time when Woolf first met her, Vita had recently published a history of the house, which had been her birthplace, and her family, *Knole and the Sackvilles* (1922).

Though Knole was Vita's birthplace, she knew it would not remain

---

[2] Nigel Nicolson, *Portrait of a Marriage* (1973; London: Orion, 1992), 186.

[3] Woolf, *The Letters of Virginia Woolf*, ed. Nigel Nicolson and Joanne Trautmann, 6 vols. (London: Hogarth Press, 1975–80), iii. 428.

[4] Virginia Woolf, *The Diary of Virginia Woolf*, ed. Anne Olivier Bell assisted by Andrew McNeillie, 5 vols. (London: Hogarth Press, 1977–84), ii. 216.

[5] V. Sackville-West, *Knole and the Sackvilles* (London: W. Heinemann, 1922), 29–30.

her home for ever. As she was female the family title (and with it, the estate) would not pass to her on her father's death; indeed, as Vita was her father's only child, the title passed to his brother. In Woolf's novel, the first two charges against Orlando on her return from her travels allude to Vita's situation. They are: '(1) that she was dead, and therefore could not hold any property whatsoever; (2) that she was a woman, which amounts to much the same thing' (p. 100). However, even before her father's death, Vita's hold on Knole was by no means secure, and here the third charge against Orlando comes in:

(3) that she was an English Duke who had married one Rosina Pepita, a dancer; and had had by her three sons, which sons now declaring that their father was deceased, claimed that all his property descended to them. (p. 100)

The narrative here draws on the life of Vita's maternal grandfather, Lionel Sackville Sackville-West (1827–1908), the 2nd Lord Sackville, who had fathered two sons and three daughters by a Spanish dancer Josefa de la Oliva, known as Pepita. He had not, however, married her. Pepita was already married, and at that time in Spain divorce was impossible. Vita's grandfather had fully acknowledged and provided for his daughters; one, Victoria, married her cousin, Lionel Edward Sackville-West (1867–1928), and Vita was their daughter. However, as Vita's grandfather neared the end of his life, Pepita's son Henry attempted to assemble documents that would prove that his father and mother had married; if that were so, Henry and not the younger Lionel would inherit the estate. Vita's grandfather died in 1908, and Henry's case came to the High Court in February 1910. As Vita's son Nigel Nicolson later put it, the case 'had everything': 'A family which belonged to the highest Edwardian society were quarrelling publicly about inheritance—the inheritance of one of the most historic houses and titles in England, and a large sum of money—all because a young diplomatist had fallen in love with a Spanish ballerina sixty years before, and made her his mistress.'[6] Given that Pepita never could have divorced her husband, Henry Sackville-West's claims were unlikely to succeed, as any marriage between Pepita and the elder Lionel would have been invalid, and the case was decided in favour of the younger Lionel, who became the 3rd Lord Sackville. On his death in 1928, the title passed to his brother Charles Sackville-West.

[6] Nicolson, *Portrait*, 65.

Vita had left Knole in 1913 on her marriage to Harold Nicolson. By 1922, they had homes in Kent, at Long Barn near Knole, and in London; two sons, Benedict and Nigel, had been born to them in 1914 and 1917. However, Vita had always been more strongly drawn to women than to men, and by the time of her marriage had had passionate relationships with Rosamund Grosvenor and Violet Keppel. In April 1918 she had resumed her relationship with Violet. In a memoir written in 1920, and published posthumously, Vita recalls the moment when the relationship came once again to life. Violet had been staying with her at Long Barn for about a week, when Vita changed into the masculine attire that had been adopted by wartime female farm-workers. She was overcome with excitement. Vita ran off, vaulting over gates and through the countryside, with Violet following after her, 'never taking her eyes off me'.[7] It was a moment of revelation: Vita recognized that there were two sides to her identity. Her 'femininity' was called out by Harold, but Violet had recognized another side. The woman who fell for Violet was 'a *different person*' from the one Harold knew. In her memoir, Vita theorized about sexuality. In years to come, she claimed, the sexes would gradually become indistinguishable, and relationships such as hers would no longer be seen as unnatural. She saw herself as an instance of a 'dual personality', 'in which the feminine and masculine elements alternately preponderate'.[8]

The days that Vita and Violet spent together at Long Barn were the beginning of a relationship that lasted through the summer of 1918, 'a mad and irresponsible summer of moonlight nights, and infinite escapades, and passionate letters, and music, and poetry'.[9] Towards the end of 1918 they travelled to Paris together, and the transvestism that seems to have enabled Vita's self-recognition continued, with Vita adopting the identity of 'Julian'.

I had done it once already in England; that was one of the boldest things I ever did. I will tell about it: I changed in my own house in London late one night (the darkened streets made me bold), and drove with Violet in a taxi as far as Hyde Park Corner. There I got out. I never felt so free as when I stepped off the kerb, down Piccadilly, alone, and knowing that if I met my own mother face to face she would take no notice of me. I walked

[7] Nicolson, *Portrait*, 99.   [8] Nicolson, *Portrait*, 100, 101–2.
[9] Nicolson, *Portrait*, 103.

along, smoking a cigarette, buying a newspaper off a little boy who called me 'sir', and being accosted now and then by women.[10]

In Paris with Violet, Vita 'practically lived' in the role of Julian; the couple travelled south to Monte Carlo, where a family befriended them, and, Vita believed, were hoping to catch 'Julian' as a husband for their daughter.

'Julian' had an afterlife as the name of a character—a man—in *Challenge*, a novel that Vita began collaboratively with Violet, and published under her own name in 1924; the character Eve is a portrait of Violet. (The novel had been due to be published in Britain in 1920, but Vita's mother persuaded her to suppress it.) Vita's cross-dressing also lies behind several scenes in *Orlando* where the protagonist goes out at night disguised: the first, in Turkey, does not involve cross-gender impersonation, but in the second (pp. 125–8), the female Orlando leaves her London home dressed as a man, and, like Vita, is propositioned by a prostitute.

Violet was persuaded by her mother to marry Denys Trefusis in June 1919, but she resumed her relationship with Vita a few days after the wedding. In early 1920 the couple went on a series of journeys together, first to Lincoln, then to France, to Amiens. Violet seemed set on leaving her husband, and Vita entertained the possibility of living with Violet. The elopement culminated in Denys Trefusis and Harold Nicolson flying to Amiens and attempting to persuade Violet and Vita to return to them. It was 'quite like a sensational novel', Vita's mother noted in her diary; Woolf gave a version of the incident in a letter to a friend in 1925, and it is alluded to in Chapter IV of *Orlando*, where the protagonist is said to have 'fled with a certain lady to the Low Countries where the lady's husband followed them' (p. 129).[11] Vita and Violet returned to their husbands, though the tone of Vita's memoir suggests they did so grudgingly. They were reunited for six weeks early in 1921, but after that the relationship faded.

If Woolf did not know of Sackville-West's sexuality on their first meeting, she soon did. After a 'surprise visit' from Vita and Harold in February 1923, Woolf recorded that 'She is a pronounced Sapphist'— Woolf's preferred term—'& may, thinks Ethel Sands, have an eye on

[10] Nicolson, *Portrait*, 105.
[11] Nicolson, *Portrait*, 160; Woolf, *Letters of Virginia Woolf*, ed. Nicolson and Trautmann, iii. 155.

me, old though I am.' Woolf's remarks about her in 1923 are dispar-
aging—she and Harold are 'incurably stupid', for example—but in
1924 a new tone creeps in. After lunching with Vita's father at Knole,
Woolf reflected that 'All these ancestors & centuries, & silver & gold,
have bred a perfect body. She is stag like, or race horse like, save for
the face, which pouts, & has no very sharp brain. But as a body hers is
perfection.'[12] Woolf's feelings about Vita's physique are echoed very
specifically in the comment that Orlando 'moved like a stag' (p. 76),
and in the frequent remarks about his/her handsome legs.

The friendship developed through 1925, and a period of illness
in October and November of that year, coupled with the prospect of
Vita leaving to join her husband in Persia, seems to have led Woolf
to a recognition of her full feelings. Leonard and Virginia Woolf
stayed with Vita at Long Barn for three days in December 1925, and
this appears to have been the beginning of Virginia's affair with Vita.
Woolf's physical attraction emerges in the recollected image of Vita
in a grocer's shop in Sevenoaks:

I like her & being with her, & the splendour—she shines in the grocers shop
in Sevenoaks with a candle lit radiance, stalking on legs like beech trees,
pink glowing, grape clustered, pearl hung. That is the secret of her glamour,
I suppose. Anyhow she found me incredibly dowdy, no woman cared less for
personal appearance—no one put on things in the way I did. [. . .] What is the
effect of all this on me? Very mixed. There is her maturity & full breastedness:
her being so much in full sail on the high tides, where I am coasting down
backwaters; her capacity I mean to take the floor in any company, to represent
her country, to visit Chatsworth [the Duke of Devonshire's stately home], to
control silver, servants, chow dogs; her motherhood [. . .] her being in short
(what I have never been) a real woman.[13]

Though the diary entry goes on to sound a familiar critical note about
Vita's intellect, the physical affection is unmistakable. The moment
in the grocer's recurs several times in Woolf's letters and diaries
with minor variations; the image of Vita as 'a ship in full sail' likewise
recurs, and appears in *Orlando* (p. 146), where Shelmerdine sees the
heroine in identical terms.

Between 20 January and 16 May 1926 Vita was abroad, travelling
through Iraq to Persia (present-day Iran) where Harold was serving
as a diplomat. The journey was recorded in *Passenger to Teheran*,

---

[12] Woolf, *Diary*, ii. 235, 306.   [13] Woolf, *Diary*, iii. 52.

which Leonard and Virginia Woolf's Hogarth Press published later in the year. Woolf and Vita wrote frequently to each other during Vita's absence, and the separation by no means ended the relationship. Shortly before being reunited with Vita, Woolf asks herself whether she is 'in love' with Vita, before, with a characteristic Bloomsbury reflex, asking herself to define what exactly she means by love.[14] However, though the affair continued after Vita's return, it cooled somewhat. In January 1927 Vita made a second journey to Persia, returning at the start of May. On her return she began a relationship with Mary Campbell, who with her husband Roy, a poet, was living in the garden cottage at Long Barn. Mindful of Virginia's feelings, Vita attempted to conceal the relationship from her, but eventually revealed it in November of that year.

Virginia Woolf's first idea for *Orlando* came while Vita was away on the second of her journeys to Persia. It began as an idea for a 'Defoe narrative': one dominated, Woolf's diary implies, by actions (in the style of Daniel Defoe) rather than a psychological conception of character. But developing out of this came the idea for a 'fantasy' called 'The Jessamy Brides': 'Two women, poor, solitary at the top of a house. One can see anything (for this is all fantasy) the Tower Bridge, clouds, aeroplanes.' The fantasy element would continue into *Orlando*, as would the house with the topographically impossible view across nineteen counties. She continued: 'Everything is to be tumbled in pall mall. It is to be written as I write letters at the top of my speed: on the ladies of Llangollen; on Mrs Fladgate; on people passing.' The Ladies of Llangollen, Lady Eleanor Butler (1739–1829) and the Hon. Sarah Ponsonby (1755–1831) had established a home together in north-east Wales in 1778; from their habit of wearing a Welsh countrywoman's riding clothes and hat, they were mistakenly believed to dress as men. Woolf continued:

No attempt is to be made to realise the character. Sapphism is to be suggested. Satire is to be the main note—satire & wildness. The Ladies are to have Constantinople in view. Dreams of golden domes. My own lyric vein is to be satirised. Everything mocked. And it is to end with three dots . . . so.[15]

[14] Woolf, *Diary*, iii. 87; for 'what exactly', see Michael H. Whitworth, *Virginia Woolf* (Oxford: Oxford University Press, 2005), 132–4.
[15] Woolf, *Diary*, iii. 131.

Woolf had already, in 1925, had the first intuition of another work, a 'very serious, mystical poetical work', which was to become *The Waves* (1931). In January 1927 she had completed writing *To the Lighthouse*, the most personal of her novels, in which the figure of Mrs Ramsay embodies much of her own mother, who had died in 1895 when Woolf was 13. After such a psychologically intense work, she felt the need of a rest, and 'The Jessamy Brides' was envisaged as relaxation before the next major project.

In June 1927 Woolf read an advance copy of Harold Nicolson's experiment in biography, *Some People*, in which he 'put real people in imaginary situations, and imaginary people in real situations'. She envied the way that he 'combine[d] the advantages of fact and fiction'.[16] His experiment almost certainly lies behind her idea, in September, to sketch 'like a grand historical picture, the outlines of all my friends. [. . .] It might be a way of writing the memoirs of one's own times during peoples lifetimes. It might be a most amusing book. The question is how to do it. Vita should be Orlando, a young nobleman.'[17] The projected work shared the fantasy quality with 'The Jessamy Brides' and the duality of *Some People*: 'it should be truthful; but fantastic'. Woolf envisaged including several of her closest circle: her friend Lytton Strachey, whose *Eminent Victorians* (1918) had broken decisively with the reverent tone and ponderousness of Victorian biography; Roger Fry, the artist and art-theorist; Duncan Grant, artist; Clive Bell; and her brother Adrian Stephen. This outline dates from 20 September 1927. A little over two weeks later, Woolf had a clearer idea: 'a biography beginning in the year 1500 & continuing to the present day, called Orlando: Vita; only with a change about from one sex to another'. She began writing three days later, prefacing her manuscript with a version of this outline, and adding a 'theory' 'that character goes on underground before we are born; & leaves something afterwords [*sic*] also'.[18] There is a suggestion here of doctrines of reincarnation. Like Vita, Woolf was theorizing about character in ways that broke with conventional Judaeo-Christian and humanist ideas about the self.

[16] Harold Nicolson, qtd. by Nigel Nicolson, Introduction to *Some People* (Oxford: Oxford University Press, 1983), p. vii; Woolf, *Letters*, iii. 392.

[17] Woolf, *Diary*, iii. 156–7.

[18] Woolf, *Diary*, iii. 161; Woolf, *Orlando: The Original Holograph Draft*, ed. S. N. Clarke (London: S. N. Clarke, 1993), 2.

'These charming people': Fame and Glory

Vita was not the only figure behind *Orlando*: as the novel gestated, other preoccupations were drawn into it. One, which has largely been overshadowed by the novel's concerns with sexuality and identity, was the question of literary fame. What survives of a writer after her death? How far should she court immediate popularity if it means compromising the literary value of her work? What sacrifices should a writer make in order to produce enduring work? These questions come into the novel through Orlando's perseverance with his/her poem 'The Oak Tree', through the figure (or figures) of Nick Greene and Sir Nicholas Greene, and less directly, through the treatment of Orlando's country house.

Nick Greene and Sir Nicholas Greene both speak out against the commercialization of literature, but both display double standards in doing so. Both agree that all the young writers are 'in the pay of the booksellers' (pp. 54, 162), but Nick Greene treats his visit to Orlando's home in an instrumental spirit, writing about it satirically to pay for the expenses of his wife's labour; and Sir Nicholas, 'sprucely dressed' and able to dine in the finest restaurants, appears to have achieved the degree of material security that enables noble sentiments. The novel itself seems more open to the idea that a writer might court popularity, though it is by no means rigidly committed to a position on the question.

Nick Greene's account of Marlowe and Shakespeare opens a window onto the contemporary context for the discussion of fame:

'Stap my vitals, Bill' (this was to Shakespeare), 'there's a great wave coming and you're on the top of it,' by which he meant, Greene explained, that they were trembling on the verge of a great age in English literature, and that Shakespeare was to be a poet of some importance. (p. 54)

The phrase about 'trembling on the verge' derives ultimately from an essay that Woolf had herself written in 1924, 'Character in Fiction'. The essay considered the prospects for fiction, distinguishing sharply between the 'materialists' like Arnold Bennett who wrote in a tradition of Victorian realism, and experimentalists like James Joyce whose work was open to the complexity and mutability of modern existence. In her final paragraph, Woolf had exhorted her readers to 'tolerate' the partial successes of those who experimented, because, she predicted, 'we are trembling on the verge of one of the great ages of English literature'.[19]

However, in *Orlando*, in quoting from her own essay Woolf was engaging with the work of another writer and friend, the critic Logan Pearsall Smith, who had doubted her prediction.[20] Smith, who had known Woolf since around 1910, had written to her in 1924 following the publication of 'Character in Fiction', taking issue with her conclusion. He argued that the present day did not have the 'great interest in words and excitement about them' that characterized 'great periods of English literature'.[21] In the autumn of the same year, he had taken issue with her decision to write for *Vogue*, which under the editorship of Dorothy Todd had extended its coverage beyond fashion, and had recruited many writers associated with the modernist movement. Smith felt that to write for such a periodical was to debase literature. Smith believed that writers should write only for highbrow weeklies, that they should court the approval of poets, and that they should write for 'prestige and posterity and to set a high example'. Woolf was not persuaded that writing for *Vogue* would debase her style, and was, moreover, pragmatic: 'What he wants is prestige; what I want, money.'[22]

Late in 1924 and early in 1925 Smith further criticized writers who courted publicity and who wrote for fashion magazines.[23] He fell silent on the question until 1927, when he offered Leonard and Virginia Woolf a pamphlet, *The Prospects of Literature*, which the Hogarth Press published in October of that year, just as Woolf's ideas for *Orlando* took shape. Smith took his starting point, once again, from Woolf's 'Character in Fiction', quoting again her words about 'trembling on the verge' of a great era, and repeating the point he had made privately about the lack of linguistic ferment. However, he also blamed the attitudes of contemporary publishers and readers. Smith

[19] Woolf, 'Character in Fiction', in *The Essays of Virginia Woolf*, ed. Andrew McNeillie and Stuart N. Clarke, 6 vols. (London: Hogarth, 1986–2011), iv. 436.

[20] My account here draws on my article 'Logan Pearsall Smith and *Orlando*', *Review of English Studies*, 55 (2004), 598–604. See also my *Virginia Woolf, Fame and* La Gloire (Southport: Virginia Woolf Society of Great Britain, 2012).

[21] Logan Pearsall Smith, *A Chime of Words: The Letters of Logan Pearsall Smith*, ed. Edwin Tribble (New York: Ticknor & Fields, 1984), 21.

[22] Woolf, *Letters*, iii. 154.

[23] Smith, 'Giant Fish', *New Statesman*, 24 (6 Dec. 1924), 265–6, and 'Preaching to Butterflies', *New Statesman*, 24 (14 Mar. 1925), 655–7.

claimed that the existence of a large market for literature meant that
clever young writers could rise to prominence without having to learn
their craft. The editors of weekly and daily papers seized on such
talent and tempted it into literary journalism. '[E]ven the fashion-
papers', he added, no doubt thinking of *Vogue*, 'pay them large sums
for their little essays.' Such easy rewards took young writers away
from the 'disinterested study' that might nourish their minds. Book
publishers were also to blame: by giving writers contracts for as many
as two books a year, they encouraged writers to write hastily and care-
lessly.[24] Smith's critique in *The Prospects of Literature* is clearly the
source for Nick Greene's and Sir Nicholas's opinion that writers are
in the pay of the booksellers.

Smith was also Woolf's source for Greene's distinctive concept of
la gloire. In *The Prospects of Literature* he outlines an ideal for the
writer who wishes to eschew short-term rewards: a life of dedication
to literary study and composition, which is 'crowned at last, if at all',
by 'that enduring fame which is the final reward of a rounded career';
only the artist who lives for his art and for such lasting fame, and who
spurns instant rewards and praise, will be able to undertake the necessary work.[25] Smith recognizes that 'high-sounding terms' like 'glory'
had been tainted by their use in the 1914–18 war, but nevertheless
wishes to find a word for 'enduring fame' that will differentiate it from
transient celebrity. He finds it in the French term *la gloire*, which for
him embodies a classical belief in recognition by a distant posterity.

While Smith's opinions are recognizable in the mouth of Nick
Greene, his physical person is not, and the transformation makes
a difference. Smith was closer to the suave Sir Nicholas, and Woolf
uses several adjectives for the later Greene that she also used for
Smith: both are 'pink' and 'spruce'.[26] Nick Greene, by contrast, is
conspicuous in his physicality: his nose is beaked, his chin receding;
his lips 'hung loose and slobbered'; his face is 'seamed, puckered,
and drawn together' (p. 52). His list of ailments includes 'the palsy,
the gout, the ague', and 'the dropsy'; he has 'an enlarged heart,
a great spleen, and a diseased liver' (p. 53). Mrs Greene has a tenth
child on the way (p. 57). While Nick Greene's physicality is in part
an index of Orlando's distaste, it also reminds us that creative work,

[24] Smith, *Prospects*, 13, 14.
[25] Smith, *Prospects*, 20, 26.
[26] Woolf, *Orlando*, p. 161; *Diary*, iii. 137; *Letters* ii. 358.

while it might aspire to spiritual values, must be done by embodied beings with material needs. Greene's insistence that he needs a pension of £300 a year in order to live for *gloire* comes across as lazy and self-interested—reading Cicero might be laudable, but doing it in bed is self-indulgent—but there is a serious point behind it. In *A Room of One's Own* (1929), a book-length essay closely connected to *Orlando*, Woolf contrasted the experience of dining at an impoverished women's college in Cambridge with the experience of dining at a rich college for men:

The human frame being what it is, heart, body and brain all mixed together, and not contained in separate compartments [. . .], a good dinner is of great importance to good talk. One cannot think well, love well, sleep well, if one has not dined well. The lamp in the spine does not light on beef and prunes.[27]

Nick Greene's pension of £300 a year anticipates the £500 a year that, in the later work, Woolf declares to be necessary for a woman to write fiction. That £300 in Elizabethan and Jacobean times was an immense sum is a measure of Nick Greene's greed, but his greed does not invalidate the argument that writers need to survive physically.

By October 1927, when Woolf began writing *Orlando*, she had been aware for some years of her growing public reputation. As far back as August 1922 she had the first inkling that she and Leonard Woolf were 'becoming celebrities'; it is significant that her awareness came from a tea party given by Logan Pearsall Smith, and that in the same diary entry she immediately goes on to make her first reference to Vita, who thought her 'the best woman writer'.[28] At that date Woolf had published two novels, *The Voyage Out* (1915) and *Night and Day* (1919), and a collection of experimental short fiction, *Monday or Tuesday* (1921); her third novel, *Jacob's Room* (1922), was completed and would shortly be published by the Hogarth Press. By 1927, when she first conceived of *Orlando*, she was more firmly established. After *Jacob's Room* she had published two further novels, *Mrs Dalloway* (1925) and *To the Lighthouse* (1927), and a collection of essays, *The Common Reader* (1925). In June 1927, a month after the appearance of *To the Lighthouse*, she turned in her diary again to the question of

[27] Woolf, *A Room of One's Own* and *Three Guineas*, ed. Morag Shiach (Oxford: Oxford University Press, 1992), 23.
[28] Woolf, *Diary*, ii. 187.

reputation, reflecting that she was 'almost an established figure', and that soon she would be 'a celebrated writer'. In the next paragraph, as if by a process of association, Woolf mentions Smith again, whom she had met in the previous week, 'pink & spruce, doing his trick of culture & urbanity & good sense very efficiently'.[29]

In July 1927, Leonard and Virginia Woolf reached an even larger audience when they undertook their first radio broadcast, a scripted dialogue, 'Are Too Many Books Written and Published?'.[30] Woolf joked with Vita that she might deviate from the script and accidentally allude to her affair with Mary Campbell, 'and ruin the chastity of 12 million homes'.[31] Although Woolf's readership was altogether more modest in scale, she was proud of her sales figures and her literary income. Later that July she quietly boasted to Vita that 'You'll be glad to hear I've sold 4000 of the L[ighthouse]: in America in a month: so they think I shall sell 8000 before the end of the year. And I shall make £800: (that is with luck.)'[32] The terms of Vita's teasing response are interesting for *Orlando*: 'you are a purely mercenary writer, like Michael Arlen, and think of nothing but your returns'.[33] Arlen, born Dikran Kouyoumdjian, had come to literary prominence with the publication of *The London Venture* (1920), a success that was rapidly followed by a collection of short stories, *The Romantic Lady* (1921), *'Piracy': A Romantic Chronicle of These Days* (1922), and the linked short stories of *These Charming People* (1923). He was the sort of novel-a-year writer that Logan Pearsall Smith despised; his light, witty narratives concerned the affairs of café society in London. With *The Green Hat: A Romance for a Few People* (1924), he reached even greater heights of success: it sold enormously well, was highly acclaimed, and was even the subject of several parodies including *The Green Mat: A Romance of Askew People* (1925) and *This Charming Green Hat-Fair* (1926). Arlen followed it up with further short stories in *May Fair* (1925) and with a novel, *Young Men in Love* (1927). It was in *The London Venture* that Arlen introduced the

[29] Woolf, *Diary*, iii. 137.

[30] Leonard and Virginia Woolf, 'Are Too Many Books Written and Published?', in *Essays*, vi. 609–16.

[31] Woolf, letter of 15 July 1927, repr. in *Essays*, vi. 609; the words about Mary Campbell are omitted in *Letters*, iii. 397, presumably because she was alive at the time of publication.

[32] Woolf, *Letters*, iii. 403.

[33] Sackville-West, letter of 25 July 1927, *Letters of VSW to VW*, 237.

character of Shelmerdene, a 'delightful adventuress'; the first-person narration is principally concerned with her and her many lovers, and with the narrator's attraction to her.[34] Shelmerdene and her circle were to return in *These Charming People* and *May Fair*, and Woolf's adoption of the heroine's name for Orlando's husband (albeit with a change of spelling) suggests that Arlen's success interested her. Her original intention to end the novel 'with three dots' may also be a gesture towards Arlen: *The London Venture* ends with the narrator rousing himself from his reveries over Shelmerdene and recognizing that he is in fact in London in March; his final thoughts likewise trail off with three dots. Initially Woolf may simply have wished to emulate Arlen's success, as well as Vita's; her desire to simplify her prose style, 'so that people will understand every word', indicates that she wished to reach a wider readership.[35] However, the allusion to Arlen's Shelmerdene, coupled with Greene's protests about writers being 'in the pay of the booksellers', invites the reader to consider the relation between *Orlando* and the fashionable popular novels of the time. Just as its hero/heroine moves across gender categories, so does *Orlando* move between the popular and the highbrow. *Orlando* is a long and charming love letter addressed from literary fiction to popular fiction.

A willingness to court popularity does not entail the abandonment of the desire to create enduring works. Throughout *Orlando* Woolf returns, in direct and indirect ways, to the question of the preservation of moments in history. In this, she develops a theme from *To the Lighthouse*, which is much concerned with memory and the power of art to endure. Among the most vivid images in the Great Frost episode are those of the old bumboat woman, frozen beneath the Thames 'for all the world as if she were about to serve a customer' (p. 23), and of the frozen figures in the roads and fields, 'all struck stark in the act of the moment' (p. 22). These images arrest time, but ultimately do not endure. The ice melts, and the bumboat woman drifts away. The figures in the fields may have turned to rocks, but they are no longer recognizable as people, and are turned to other uses, as landmarks, as 'scratching-posts for sheep', or as 'drinking troughs for cattle' (p. 22). Similarly, in Orlando's great house, the narrator reports

---

[34] Michael Arlen, *These Charming People* (London: Heinemann, 1920), 28.
[35] Woolf, *Diary*, iii. 131, 162.

that the remains of those accidentally locked in hidden rooms are frequently discovered 'in attitudes of great agony' (p. 43). Orlando's melancholy fascination with the family tombs introduces a variant of the theme. Considering the exploits of his ancestors, Orlando is moved to ask, 'But of all that killing and campaigning, that drinking and love-making, that spending and hunting and riding and eating, what remained? A skull; a finger' (p. 49). Likewise, Mary, Queen of Scots is reduced to what is supposedly a bloodstain on her prayer book, and, inside it, 'a lock of hair and a crumb of pastry', to which Orlando adds 'a flake of tobacco' (p. 102).

What endures? One answer is that human structures and monuments endure. There is a brief glimpse of this answer in the almshouses that Orlando endows as repentance for his dalliance with Sukey; they are 'still standing' as 'the visible fruit' of that moment (p. 20). A more sustained version of it comes when, in Chapter II, Orlando becomes disillusioned with the literary life and with the pursuit of fame. The narrator paraphrases Orlando's extravagant images: 'The pith of his phrases was that while fame impedes and constricts, obscurity wraps about a man like a mist; obscurity is dark, ample, and free; obscurity lets the mind take its way unimpeded' (p. 62). Orlando delights in the prospect of 'being like a wave which returns to the deep body of the sea' (p. 62). In this moment, there appears before him like a revelation the sight of his ancestral home, more like a town than a house. Although the narrator says it was built 'by a single architect with one idea in his head' (p. 63), the description emphasizes the multifariousness of the buildings and the anonymity of the workmen who built it. The building was made, 'Orlando thought, by workmen whose names are unknown. [. . .] Not one of these Richards, Johns, Annes, Elizabeths has left a token of himself behind him, yet all, working together with their spades and their needles, their love-making and their child-bearing, have left this' (p. 63). In its praise of anonymous labour the passage anticipates Woolf's remarks about the literary tradition in *A Room of One's Own*: 'masterpieces are not single and solitary births; they are the outcome of many years of thinking in common, of thinking by the body of the people, so that the experience of the mass is behind the single voice'.[36] But just as that passage implicitly sees the masterpiece as

[36] Woolf, *A Room of One's Own and Three Guineas*, 85.

more valuable than the anonymous work, so too Orlando returns after his years spent building to writing 'The Oak Tree'. And in the passage where Orlando considers the tombs of his ancestors, he realizes that while 'they and their deeds were dust', the words of Sir Thomas Browne that he has just read 'were immortal' (p. 50).

Orlando: A Biography

When *Orlando* was first published, its jacket and title page gave prominence to its subtitle: *A Biography*. Unlike Woolf's three previous novels, which had been published in the United Kingdom in jackets designed by her sister Vanessa Bell, *Orlando* appeared with a jacket which attempted to mimic a respectable work of biography or history: the Roman typeface was austere, as was the black-and-white portrait of a bearded nobleman holding his sword aloft. Inside, *Orlando* has all the conventional elements of a biography. Woolf recruited her niece and Vita to pose for black-and-white illustrations of Orlando, as well as using other paintings. She included a Preface, which appears to thank those who assisted her in her research, though the novel had not been researched in any meaningful sense of the word; she included a Contents page and even an Index.

As the novel neared its publication day, Woolf feared that she and the Hogarth Press would regret their efforts at mimicry. Alice Ritchie, responsible for taking samples of the Press's new works to bookshops, reported back that 'No one wants biography'. Though she protested that it was a novel, the booksellers responded that, as it called itself a biography on the title page, it would have to go on their biography shelves. 'I doubt', recorded Woolf, 'that we shall do more than cover expenses—a high price to pay for the fun of calling it a biography. And I was so sure that it was going to be the one popular book!'[37] Although in fact the book sold well, its generic identity also roused the interest of critics. Not only does it cross boundaries between the popular and the highbrow, but it crosses boundaries between genres. As Conrad Aiken wrote, 'In England as well as in America it has set the critics by the ears. They have not known quite how to take it—whether to regard it as a biography, or a satire on biography; as a history, or a satire on history; as a novel, or as an

---

[37] Woolf, *Diary*, iii. 198.

allegory.'[38] For other reviewers it was 'fantasy', or a 'play of fancy, a wild fantasia, a romance, a high-brow lark'.[39] What the reviewers meant by 'fantasy' was not always defined, but the term had different parameters from present-day definitions of the genre: certainly the associations that accrued to 'fantasy' after J. R. R. Tolkien's *The Hobbit* (1937) were not known in the 1920s. Aiken felt *Orlando* had something in common with *Alice in Wonderland*; J. C. Squire compared it to Enid Bagnold's *Serena Blandish* (1924), to Elinor Wylie's *The Venetian Glass Nephew* (1925), which Vita had lent Virginia in July 1926, and to the tales of David Garnett, among which he was almost certainly thinking of *Lady into Fox* (1922), a novella in which the narrator treats a fantastic transformation with a matter-of-factness that anticipates *Orlando*.[40] One might also note Vita Sackville-West's own *Seducers in Ecuador* (1924), published by the Hogarth Press, in which Arthur Lomax's perceptions and decisions are shaped by the tinted sunglasses that he wears; Sylvia Townsend Warner's *Lolly Willowes* (1926), in which a woman sells her soul to the devil; or, slightly post-dating *Orlando*, Rebecca West's *Harriet Hume: A London Fantasy* (1929). Brian Richardson has suggested that *Seducers in Ecuador* might be termed an 'intellectual fable', a form deriving from the eighteenth-century French *contes philosophiques* ('philosophic tales'), of which Voltaire was the best-known practitioner.[41] In the late nineteenth- and early twentieth-century revival of the form he includes works more often classified as Gothic—Robert Louis Stevenson's *Dr Jekyll and Mr Hyde* (1886) and Oscar Wilde's *The Picture of Dorian Gray* (1890)—and others like G. K. Chesterton's *The Man Who Was Thursday: A Nightmare* (1908) that have largely escaped categorization. The term 'romance', invoked by Arnold Bennett in his review of *Orlando*, covers similar territory: in the jacket copy for *The Green Child*:

[38] Conrad Aiken, repr. in Robin Majumdar and Allen McLaurin (eds.), *Virginia Woolf: The Critical Heritage* (London: Routledge & Kegan Paul, 1975), 234.

[39] Desmond MacCarthy and Arnold Bennett, repr. in Majumdar and McLaurin (eds.), *Critical Heritage*, 222, 232; see also Anon. [Arthur Sydney McDowall], 'Orlando', *TLS*, 11 Oct. 1928, 729.

[40] Aiken and J. C. Squire, reprinted in Majumdar and McLaurin (eds.), *Critical Heritage*, 235, 227. Squire writes 'The Venetian Glass Lady', but presumably intends Wylie's novel; for Woolf's reading it, see *Letters*, iii. 279–80, 282, 284.

[41] Brian Richardson, 'Remapping the Present: The Master Narrative of Modern Literary History and the Lost Forms of Twentieth-Century Fiction', *Twentieth Century Literature*, 43/3 (Autumn 1997), 300.

A Romance (1935), Herbert Read explained further that 'The author deliberately rejects the naturalistic conception of fiction, with its dependence on character-building, psychology, truth-to-life, etc., in favour of a more metaphysical conception depending on phantasy, ideas, and the life of the imagination.'[42] These works of modernist fantasy share with high modernist fiction a dissatisfaction with realism, but reach a solution that makes gentler demands on its readers.

The capaciousness of the fantasy-romance mode allows Woolf to incorporate and mock other genres. Above all, *Orlando* mocks biography, a mode that Woolf was deeply familiar with from her earliest childhood, her father having begun work on the *Dictionary of National Biography* in the year of her birth, 1882. The *Dictionary*, which by 1900 had run to sixty-three volumes covering over 29,000 people, aimed to provide a comprehensive record of the great figures of British history. *Orlando* questions whether its scrupulously scholarly approach to fact reaches the truth: 'The true length of a person's life, whatever the *Dictionary of National Biography* may say, is always a matter of dispute' (p. 177). Woolf also takes aim at conventional book-length biography, and particularly the reverential and at times censorious attitudes that it embodied. Her friend Lytton Strachey had already demonstrated the need for innovation in his *Eminent Victorians* (1918). Woolf's first truly experimental novel, *Jacob's Room*, has been termed by Judy Little a parodic *Bildungsroman*, but can also be seen as parodic biography, and thus a forerunner to *Orlando*. Like the narrator of *Orlando*, the narrator of *Jacob's Room* at times seems unable to penetrate to the essence of his subject and unable to provide a comprehensive account of his life; he attempts to conceal his ignorance with generic scenes and even with outright denials: 'But there is no need to think of them grown old', he remarks of a group of students, by way of attempting to conceal the recognition that they have died in the 1914–18 war.[43] While in *Jacob's Room* the parody is conducted in a spirit of bitterness, in *Orlando* the tone is much lighter. The conventional role of the biographer is set out by the narrator in the opening pages: Orlando, as one destined for the conventional career of a great man, is a biographer's ideal: 'From deed to deed, from glory to glory, from office to office he must go, his

[42] Jacket copy on Heinemann's 1935 edition of *The Green Child: A Romance*, by Herbert Read.
[43] Woolf, *Jacob's Room*, ed. Kate Flint (Oxford: Oxford University Press, 1992), 55.

scribe following after, till they reach whatever seat it may be that is
the height of their desire' (p. 12). Later, the narrator reiterates that
it is the duty of a biographer 'to plod, without looking to right or
left, in the indelible footprints of truth' (p. 41). However, Orlando's
eyes 'like drenched violets' suggest a different side to his nature, one
of those 'thousand disagreeables which it is the aim of every good
biographer to ignore' (p. 12). For Vita and those in her circle, the
phrase about 'drenched violets' glances at Violet Trefusis, and the
'disagreeable' is lesbianism; but for the general reader the sentence
refers to any inaccessible aspect of the human self. The biographer's
subject will always, it seems, escape the ability of language and the
conventions of biography. The self is plural, but biography, to render
a coherent narrative, must simplify it: Orlando is 'compounded of
many humours' (p. 45). At times the narrator hints that the problem
is a wider one, that 'Nature and letters' have 'a natural antipathy'
(p. 13). Other subjects, particularly female ones, escape the biographer's sights altogether: of Orlando's lover, 'we know no more than
Queen Elizabeth herself did what her name was' (p. 19). Woolf here
hints at a theme that runs throughout her writing, and which she
expounds with particular force in *A Room of One's Own*, the omission
of women from literary and social history. The writer, too, can easily escape the biographer's attention, as we see in the passage in the
final chapter when Orlando finally settles down to work on 'The Oak
Tree': 'Life . . . is the only fit subject for novelist or biographer', but
life 'has nothing whatever to do with sitting still in a chair and thinking' (p. 155). If there is an inner logic connecting the novel's concerns
with sexuality and its concerns with writing, it is that the 'poet' can,
in an ideal world, reconcile her innermost identity with her public
utterances and public persona; in that ideal world, the poet's innermost identity is accepted and understood for what it is, not tolerated
or patronized. In this ideal world, the poet does not feel 'some power
. . . reading over her shoulder' telling her what is acceptable and what
is 'contraband' (p. 154); in this ideal world, the poet does not have
her life distorted or censored to fit preconceptions of a life-narrative.

   The claims of biography to penetrate to the essence of a biographical subject are called into question by the notion that the self is never
truly authentic, but is always in some sense performative. Woolf's
concern with costume and transvestism in *Orlando* serves to fore-
ground this sense of the self, which in many ways anticipates later

twentieth-century literary theory.[44] There had been hints of this idea in Woolf's earlier novels, and there the interior mode of presentation makes it hard to distinguish between deception of others and self-deception: in *Mrs Dalloway* Peter Walsh sees himself as swaggering 'buccaneer', as a young man (although he is in his fifties), and a man of great 'susceptibility'; but he also acknowledges the artificiality of his fantasies about himself, and that one is constantly 'making oneself up'.[45] In *To the Lighthouse*, the philosopher Mr Ramsay imagines himself as an explorer and mountaineer, and unlike Peter Walsh, he offers us no commentary on this identity. *Orlando*'s external narrative focus allows a different perspective on performativity. The ambiguity of Orlando's clothes in the opening scene and the more pronounced ambiguity of Sasha's attire in the Great Frost scenes both hint that gender identity might be a performance, that the clothes do not so much express identity as create it. The idea is confirmed when the Archduchess Harriet removes her riding habit and reveals herself to be the Archduke Harry; whereas before, the female Orlando had been politely veiling her antipathy to Harriet, on first seeing Harry she stereotypically feels faint, while Harry goes down on bended knee and begs for forgiveness: as the narrator comments, 'they acted the parts of man and woman for ten minutes with great vigour' (p. 106). When Harry proposes marriage and bursts into tears, the performativity is expressed as a social imperative: Orlando 'was beginning to be aware that women should be shocked when men display emotion in their presence, and so, shocked she was' (p. 106). Social class is also presented as a performance: the sprucely dressed Sir Nicholas Greene, with his pink flower in his buttonhole and his grey suede gloves, is dressed as a gentleman; when he bows, Orlando reflects that the bow might have been 'a thought overdone', but 'the imitation of fine breeding was creditable' (p. 161). However, whereas for some theorists of performativity the self is a performance to its very depths, for Woolf there is some sort of true self beneath the façade: after Orlando and Harry have acted the parts of man and woman, they fall into 'natural discourse' (p. 106). The natural self, it appears, is without gender. Although, as Pamela Caughie has cautioned, Orlando is

---

[44] Most prominently, Judith Butler's account of performative identity in her *Gender Trouble: Feminism and the Subversion of Identity* (New York and London: Routledge, 1990).
[45] Woolf, *Mrs Dalloway*, 46.

not theoretically consistent, questioning but never quite endorsing models of identity, whether they concern transvestism, androgyny, or transsexuality,[46] at this point *Orlando* anticipates *A Room of One's Own* and its speculation as to whether 'there are two sexes in the mind corresponding to the two sexes in the body', and its suggestion that Coleridge was right in saying that 'a great mind is androgynous'.[47] In an ideal world, this implies, there would be no performances of gender. The task of the biographer is not impossible, but he or she must aim to see beyond the superficial trappings of gender.

As well as questioning the veracity of biography, *Orlando* mocks historical writing. As with biography, it does so from a well-informed position. Woolf had been a voracious reader of history in her teenage years, reading in 1897 at least nine of the twelve volumes of J. A. Froude's *History of England from the Fall of Wolsey to the Defeat of the Spanish Armada* (1856–70); one of her earliest ambitions had been to write a solid historical work.[48] She may well have read J. R. Green's *History of the English People* (1877–80), which is one possible source for the anecdote about Queen Elizabeth rebuking Robert Cecil as a 'little man' (p. 136). In more specific preparation for writing *Orlando*, Woolf read Vita Sackville-West's *Knole and the Sackvilles*.[49] It gave her numerous details about the house and family, some of which are noted in the annotations to the present edition, and also gave her an example of scrupulously documented historical writing to mock. The 'tedious' catalogues of expenditure on Orlando's home (p. 65) are drawn almost verbatim from *Knole and the Sackvilles*, though Woolf's persistent tendency is to inflation: for the pair of Spanish blankets in Vita's text, Woolf has fifty; Vita's single box containing '3 dozen of Venice glasses' becomes 'seventeen dozen boxes containing each dozen five dozen of Venice glasses'.[50] As well as making such highly specific and almost private jokes, Woolf engages more broadly with historical writing. Her narratorial voice parodies that of a moralizing historian, warning the reader 'that crime and poverty

---

[46] Pamela Caughie, *Virginia Woolf and Postmodernism: Literature in Quest & Question of Itself* (Urbana : University of Illinois Press, 1991).

[47] Woolf, *A Room of One's Own and Three Guineas*, 127–8.

[48] Woolf, *A Passionate Apprentice*, ed. Mitchell A. Leaska (1990), 117, 128; Katherine C. Hill, 'Virginia Woolf and Leslie Stephen: History and Literary Revolution', *PMLA* 96 (1981), 354.

[49] Woolf, letter to VSW, 9 Oct. 1927, *Letters*, iii. 429.

[50] Vita Sackville-West, *Knole and the Sackvilles*, 95–6.

had none of the attraction for the Elizabethans that they have
for us' (p. 20), and that Elizbethan morals were not ours (p. 18).
Moreover, although at times one historical epoch succeeds another
almost imperceptibly, the passage of time being mentioned only par-
enthetically, at the transition from the eighteenth to the nineteenth
century, the transition is prominent and parodically instantaneous:
the former is understood as light, clarity, and order, while the latter
is cloudiness, confusion, and damp. The division of the flux of history into distinct epochs may be convenient for writers of histories,
but it distorts the reality of time. In this, the chapter division is
cousin to the clocks of Harley Street in *Mrs Dalloway*, '[s]hredding
and slicing, dividing and subdividing' time.[51] Woolf's sprinkling of
the text with archaic terms might be read as producing authenti-
city, but can produce the effect of setting Orlando's life not in real
history, but in a received version of history, a costume pageant of
'our island story'.[52] One prominent instance of such shaping comes
when Captain Bartolus believes he has seen Joseph Addison, John
Dryden, and Alexander Pope taking coffee at the same coffee house.
Improbable in terms of their relative ages and their political affili-
ations, the conjunction of three great writers of the late seventeenth
and early eighteenth centuries is a fact of literary periodization, not
actual events. At times the narrator appears to subscribe to ideas of
periodization, as in the passage where he explains that Orlando had
been naturally inclined to 'the Elizabethan spirit, to the Restoration
spirit, to the spirit of the eighteenth century', and was antipathetic to
the spirit of the nineteenth century. But the general effect is to leave
the confident generalizations of the historian looking as questionable
as those of the biographer.

'Why not simply say what one means and leave it?'

In writing *Orlando*, Woolf deliberately adopted a prose style more
suited to its comic tone, its emphasis on exterior events, and her
desire to reach a wider audience. 'I am writing Orlando half in a mock
style very clear & plain, so that people will understand every word',
she wrote in her diary in October 1927. A month later she reflected

---

[51] Woolf, *Mrs Dalloway*, 87.
[52] The phrase was the title of 'a child's history' of England by H. E. Marshall, published 1905.

that she liked the 'plain sentences' she had found herself writing, and, shortly after its publication, she recorded that writing it had taught her 'how to write a direct sentence'.[53]

The idea that every word might be understood is generous in its expectations of her audience's vocabulary. In practice, Woolf brings an air of period flavour to some chapters, particularly the Elizabethan, by employing archaic vocabulary, some of it familiar even to readers not directly acquainted with Elizabethan texts (for example '"Twas' (p. 23) and 'popinjay' (p. 26)), and others less common, such as 'sennight' (p. 31), 'orgulous' (p. 30), the '*massy* square of the Tower buildings' (p. 32). She uses relatively obscure terms for fabrics ('drugget' and 'hodden') and for dances (the 'corantoe' and 'lavolta'). The novel is particularly rich in terms for outmoded forms of transport, from the palanquin of the Jacobean era to the barouches and broughams of Victorian and Edwardian England, all building up to Orlando's climactic car journey home.

Woolf not only introduces archaic words, but at times aims to reproduce archaic phrasing: the inversions of 'hodden brown' (p. 15) and 'Many a time did Orlando . . . hold his heart' (p. 36) for example, and idioms such as 'not a straw' (p. 31), a phrase familiar from Shakespeare's *The Winter's Tale*. In her doubling of epithets—'the hard and consolidated sky' (p. 37), 'the huge and massy fragments' (p. 38), 'the whole boundary and circumference' (p. 45)—she mimics a distinctive feature of Shakespeare's style, the pairing of almost synonymous words, one deriving from Anglo-Saxon, the other from Latin. Woolf happily breaks the rule about derivation—'huge' and 'massy' both come from French—suggesting that her aim is more to evoke Shakespearean style than scrupulously to recreate it. As Orlando leaves behind the Shakespearean age, he grows suspicious of his own stylistic devices, and through him Woolf turns to mocking the device she had deployed. '"And if literature is not the Bride and Bedfellow of Truth, what is she? Confound it all," he cried, "why say Bedfellow when one's already said Bride? Why not simply say what one means and leave it?"' (pp. 60–1).

A similar scepticism creeps into the text in relation to simile. As a young man, Orlando is delighted to compare Sasha to 'a melon, a pineapple, an olive tree, an emerald, and a fox in the snow' (p. 24),

[53] Woolf, *Diary*, iii. 162, 164, 203.

but when as a woman of 30 or more she exercises the same facility, the text is more explicit about the shortcomings of comparison:

She likened the hills to ramparts, to the breasts of doves, and the flanks of kine. She compared the flowers to enamel and the turf to Turkey rugs worn thin. Trees were withered hags, and sheep were grey boulders. Everything, in fact, was something else (p. 86)

The narrator grows weary of such comparison making, and a few pages later remarks that 'if we must compare the landscape to anything, it would have been to a dry bone; to a sheep's skeleton; to a gigantic skull' (pp. 89–90). In passages like these, through its self-awareness about style, *Orlando* sensitizes the reader to stylistic effect and to the artificiality of style.

In *Orlando*, Woolf's prose delights in multifariousness and accumulated detail. Whereas in *To the Lighthouse* her syntax had been intricate, registering in subordinated clauses the complex working of minds, here, even in long sentences, the syntactic skeleton is relatively simple, consisting of one phrase placed in parallel to another. A simple example occurs in the epithets Orlando heaps upon Sasha: the list could continue indefinitely; the reader soon recognizes the interchangeability of the epithets and the simplicity of the syntax. Or take a longer sentence from Chapter II:

He lay as if in a trance, without perceptible breathing; and though dogs were set to bark under his window; cymbals, drums, bones beaten perpetually in his room; a gorse bush put under his pillow; and mustard plasters applied to his feet, still he did not wake, take food, or show any sign of life for seven whole days. (p. 41)

The ultimate outcome of the sentence is clearly signalled by 'and though'; we can easily guess that, though various things were done, Orlando remained in a trance, and so we are free for the rest of the sentence to enjoy the diverse absurdities visited upon him. Each of the four passive verbs ('set', 'beaten', 'put', and 'applied') is followed by a preposition indicating where the activity took place: once again, consciously or otherwise, we recognize the pattern. Throughout the novel Woolf makes extensive use of antithesis, not as a means of establishing sharp contrasts, but to create a sense of the breadth of her canvas. In the long passage at the end of Chapter I describing the melting of the Frost Fair, the various fates of those carried away in the

melting ice are lightly framed by 'Some . . . others', then 'Sometimes
. . . At other times', and by contrasts between individuals ('One old
man', 'a solitary wretch', 'An old nobleman') and generalized groups
('Others', 'Many') (pp. 38–9).

Woolf recognized and distrusted her own facility as she wrote the
novel, and in places in *Orlando* her distrust is channelled into self-
mockery. As Orlando examines the bones of his ancestors, he specu-
lates who one particular bone belonged to:

'Whose hand was it?' he went on to ask. 'The right or the left? The hand
of man or woman, of age or youth? Had it urged the war horse, or plied the
needle? Had it plucked the rose, or grasped cold steel? Had it——' but
here either his invention failed him or, what is more likely, provided him
with so many instances of what a hand can do that he shrank, as his wont
was, from the cardinal labour of composition, which is excision (p. 44)

The remark about 'the cardinal labour of composition' does not
appear in the manuscript, though the uncontrollably multiplying
examples do, and may belong to the revision stage. After she had
completed the first draft, Woolf was concerned that the work had
grown 'too long for a joke, & too frivolous for a serious book'; after
correcting the proofs in June 1928, she found that she detested her
own volubility: 'Why be always spouting words'.[54] Yet, at least in the
passage just quoted, the revision process led to Woolf spouting more
words in comment on the existing ones. The spirit of *Orlando* is one
of generous superfluity.

Reception

In numerical terms, *Orlando* achieved the popularity that Woolf had
sought. In its first six months it sold twice as many as *To the Lighthouse*
had done in its first year, and it was highly successful in the United
States.[55] Looking back, Leonard Woolf saw it as 'the turning point'
in Woolf's career as 'a successful novelist'.[56] The financial success of

---

[54] Woolf, *Diary*, iii. 177, 186.
[55] B. J. Kirkpatrick and Stuart N. Clarke, *A Bibliography of Virginia Woolf*, 4th edn.
(Oxford: Clarendon Press, 1997), 60–3; Julia Briggs, *Virginia Woolf: An Inner Life*
(London: Allen Lane, 2005), 212. See the Note on the Text for further details.
[56] Leonard Woolf, *An Autobiography*, 2 vols. (Oxford: Oxford University Press, 1980),
ii. 292.

the novel had an immediate impact on Virginia's life: in April 1929 she and Leonard had an additional two rooms built at Monks House, and in June 1929 briefly contemplated buying a tumbledown house in the south of France; her earnings were a source of pride.[57] Quite apart from the financial aspects, the success of *Orlando* gave Woolf a greater sense of her place as a writer: 'I have become two inches & a half higher in the public view', she wrote in her diary soon after publication; 'I am now among the well known writers.'[58]

Immediate critical reactions were more mixed, though as Woolf had always had her detractors and admirers, this was not unexpected. Most critics recognized that *Orlando* broke away from the line of development established from *Jacob's Room* through *To the Lighthouse*, though they differed on how complete the break was. For Henry Seidel Canby, there was a continuity with the earlier novels, 'in which time is made to move at a snail's pace'.[59] Dorothy Brewster took her cue from Woolf's essay 'Mr Bennett and Mrs Brown', and felt that many of her earlier novels had an equivalent to the elusive Mrs Brown, challenging novelist and reader to 'come and catch me if you can'; Orlando was merely the latest incarnation, and demonstrated that Woolf was 'not seeking to capture characters, but life'.[60] For Woolf's friend Desmond MacCarthy, who confessed to having been 'a reluctant admirer' of the earlier novels, the break with the 'raw stuff of life' allowed Woolf to escape from something that had previously burdened her, and allowed her 'lyric fantasy' and her 'power of soaring or ironic description' to reach their 'greatest perfection'.[61] By implication there was continuity with the moments of fantasy and description in the earlier novels. For J. C. Squire, on the other hand, Woolf was a writer who had 'not previously inclined to fairy tale or phantasy', and the novel appeared something of an anomaly. Squire acknowledged many of the novel's strengths, such as the readable quality of her prose and the inventiveness of her stylistic

---

[57] Woolf, *Diary*, iii. 232.

[58] Woolf, *Diary*, iii. 201.

[59] Henry Seidel Canby, 'Orlando, a Biography', *Saturday Review of Literature*, 3 November 1928; repr. in Eleanor McNees (ed.), *Virginia Woolf: Critical Assessments*, 4 vols. (Mountfield: Helm Information, 1994), 416–21.

[60] Dorothy Brewster, 'The Wild Goose', *The Nation* [New York], 28 Nov. 1928, 577–8; repr. in McNees (ed.), *Virginia Woolf*, 424–5.

[61] Desmond MacCarthy, review for *The Sunday Times*, repr. in Majumdar and McLaurin (eds.), *Virginia Woolf: The Critical Heritage*, 225.

flexibility; his praise of it as 'a thread on which many bright beads are strung' suggests that the accumulative, appositive quality of the prose noted earlier is also a quality of the plot: it is loosely knit and episodic. However, ultimately, he felt that Woolf seemed unconvinced by her own joke: the novel had a quality of 'fatigued grace' and a lack of 'gusto'. Although this view chimed with Woolf's own doubts about the novel, she was unmoved by it: 'I felt the rock of self esteem untouched in me.'[62] She was further buoyed up by reviews from Rebecca West and Hugh Walpole: the former termed it 'a poetic masterpiece of the first rank', terms of praise which suggest a continuity with the lyricism of the earlier novels; the latter was so confident of its place in literary history that his review, 'On a Certain New Book', praised it without giving either the title or the author.[63]

Vita Sackville-West, the recipient of 'the longest and most charming love letter in history', responded almost immediately after publication. 'I can't say anything except that I am completely dazzled, bewitched, enchanted, under a spell. It seems to me the loveliest, wisest, *richest* book that I have ever read. [. . .] I feel like one of those wax figures in a shop window, on which you have hung a robe stitched with jewels. It is like being alone in a dark room with a treasure chest full of rubies and nuggets and brocades.' As a *post scriptum* she added 'You made me cry with your passages about Knole, you wretch.'[64] Harold Nicolson was also pleased with it, writing to Vita that 'The whole world of life has been poured into it, flashing with molten flames', and saying a few days later that 'It really *is* Vita—her puzzled concentration, her absent-minded tenderness . . . She strides magnificent and clumsy through 350 years.'[65] Vita's mother took against it, writing to Woolf that she had been cruel, and that Vita had been still crueller. In her own copy she pasted a photograph of Virginia, describing it as 'The awful face of a mad woman whose successful mad desire is to separate people who care for each other.'[66]

    [62] J. C. Squire, repr. in Majumdar and McLaurin (eds.), *Virginia Woolf: The Critical Heritage*, 227, 229; Woolf, *Diary*, iii. 2000.

    [63] Woolf, *Diary*, iii. 2000 (n. 3).

    [64] Vita Sackville-West, letter to Virginia Woolf, 11 Oct. 1928, *Letters of VSW to VW*, 304–6.

    [65] Vita Sackville-West, letter to Virginia Woolf, 15 Oct. 1928, *Letters of VSW to VW*, 307; Harold Nicolson, letter to Virginia Woolf, 15 Oct. 1928, quoted in Woolf, *Letters*, iii. 548 (n. 1).

    [66] Lady Sackville, quoted in Woolf, *Letters*, iii. 548.

As Logan Pearsall Smith was one of the models for Nick and Sir Nicholas Greene, it would be valuable to know his reaction, but, if he recorded it, it has not survived. (One of the other possible models, Sir Edmund Gosse, had died earlier in 1928, before the novel was published.) However, at the time of its publication his friend Cyril Connolly recorded in his journal the names of twelve friends who were 'Against *Orlando*', and Smith's name appeared at the head of the list.[67] Moreover, there appears to have been a distinct cooling of relations between Woolf and Smith that lasted until 1932.

Given the initial success of *Orlando*, one might have expected its place in Woolf's canon of works to be assured. However, for several reasons it endured a long period of critical neglect, before rising in critical prominence in the 1980s. Although Woolf's publication of her mock-biography of Elizabeth Barrett Browning's spaniel, *Flush* (1933), did something to make *Orlando* seem less anomalous in her oeuvre, by creating a subcategory of biographies among her works, it equally furthered the separation of *Orlando* from the other novels. Although the Hogarth Press's lists of Woolf's works included *Orlando* among the novels, not all critics agreed. Joan Bennett's influential early critical book (1945) scarcely mentions it, and lists it not under 'The Novels', but (along with *Flush* and Woolf's collections of essays), under 'Other Works'. It was not until 1955 that any scholarly work appeared on it, in the form of notes that treated the novel as a *roman-à-clef*, and suggested that there were real-life sources in the Sackville family for several of the characters.[68] It is clear that to discuss *Orlando* is to discuss sexuality, and almost unavoidably to touch on Woolf's relationship with Vita Sackville-West. It may be that while Vita lived critics felt unable to acknowledge the obvious. Jean Guiguet's study, first published in French in 1962, the year of Vita's death, is delicately indirect in referring to Virginia's bisexuality. Moreover, the dominance of the New Criticism, and in particular its belief that literary works should be studied in themselves, separately from biographical information about their authors, inhibited the study of works that needed to be informed by a particular biographical context.

The publication of Vita's memoir about Violet Trefusis, as part of Nigel Nicolson's *Portrait of a Marriage*, along with a liberalization of

[67] D. Pryce-Jones (ed.), *Cyril Connolly: Journal and Memoir* (London, 1983), 180.
[68] Frank Baldanza, 'Orlando and the Sackvilles', *PMLA* 70 (1955), 274–9; David Bonnell Green, 'Orlando and the Sackvilles: Addendum', *PMLA* 71 (1956), 268–9.

social attitudes to sexuality in the English-speaking world, made possible a more complete understanding of *Orlando*. In the first instance the effect was to encourage the treatment of *Portrait of a Marriage* as a new key to the novel.[69] But larger assessments soon began to appear: among the earliest to see the novel as part of a lost tradition of lesbian writing was Blanche Wiesen Cook; other accounts emphasizing Woolf's sexuality came from Jane Marcus and Sherron E. Knopp.[70]

By the late 1980s, *Orlando*'s parodies of biography and history made it seem a work that anticipated postmodern writing; its questioning of categories of fact and fiction seemed to align it with writers of metafiction from the 1960s and 1970s such as John Barth; its awareness that we see the world through the categories of language anticipates the post-structuralist form of the 'linguistic turn' in philosophy; in its matter-of-fact treatment of fantastic events it seemed to anticipate magic realist fiction. If there is a problem with such approaches, it is that they find *Orlando* valuable for its anticipation of later movements, rather than for its relation to its contemporary culture. More recent critical works have tended to return *Orlando* to its historical moment, while recognizing qualities more commonly associated with other eras. The Turkish episodes speak to twenty-first-century concerns with nationhood and national identity, and—as it is notable that Orlando's transformation occurs while he is abroad—with their relation to gender and sexuality. Although Woolf chose to end the narrative in her present moment, 1928, *Orlando* has the potential to live on for many more centuries.

[69] Frederick Kellermann, 'A New Key to Virginia Woolf's *Orlando*', *English Studies*, 59 (1978), 138–50.
[70] See Select Bibliography.

NOTE ON THE TEXT

THIS text follows the first trade edition of *Orlando*, published in London in 1928 by the Hogarth Press. It makes minor adjustments to hyphenation and word division (for example, 'tomorrow', 'tonight', 'someone'), uses '-ize' forms for '-ise', drops the full point after 'Mr' and 'Mrs', and uses single rather than double quotation marks, in keeping with Oxford World's Classics style.

As noted in the Introduction, *Orlando* significantly outsold Woolf's previous novels. The first impression of 5,080 copies was sold out within weeks of publication; it was followed by a second impression of 3,000 copies in October 1928, and a third of 3,000 copies in January 1929. The third impression had been exhausted by October 1933, when a further impression of 3,000 copies was produced. The novel sold equally well in the United States of America, where the first impression of 6,350 copies sold out in the first month; five further impressions totalling 14,950 copies were produced between November 1928 and February 1933.

To date the most comprehensive scholarly edition of the text is that edited by J. H. Stape for the Shakespeare Head Press (1998); another scholarly edition is in preparation for the Cambridge Edition of the Works of Virginia Woolf. Woolf's manuscript of the text has been edited by Stuart N. Clarke (1993); the original is at Knole in Kent, the Sackville-West home.

SELECT BIBLIOGRAPHY

Bibliography

Kirkpatrick, B. J., and Clarke, Stuart N., *A Bibliography of Virginia Woolf* (4th edn., Oxford: Clarendon Press, 1997).

Biography

Briggs, Julia, *Virginia Woolf: An Inner Life* (London: Allen Lane, 2005).
Lee, Hermione, *Virginia Woolf* (London: Chatto and Windus, 1996).
Mepham, John, *Virginia Woolf: A Literary Life* (London and Basingstoke: Macmillan, 1991).

Editions

The Complete Shorter Fiction of Virginia Woolf, ed. Susan Dick (1985; London: Hogarth Press, rev. edn., 1989).
The Diary of Virginia Woolf, ed. Anne Olivier Bell assisted by Andrew McNeillie, 5 vols. (London: Hogarth Press, 1977–84).
The Essays of Virginia Woolf, 6 vols., ed. Andrew McNeillie (vols. i–iv) and Stuart N. Clarke (vols. v–vi) (London: Hogarth Press, 1984–2012).
The Letters of Virginia Woolf, ed. Nigel Nicolson and Joanne Trautmann, 6 vols. (London: Hogarth Press, 1975–80).
A Passionate Apprentice: The Early Journals 1897–1909, ed. Mitchell Leaska (London: Hogarth Press, 1990).
Moments of Being, ed. Jean Schulkind (1976; London: Pimlico, 2002).

General Criticism

Beer, Gillian, *Virginia Woolf: The Common Ground* (Edinburgh: Edinburgh University Press, 1996).
Bowlby, Rachel, *Feminist Destinations and Further Essays on Virginia Woolf* (Edinburgh: Edinburgh University Press, 1997).
—— (ed.), *Virginia Woolf*, Longman Critical Readers (London: Longman, 1992).
Goldman, Jane, and Randall, Bryony (eds.), *Virginia Woolf in Context* (Cambridge: Cambridge University Press, 2012).
Majumdar, Robin, and McLaurin, Allen (eds.), *Virginia Woolf: The Critical Heritage* (1975; London: Routledge, 1997).
Marcus, Jane (ed.), *New Feminist Essays on Virginia Woolf* (London: Macmillan, 1981).
—— *Virginia Woolf and the Languages of Patriarchy* (Bloomington: Indiana University Press, 1987).

—— (ed.), *Virginia Woolf and Bloomsbury: A Centenary Celebration* (Macmillan, 1987).

Sellers, Susan (ed.), *The Cambridge Companion to Virginia Woolf* (2nd edn., Cambridge: Cambridge University Press, 2010).

Zwerdling, Alex, *Virginia Woolf and the Real World* (Berkeley and Los Angeles: University of California Press, 1986).

Vita Sackville-West and Harold Nicolson

Glendinning, Victoria, *Vita: The Life of V. Sackville-West* (London: Weidenfeld and Nicolson, 1983).

Nicolson, Harold, *The Development of English Biography* (London: Hogarth Press, 1927).

—— *Some People* (London: Constable, 1927).

Nicolson, Nigel, *Portrait of a Marriage* (London: Weidenfeld and Nicolson, 1973).

Sackville-West, Vita, *Knole and the Sackvilles* (London: William Heinemann, 1922).

—— *The Land* (London: William Heinemann, 1926).

—— *The Letters of Vita Sackville-West to Virginia Woolf*, ed. Louise DeSalvo and Mitchell A. Leaska (London: Hutchinson, 1984).

—— *Passenger to Teheran* (London: Hogarth Press, 1926).

Criticism of Orlando

Benzel, Kathryn N., 'Reading Readers in Virginia Woolf's *Orlando: A Biography*', *Style*, 28/2 (Summer 1994), 169–82.

Boehm, Beth A., 'Fact, Fiction, and Metafiction: Blurred Gen(d)res in *Orlando* and *A Room of One's Own*', *Journal of Narrative Technique*, 22/3 (Fall 1992), 191–204.

Caughie, Pamela, *Virginia Woolf & Postmodernism: Literature in Quest & Question of Itself* (Urbana: University of Illinois Press, 1991). (The chapter on *Orlando* had previously appeared as 'Virginia Woolf's Double Discourse', in Marleen S. Barr and Richard Feldstein (eds.), *Discontented Discourses: Feminism/Textual Intervention/Psychoanalysis* (Urbana: University of Illinois Press, 1989), 41–53.)

Clarke, Stuart N. (ed.), *Orlando: The Original Holograph Draft* (London: S. N. Clarke, 1993).

Collier, Patrick, 'Virginia Woolf in the Pay of Booksellers: Commerce, Privacy, Professionalism, *Orlando*', *Twentieth Century Literature*, 48/4 (Winter, 2002), 363–92.

Cook, Blanche Wiesen, 'Women Alone Stir My Imagination', *Signs*, 4 (1979), 718–39.

Horner, Avril, 'Virginia Woolf, History and the Metaphors of *Orlando*', *Essays and Studies*, 44 (1991), 70–87.

Kaivola, Karen, 'Virginia Woolf, Vita Sackville-West, and the Question of Sexual Identity', *Woolf Studies Annual*, 4 (1998), 18–40.

Johnson, Erica L., 'Giving up the Ghost: National and Literary Haunting in *Orlando*', *Modern Fiction Studies*, 50/1 (2004), 110–28.

Knopp, Sherron E., ' "If I Saw You Would You Kiss Me?": Sapphism and the Subversiveness of Virginia Woolf's Orlando', *PMLA* 103/1 (Jan. 1988), 24–33.

Lawrence, Karen R., '*Orlando*'s Voyage Out', *Modern Fiction Studies*, 38/1 (Spring 1992), 253–77.

Lewis, Thomas S. W., 'Combining the Advantages of Fact and Fiction', in Elaine K. Ginsberg and Laura Moss Gottlieb (eds.), *Virginia Woolf: Centennial Essays* (Troy, NY: Whitston, 1983), 295–324.

Little, Judy, '(En)gendering Laughter: Woolf's *Orlando* as Contraband in the Age of Joyce', in Regina Barreca (ed.), *Last Laughs: Perspectives on Women and Comedy* (New York: Gordon and Breach, 1988), 179–92.

Lokke, Kari Elise, '*Orlando* and Incandescence: Virginia Woolf's Comic Sublime', *Modern Fiction Studies*, 38/1 (Spring 1992), 235–52.

Marcus, Jane, 'Sapphistry: Narration as Lesbian Seduction', in Marcus, *Virginia Woolf and the Languages of Patriarchy*, 163–87.

Parkes, Adam, 'Lesbianism, History, and Censorship: *The Well of Loneliness* and the Suppressed Randiness of Virginia Woolf's *Orlando*', *Twentieth Century Literature*, 40/4 (Winter 1994), 434–60; another version appears in Parkes's *Modernism and the Theater of Censorship* (New York: Oxford University Press, 1996), 144–79.

Rosenbaum, S. P., 'Virginia Woolf and the Proper Writing of Lives', in Rosenbaum, *Edwardian Bloomsbury* (Basingstoke: Macmillan, 1994), 339–90.

Thompson, Nicola, 'Some Theories of One's Own: *Orlando* and the Novel', *Studies in the Novel*, 25/3 (Fall 1993), 306–17.

Webb, Caroline, 'Listening to the Right: Authority and Inheritance in *Orlando* and *Ulysses*', *Twentieth Century Literature*, 40/2 (Summer 1994), 190–205.

Whitworth, Michael H., 'Logan Pearsall Smith and *Orlando*', *Review of English Studies*, 55 (2004), 598–604.

Wilson, J. J., 'Why Is *Orlando* Difficult?', in Marcus (ed.), *New Feminist Essays on Virginia Woolf*, 170–84.

Further Reading in Oxford World's Classics

Woolf, Virginia, *Between the Acts*, ed. Frank Kermode.

—— *Flush*, ed. Kate Flint.

—— *Jacob's Room*, ed. Kate Flint.

—— *The Mark on the Wall and Other Short Fiction*, ed. David Bradshaw.

—— *Mrs Dalloway*, ed. David Bradshaw.

—— *Night and Day*, ed. Suzanne Raitt.

—— *A Room of One's Own* and *Three Guineas*, ed. Morag Shiach.

—— *Selected Essays*, ed. David Bradshaw.

—— *To the Lighthouse*, ed. David Bradshaw.

—— *The Voyage Out*, ed. Lorna Sage.

—— *The Waves*, ed. David Bradshaw.

—— *The Years*, ed. Hermione Lee, with notes by Sue Ashbee.

A CHRONOLOGY OF VIRGINIA WOOLF

Life	*Historical and Cultural Background*
1882 (25 Jan.) Adeline Virginia Stephen (VW) born at 22 Hyde Park Gate, London.	Deaths of Darwin, Trollope, D. G. Rossetti; Joyce born; Stravinsky born; Married Women's Property Act; Society for Psychical Research founded.
1895 (5 May) Death of mother, Julia Stephen; VW's first breakdown occurs soon afterwards.	Death of T. H. Huxley; X-rays discovered; invention of the cinematograph; wireless telegraphy invented; arrest, trials, and conviction of Oscar Wilde. Wilde, *The Importance of Being Earnest* and *An Ideal Husband* Wells, *The Time Machine*
1896 (Nov.) Travels in France with sister Vanessa.	Death of William Morris; *Daily Mail* started. Hardy, *Jude the Obscure* Housman, *A Shropshire Lad*
1897 (10 April) Marriage of half-sister Stella; (19 July) death of Stella; (Nov.) VW learning Greek and history at King's College, London.	Queen Victoria's Diamond Jubilee; Tate Gallery opens. Stoker, *Dracula* James, *What Maisie Knew*
1898	Deaths of Gladstone and Lewis Carroll; radium and plutonium discovered. Wells, *The War of the Worlds*
1899 (30 Oct.) VW's brother Thoby goes up to Trinity College, Cambridge, where he forms friendships with Lytton Strachey, Leonard Woolf, Clive Bell, and others of the future Bloomsbury Group (VW's younger brother Adrian follows him to Trinity in 1902).	Boer War begins. Births of Bowen and Coward. Symons, *The Symbolist Movement in Literature* James, *The Awkward Age* Freud, *The Interpretation of Dreams*
1900	Deaths of Nietzsche, Wilde, and Ruskin; *Daily Express* started; Planck announces quantum theory; Boxer Rising. Conrad, *Lord Jim*

Life	Historical and Cultural Background
1901	Death of Queen Victoria; accession of Edward VII; first wireless communication between Europe and USA; 'World's Classics' series begun. Kipling, *Kim*
1902 VW starts private lessons in Greek with Janet Case.	End of Boer War; British Academy founded; *Encyclopaedia Britannica* (10th edn.); *TLS* started. Bennett, *Anna of the Five Towns* James, *The Wings of the Dove*
1903	Deaths of Gissing and Spencer; *Daily Mirror* started; Wright brothers make their first aeroplane flight; Emmeline Pankhurst founds Women's Social and Political Union. Butler, *The Way of All Flesh* James, *The Ambassadors* Moore, *Principia Ethica*
1904 (22 Feb.) Death of father, Sir Leslie Stephen. In spring, VW travels to Italy with Vanessa and friend Violet Dickinson. (10 May) VW has second nervous breakdown and is ill for three months. Moves to 46 Gordon Square. (14 Dec.) VW's first publication appears.	Deaths of Christina Rossetti and Chekhov; Russo-Japanese War; *Entente Cordiale* between Britain and France. Chesterton, *The Napoleon of Notting Hill* Conrad, *Nostromo* James, *The Golden Bowl*
1905 (March, April) Travels in Portugal and Spain. Writes reviews and teaches once a week at Morley College, London	Einstein, *Special Theory of Relativity*; Sartre born Shaw, *Major Barbara and Man and Superman* Wells, *Kipps* Forster, *Where Angels Fear to Tread*
1906 (Sept. and Oct.) Travels in Greece. (20 Nov.) Death of Thoby Stephen.	Death of Ibsen; Beckett born; Liberal Government elected; Campbell-Bannerman Prime Minister; launch of HMS *Dreadnought*.
1907 (7 Feb.) Marriage of Vanessa to Clive Bell. VW moves with Adrian to 29 Fitzroy Square. At work on her first novel, 'Melymbrosia' (working title for *The Voyage Out*).	Auden born; Anglo-Russian Entente. Synge, *The Playboy of the Western World* Conrad, *The Secret Agent* Forster, *The Longest Journey*

Life	*Historical and Cultural Background*
1908 (Sept.) Visits Italy with the Bells.	Asquith Prime Minister; Old Age Pensions Act; Elgar's First Symphony. Bennett, *The Old Wives' Tale* Forster, *A Room with a View* Chesterton, *The Man Who Was Thursday*
1909 (17 Feb.) Lytton Strachey proposes marriage. (30 March) First meets Lady Ottoline Morrell. (April) Visits Florence. (Aug.) Visits Bayreuth and Dresden.	Death of Meredith; 'People's Budget'; English Channel flown by Blèriot. Wells, *Tono-Bungay* Masterman, *The Condition of England* Marinetti, *Futurist Manifesto*
1910 (Jan.) Works for women's suffrage. (June–Aug.) Spends time in a nursing home at Twickenham.	Deaths of Edward VII, Tolstoy, and Florence Nightingale; accession of George V; *Encyclopaedia Britannica* (11th edn.); Roger Fry's Post-Impressionist Exhibition. Bennett, *Clayhanger* Forster, *Howards End* Yeats, *The Green Helmet* Wells, *The History of Mr Polly*
1911 (April) Travels to Turkey, where Vanessa is ill. (Nov.) Moves to 38 Brunswick Square, sharing house with Adrian, John Maynard Keynes, Duncan Grant, and Leonard Woolf.	National Insurance Act; Suffragette riots. Conrad, *Under Western Eyes* Wells, *The New Machiavelli* Lawrence, *The White Peacock*
1912 Rents Asheham House. (Feb.) Spends some days in Twickenham nursing home. (10 Aug.) Marriage to Leonard Woolf. Honeymoon in Provence, Spain, and Italy. (Oct.) Moves to 13 Clifford's Inn, London.	Second Post-Impressionist Exhibition; Suffragettes active; strikes by dockers, coal-miners, and transport workers; Irish Home Rule Bill again rejected by Lords; sinking of SS *Titanic*; death of Scott in the Antarctic; *Daily Herald* started. English translations of Chekhov and Dostoevsky begin to appear.
1913 (March) MS of *The Voyage Out* delivered to publisher. Unwell most of summer. (9 Sept.) Suicide attempt. Remains under care of nurses and husband for rest of year.	*New Statesman* started; Suffragettes active. Lawrence, *Sons and Lovers*
1914 (16 Feb.) Last nurse leaves. Moves to Richmond, Surrey.	Irish Home Rule Bill passed by Parliament; First World War begins (4 Aug.); Dylan Thomas born. Lewis, *Blast*

	Life	*Historical and Cultural Background*
1914		Joyce, *Dubliners* Yeats, *Responsibilities* Hardy, *Satires of Circumstance* Bell, *Art*
1915	Purchase of Hogarth House, Richmond. (26 March) *The Voyage Out* published. (April, May) Bout of violent madness; under care of nurses until November.	Death of Rupert Brooke; Einstein, *General Theory of Relativity*; Second Battle of Ypres; Dardanelles Campaign; sinking of SS *Lusitania*; air attacks on London. Ford, *The Good Soldier* Lawrence, *The Rainbow* Brooke, *1914 and Other Poems* Richardson, *Pointed Roofs*
1916	(17 Oct.) Lectures to Richmond branch of the Women's Co-operative Guild. Regular work for *TLS*.	Death of James; Lloyd George Prime Minister; First Battle of the Somme; Battle of Verdun; Gallipoli Campaign; Easter Rising in Dublin. Joyce, *Portrait of the Artist as a Young Man*
1917	(July) Hogarth Press commences publication with *The Mark on the Wall*. VW begins work on *Night and Day*.	Death of Edward Thomas. Third Battle of Ypres (Passchendaele); T. E. Lawrence's campaigns in Arabia; USA enters the War; Revolution in Russia (Feb., Oct.); Balfour Declaration. Eliot, *Prufrock and Other Observations*
1918	Writes reviews and *Night and Day*; also sets type for the Hogarth Press. (15 Nov.) First meets T. S. Eliot.	Death of Owen; Second Battle of the Somme; final German offensive collapses; Armistice with Germany (11 Nov.); Franchise Act grants vote to women over 30; influenza pandemic kills millions. Lewis, *Tarr* Hopkins, *Poems* Strachey, *Eminent Victorians*
1919	(1 July) Purchase of Monk's House, Rodmell, Sussex. (20 Oct.) *Night and Day* published.	Treaty of Versailles; Alcock and Brown fly the Atlantic; National Socialists founded in Germany. Sinclair, *Mary Olivier* Shaw, *Heartbreak House*
1920	Works on journalism and *Jacob's Room*.	League of Nations established. Pound, *Hugh Selwyn Mauberley* Lawrence, *Women in Love* Eliot, *The Sacred Wood* Fry, *Vision and Design*

Life	Historical and Cultural Background
1921 Ill for summer months. (4 Nov.) Finishes *Jacob's Room*.	Irish Free State founded. Huxley, *Crome Yellow*
1922 (Jan. to May) Ill. (24 Oct.) *Jacob's Room* published. (14 Dec.) First meets Vita Sackville-West.	Bonar Law Prime Minister; Mussolini forms Fascist Government in Italy; death of Proust; *Encyclopaedia Britannica* (12th edn.); *Criterion* founded; BBC founded; Irish Free State proclaimed. Eliot, *The Waste Land* Galsworthy, *The Forsyte Saga* Joyce, *Ulysses* Mansfield, *The Garden Party* Wittgenstein, *Tractatus Logico-Philosophicus*
1923 (March, April) Visits Spain. Works on 'The Hours', the first version of *Mrs Dalloway*.	Baldwin Prime Minister; BBC radio begins broadcasting (Nov.); death of K. Mansfield.
1924 Purchase of lease on 52 Tavistock Square, Bloomsbury. Gives lecture that becomes 'Mr Bennett and Mrs Brown'. (8 Oct.) Finishes *Mrs Dalloway*.	First (minority) Labour Government; Ramsay MacDonald Prime Minister; deaths of Lenin, Kafka, and Conrad. Ford, *Some Do Not* Forster, *A Passage to India* O'Casey, *Juno and the Paycock* Coward, *The Vortex*
1925 (23 April) *The Common Reader* published. (14 May) *Mrs Dalloway* published. Ill during summer.	Gerhardie, *The Polyglots* Ford, *No More Parades* Huxley, *Those Barren Leaves* Whitehead, *Science and the Modern World*
1926 (Jan) Unwell with German measles. Writes *To the Lighthouse*.	General Strike (3–12 May); *Encyclopaedia Britannica* (13th edn.); first television demonstration. Ford, *A Man Could Stand Up* Tawney, *Religion and the Rise of Capitalism*
1927 (March, April) Travels in France and Italy. (5 May) *To the Lighthouse* published. (5 Oct.) Begins *Orlando*.	Lindburgh flies solo across the Atlantic; first 'talkie' films.
1928 (11 Oct.) *Orlando* published. Delivers lectures at Cambridge on which she bases *A Room of One's Own*.	Death of Hardy; votes for women over 21. Yeats, *The Tower* Lawrence, *Lady Chatterley's Lover* Waugh, *Decline and Fall* Sherriff, *Journey's End* Ford, *Last Post* Huxley, *Point Counter Point* Bell, *Civilization*

Life	*Historical and Cultural Background*
1929 (Jan.) Travels to Berlin. (24 Oct.) *A Room of One's Own* published.	2nd Labour Government, MacDonald Prime Minister; collapse of New York Stock Exchange; start of world economic depression. Graves, *Goodbye to All That* Aldington, *Death of a Hero* Green, *Living*
1930 (20 Feb.) First meets Ethel Smyth; (29 May) Finishes first version of *The Waves*.	Mass unemployment; television starts in USA; deaths of Lawrence and Conan Doyle. Auden, *Poems* Eliot, *Ash Wednesday* Waugh, *Vile Bodies* Coward, *Private Lives* Lewis, *Apes of God*
1931 (April) Car tour through France. (8 Oct.) *The Waves* published. Writes *Flush*.	Formation of National Government; abandonment of Gold Standard; death of Bennett; Japan invades China.
1932 (21 Jan.) Death of Lytton Strachey. (13 Oct.) *The Common Reader*, 2nd series, published. Begins *The Years*, at this point called 'The Pargiters'.	Roosevelt becomes President of USA; hunger marches start in Britain; *Scrutiny* starts. Huxley, *Brave New World*
1933 (May) Car tour of France and Italy. (5 Oct.) *Flush* published.	Deaths of Galsworthy and George Moore; Hitler becomes Chancellor of Germany. Orwell, *Down and Out in Paris and London* Wells, *The Shape of Things to Come*
1934 Works on *The Years*. (9 Sept.) Death of Roger Fry.	Waugh, *A Handful of Dust* Graves, *I, Claudius* Beckett, *More Pricks than Kicks* Toynbee, *A Study of History*
1935 Rewrites *The Years*. (May) Car tour of Holland, Germany, and Italy.	George V's Silver Jubilee; Baldwin Prime Minister of National Government; Germany re-arms; Italian invasion of Abyssinia (Ethiopia). Isherwood, *Mr Norris Changes Trains* T. S. Eliot, *Murder in the Cathedral*
1936 (May–Oct.) Ill. Finishes *The Years*. Begins *Three Guineas*.	Death of George V; accession of Edward VIII; abdication crisis; accession of George VI; Civil War breaks out in Spain; first of the

Life	*Historical and Cultural Background*
1936	Moscow show trials; Germany re-occupies the Rhineland; BBC television begins (2 Nov.); deaths of Chesterton, Kipling, and Housman. Orwell, *Keep the Aspidistra Flying*
1937 (15 March) The Years published. Begins *Roger Fry: A Biography*. (18 July) Death in Spanish Civil War of Julian Bell, son of Vanessa.	Chamberlain Prime Minister; destruction of Guernica; death of Barrie. Orwell, *The Road to Wigan Pier*
1938 (2 June) *Three Guineas* published. Works on *Roger Fry*, and begins to envisage *Between the Acts*.	German *Anschluss* with Austria; Munich agreement; dismemberment of Czechoslovakia; first jet engine. Beckett, *Murphy* Bowen, *The Death of the Heart* Greene, *Brighton Rock*
1939 VW moves to 37 Mecklenburgh Square, but lives mostly at Monk's House. Works on *Between the Acts*. Meets Freud in London.	End of Civil War in Spain; Russo–German pact; Germany invades Poland (Sept.); Britain and France declare war on Germany (3 Sept.); deaths of Freud, Yeats, and Ford. Joyce, *Finnegans Wake* Isherwood, *Goodbye to Berlin*
1940 (25 July) *Roger Fry* published. (10 Sept.) Mecklenburgh Square house bombed. (18 Oct.) witnesses the ruins of 52 Tavistock Square, destroyed by bombs. (23 Nov.) Finishes *Between the Acts*.	Germany invades north-west Europe; fall of France; evacuation of British troops from Dunkirk; Battle of Britain; beginning of 'the Blitz'; National Government under Churchill.
1941 (26 Feb.) Revises *Between the Acts*. Becomes ill. (28 March) Drowns herself in River Ouse, near Monk's House. (July) *Between the Acts* published.	Germany invades USSR; Japanese destroy US Fleet at Pearl Harbor; USA enters war; death of Joyce.

ORLANDO

A Biography

ORLANDO AS A BOY

TO
V. SACKVILLE WEST

PREFACE

MANY friends have helped me in writing this book. Some are dead and so illustrious that I scarcely dare name them, yet no one can read or write without being perpetually in the debt of Defoe, Sir Thomas Browne, Sterne, Sir Walter Scott, Lord Macaulay, Emily Brontë, De Quincey, and Walter Pater,—to name the first that come to mind. Others are alive, and though perhaps as illustrious in their own way, are less formidable for that very reason. I am specially indebted to Mr C. P. Sanger, without whose knowledge of the law of real property this book could never have been written. Mr Sydney-Turner's wide and peculiar erudition has saved me, I hope, some lamentable blunders. I have had the advantage—how great I alone can estimate—of Mr Arthur Waley's knowledge of Chinese. Madame Lopokova (Mrs J. M. Keynes) has been at hand to correct my Russian. To the unrivalled sympathy and imagination of Mr Roger Fry I owe whatever understanding of the art of painting I may possess. I have, I hope, profited in another department by the singularly penetrating, if severe, criticism of my nephew Mr Julian Bell. Miss M. K. Snowdon's indefatigable researches in the archives of Harrogate and Cheltenham were none the less arduous for being vain. Other friends have helped me in ways too various to specify. I must content myself with naming Mr Angus Davidson; Mrs Cartwright; Miss Janet Case; Lord Berners (whose knowledge of Elizabethan music has proved invaluable); Mr Francis Birrell; my brother, Dr Adrian Stephen; Mr F. L. Lucas; Mr and Mrs Desmond Maccarthy; that most inspiriting of critics, my brother-in-law, Mr Clive Bell; Mr G. H. Rylands; Lady Colefax; Miss Nellie Boxall; Mr J. M. Keynes; Mr Hugh Walpole; Miss Violet Dickinson; the Hon. Edward Sackville West; Mr and Mrs St John Hutchinson; Mr Duncan Grant; Mr and Mrs Stephen Tomlin; Mr and Lady Ottoline Morrell; my mother-in-law, Mrs Sidney Woolf; Mr Osbert Sitwell; Madame Jacques Raverat; Colonel Cory Bell; Miss Valerie Taylor; Mr J. T. Sheppard; Mr and Mrs T. S. Eliot; Miss Ethel Sands; Miss Nan Hudson; my nephew Mr Quentin Bell (an old and valued collaborator in fiction); Mr Raymond Mortimer; Lady Gerald Wellesley; Mr Lytton Strachey; the Viscountess Cecil; Miss Hope Mirrlees; Mr E. M. Forster; the Hon. Harold Nicolson;

and my sister, Vanessa Bell—but the list threatens to grow too long and is already far too distinguished. For while it rouses in me memories of the pleasantest kind it will inevitably wake expectations in the reader which the book itself can only disappoint. Therefore I will conclude by thanking the officials of the British Museum and Record Office for their wonted courtesy; my niece Miss Angelica Bell, for a service which none but she could have rendered; and my husband* for the patience with which he has invariably helped my researches and for the profound historical knowledge to which these pages owe whatever degree of accuracy they may attain. Finally, I would thank, had I not lost his name and address, a gentleman in America,* who has generously and gratuitously corrected the punctuation, the botany, the entomology, the geography, and the chronology of previous works of mine and will, I hope, not spare his services on the present occasion.

CONTENTS

LIST OF ILLUSTRATIONS

CHAPTER I

HE—for there could be no doubt of his sex, though the fashion of the time did something to disguise it—was in the act of slicing at the head of a Moor* which swung from the rafters. It was the colour of an old football, and more or less the shape of one, save for the sunken cheeks and a strand or two of coarse, dry hair, like the hair on a cocoanut. Orlando's father, or perhaps his grandfather, had struck it from the shoulders of a vast Pagan who had started up under the moon in the barbarian fields of Africa; and now it swung, gently, perpetually, in the breeze which never ceased blowing through the attic rooms of the gigantic house of the lord who had slain him.

Orlando's fathers had ridden in fields of asphodel,* and stony fields, and fields watered by strange rivers, and they had struck many heads of many colours off many shoulders, and brought them back to hang from the rafters. So too would Orlando, he vowed. But since he was sixteen only, and too young to ride with them in Africa or France, he would steal away from his mother and the peacocks in the garden and go to his attic room and there lunge and plunge and slice the air with his blade. Sometimes he cut the cord so that the skull bumped on the floor and he had to string it up again, fastening it with some chivalry almost out of reach so that his enemy grinned at him through shrunk, black lips* triumphantly. The skull swung to and fro, for the house, at the top of which he lived, was so vast that there seemed trapped in it the wind itself, blowing this way, blowing that way, winter and summer. The green arras with the hunters on it moved perpetually. His fathers had been noble since they had been at all. They came out of the northern mists wearing coronets on their heads. Were not the bars of darkness in the room, and the yellow pools which chequered the floor, made by the sun falling through the stained glass of a vast coat of arms in the window? Orlando stood now in the midst of the yellow body of an heraldic leopard. When he put his hand on the window-sill to push the window open, it was instantly coloured red, blue, and yellow like a butterfly's wing.* Thus, those who like symbols, and have a turn for the deciphering of them, might observe that though the shapely legs, the handsome body, and the well-set shoulders were all of them decorated with various tints of heraldic light, Orlando's face, as he threw the window open, was lit solely by the sun itself. A more candid, sullen face it would be impossible to find. Happy the mother who bears, happier still the biographer who records the life of such a one! Never need she vex herself, nor he invoke the help of novelist or poet. From deed to deed, from glory to glory, from office to office he must go, his scribe following after, till they reach whatever seat it may be that is the height of their desire. Orlando, to look at, was cut out precisely for some such career. The red of the cheeks was covered with peach down; the down on the lips was only a little thicker than the down on the cheeks. The lips themselves were short and slightly drawn back over teeth of an exquisite and almond whiteness. Nothing disturbed the arrowy nose in its short, tense flight; the hair was dark, the ears small, and fitted closely to the head. But, alas, that these catalogues of youthful beauty cannot end without mentioning fore-head and eyes. Alas, that people are seldom born devoid of all three; for directly we glance at Orlando standing by the window, we must admit that he had eyes like drenched violets, so large that the water seemed to have brimmed in them and widened them; and a brow like the swelling of a marble dome pressed between the two blank medal-lions which were his temples. Directly we glance at eyes and forehead, thus do we rhapsodize. Directly we glance at eyes and forehead, we have to admit a thousand disagreeables which it is the aim of every good biographer to ignore. Sights disturbed him, like that of his mother, a very beautiful lady in green walking out to feed the pea-cocks with Twitchett, her maid, behind her; sights exalted him—the birds and the trees; and made him in love with death—the evening sky, the homing rooks; and so, mounting up the spiral stairway into his brain—which was a roomy one—all these sights, and the garden sounds too, the hammer beating, the wood chopping, began that riot and confusion of the passions and emotions which every good biog-rapher detests. But to continue—Orlando slowly drew in his head, sat down at the table, and, with the half-conscious air of one doing what they do every day of their lives at this hour, took out a writing book labelled 'Æthelbert: A Tragedy in Five Acts',* and dipped an old stained goose quill in the ink.

Soon he had covered ten pages and more with poetry. He was fluent, evidently, but he was abstract. Vice, Crime, Misery were the personages of his drama; there were Kings and Queens of impossible territories; horrid plots confounded them; noble sentiments suffused them; there was never a word said as he himself would have said it, but all was turned with a fluency and sweetness which, considering his age—he was not yet seventeen—and that the sixteenth century had still some years of its course to run, were remarkable enough. At last, however, he came to a halt. He was describing, as all young poets are for ever describing, nature, and in order to match the shade of green precisely he looked (and here he showed more audacity than most) at the thing itself, which happened to be a laurel bush growing beneath the window. After that, of course, he could write no more. Green in nature is one thing, green in literature another. Nature and letters seem to have a natural antipathy; bring them together and they tear each other to pieces. The shade of green Orlando now saw spoilt his rhyme and split his metre. Moreover, nature has tricks of her own. Once look out of a window at bees among flowers, at a yawning dog, at the sun setting, once think 'how many more suns shall I see set', etc. etc. (the thought is too well known to be worth writing out*) and one drops the pen, takes one's cloak, strides out of the room, and catches one's foot on a painted chest as one does so. For Orlando was a trifle clumsy.*

He was careful to avoid meeting anyone. There was Stubbs,* the gardener, coming along the path. He hid behind a tree till he had passed. He let himself out at a little gate in the garden wall. He skirted all stables, kennels, breweries, carpenters' shops, washhouses, places where they make tallow candles, kill oxen, forge horse-shoes, stitch jerkins—for the house was a town ringing with men at work at their various crafts—and gained the ferny path leading uphill through the park unseen. There is perhaps a kinship among qualities; one draws another along with it; and the biographer should here call attention to the fact that this clumsiness is often mated with a love of solitude. Having stumbled over a chest, Orlando naturally loved solitary places, vast views, and to feel himself for ever and ever and ever alone.

So, after a long silence, 'I am alone', he breathed at last, opening his lips for the first time in this record. He had walked very quickly uphill through ferns and hawthorn bushes, startling deer and wild birds, to a place crowned by a single oak tree. It was very high, so high indeed that nineteen English counties could be seen beneath; and on clear days thirty or perhaps forty, if the weather was very fine. Sometimes one could see the English Channel,* wave reiterating upon wave. Rivers could be seen and pleasure boats gliding on them; and galleons setting out to sea; and armadas with puffs of smoke from which came the dull thud of cannon firing; and forts on the coast; and castles among the meadows; and here a watch tower; and there a fortress; and again some vast mansion like that of Orlando's father, massed like a town in the valley circled by walls. To the east there were the spires of London and the smoke of the city; and perhaps on the very sky line, when the wind was in the right quarter, the craggy top and serrated edges of Snowdon herself showed mountainous among the clouds. For a moment Orlando stood counting, gazing, recognizing. That was his father's house; that his uncle's. His aunt owned those three great turrets among the trees there. The heath was theirs and the forest; the pheasant and the deer, the fox, the badger, and the butterfly.

He sighed profoundly, and flung himself—there was a passion in his movements which deserves the word—on the earth at the foot of the oak tree. He loved, beneath all this summer transiency, to feel the earth's spine beneath him; for such he took the hard root of the oak tree to be; or, for image followed image, it was the back of a great horse that he was riding; or the deck of a tumbling ship—it was anything indeed, so long as it was hard, for he felt the need of something which he could attach his floating heart to; the heart that tugged at his side; the heart that seemed filled with spiced and amorous gales every evening about this time when he walked out. To the oak tree he tied it and as he lay there, gradually the flutter in and about him stilled itself; the little leaves hung, the deer stopped; the pale summer clouds stayed; his limbs grew heavy on the ground; and he lay so still that by degrees the deer stepped nearer and the rooks wheeled round him and the swallows dipped and circled and the dragon-flies shot past, as if all the fertility and amorous activity of a summer's evening were woven web-like about his body.

After an hour or so—the sun was rapidly sinking, the white clouds had turned red, the hills were violet, the woods purple, the valleys black—a trumpet sounded. Orlando leapt to his feet. The shrill sound came from the valley. It came from a dark spot down there; a spot compact and mapped out; a maze; a town, yet girt about with walls; it came from the heart of his own great house in the valley, which, dark before, even as he looked and the single trumpet duplicated and reduplicated itself with other shriller sounds, lost its darkness and became pierced with lights. Some were small hurrying lights, as if

servants dashed along corridors to answer summonses; others were
high and lustrous lights, as if they burnt in empty banqueting-halls
made ready to receive guests who had not come; and others dipped
and waved and sank and rose, as if held in the hands of troops of serving men, bending, kneeling, rising, receiving, guarding, and escorting
with all dignity indoors a great Princess alighting from her chariot.
Coaches turned and wheeled in the courtyard. Horses tossed their
plumes. The Queen had come.*

Orlando looked no more. He dashed downhill. He let himself in
at a wicket gate. He tore up the winding staircase. He reached his
room. He tossed his stockings to one side of the room, his jerkin to
the other. He dipped his head. He scoured his hands. He pared his
finger nails. With no more than six inches of looking-glass and a pair
of old candles to help him, he had thrust on crimson breeches, lace
collar, waistcoat of taffeta, and shoes with rosettes on them as big as
double dahlias in less than ten minutes by the stable clock. He was
ready. He was flushed. He was excited. But he was terribly late.

By short cuts known to him, he made his way now through the
vast congeries of rooms and staircases to the banqueting-hall, five
acres distant on the other side of the house. But half-way there, in the
back quarters where the servants lived, he stopped. The door of Mrs
Stewkley's* sitting-room stood open—she was gone, doubtless, with
all her keys to wait upon her mistress. But there, sitting at the servants'
dinner table with a tankard beside him and paper in front of him, sat
a rather fat, rather shabby man,* whose ruff was a thought dirty, and
whose clothes were of hodden brown.* He held a pen in his hand, but
he was not writing. He seemed in the act of rolling some thought up
and down, to and fro in his mind till it gathered shape or momentum
to his liking. His eyes, globed and clouded like some green stone of
curious texture,* were fixed. He did not see Orlando. For all his hurry,
Orlando stopped dead. Was this a poet? Was he writing poetry? 'Tell
me', he wanted to say, 'everything in the whole world'—for he had the
wildest, most absurd, extravagant ideas about poets and poetry—but
how speak to a man who does not see you? who sees ogres, satyrs,
perhaps the depths of the sea instead? So Orlando stood gazing while
the man turned his pen in his fingers, this way and that way; and
gazed and mused; and then, very quickly, wrote half-a-dozen lines
and looked up. Whereupon Orlando, overcome with shyness, darted
off and reached the banqueting-hall only just in time to sink upon his

knees and, hanging his head in confusion, to offer a bowl of rose water to the great Queen herself.

Such was his shyness that he saw no more of her than her ringed hands in water; but it was enough. It was a memorable hand; a thin hand with long fingers always curling as if round orb or sceptre; a nervous, crabbed, sickly hand; a commanding hand too; a hand that had only to raise itself for a head to fall; a hand, he guessed, attached to an old body that smelt like a cupboard in which furs are kept in camphor; which body was yet caparisoned in all sorts of brocades and gems; and held itself very upright though perhaps in pain from sciatica; and never flinched though strung together by a thousand fears; and the Queen's eyes were light yellow. All this he felt as the great rings flashed in the water and then something pressed his hair—which, perhaps, accounts for his seeing nothing more likely to be of use to a historian. And in truth, his mind was such a welter of opposites—of the night and the blazing candles, of the shabby poet and the great Queen, of silent fields and the clatter of serving men—that he could see nothing; or only a hand.

By the same showing, the Queen herself can have seen only a head. But if it is possible from a hand to deduce a body, informed with all the attributes of a great Queen, her crabbedness, courage, frailty, and terror, surely a head can be as fertile, looked down upon from a chair of state by a lady whose eyes were always, if the waxworks at the Abbey* are to be trusted, wide open. The long, curled hair, the dark head bent so reverently, so innocently before her, implied a pair of the finest legs that a young nobleman has ever stood upright upon; and violet eyes; and a heart of gold; and loyalty and manly charm—all qualities which the old woman loved the more the more they failed her. For she was growing old and worn and bent before her time. The sound of cannon was always in her ears. She saw always the glistening poison drop and the long stiletto.* As she sat at table she listened; she heard the guns in the Channel;* she dreaded—was that a curse, was that a whisper? Innocence, simplicity, were all the more dear to her for the dark background she set them against. And it was that same night, so tradition has it, when Orlando was sound asleep, that she made over formally, putting her hand and seal finally to the parchment, the gift of the great monastic house* that had been the Archbishop's and then the King's to Orlando's father.

Orlando slept all night in ignorance. He had been kissed by a queen without knowing it. And perhaps, for women's hearts are intricate, it was his ignorance and the start he gave when her lips touched him that kept the memory of her young cousin (for they had blood in common) green in her mind. At any rate, two years of this quiet country life had not passed, and Orlando had written no more perhaps than twenty tragedies and a dozen histories and a score of sonnets when a message came that he was to attend the Queen at Whitehall.*

'Here', she said, watching him advance down the long gallery towards her, 'comes my innocent!' (There was a serenity about him always which had the look of innocence when, technically, the word was no longer applicable.)

'Come!' she said. She was sitting bolt upright beside the fire. And she held him a foot's pace from her and looked him up and down. Was she matching her speculations the other night with the truth now visible? Did she find her guesses justified? Eyes, mouth, nose, breast, hips, hands—she ran them over; her lips twitched visibly as she looked; but when she saw his legs she laughed out loud. He was the very image of a noble gentleman. But inwardly? She flashed her yellow hawk's eyes upon him as if she would pierce his soul. The young man withstood her gaze blushing only a damask rose as became him. Strength, grace, romance, folly, poetry, youth—she read him like a page. Instantly she plucked a ring from her finger (the joint was swollen rather) and as she fitted it to his, named him her Treasurer and Steward;* next hung about him chains of office; and bidding him bend his knee, tied round it at the slenderest part the jewelled order of the Garter.* Nothing after that was denied him. When she drove in state he rode at her carriage door. She sent him to Scotland on a sad embassy to the unhappy Queen.* He was about to sail for the Polish wars* when she recalled him. For how could she bear to think of that tender flesh torn and that curly head rolled in the dust? She kept him with her. At the height of her triumph when the guns were booming at the Tower and the air was thick enough with gunpowder to make one sneeze and the huzzas of the people rang beneath the windows, she pulled him down among the cushions where her women had laid her (she was so worn and old) and made him bury his face in that astonishing composition—she had not changed her dress for a month—which smelt for all the world, he thought, recalling his boyish memory, like some old cabinet at home where his mother's furs were stored. He rose, half suffocated from the embrace. 'This', she breathed, 'is my victory!'—even as a rocket roared up and dyed her cheeks scarlet.

For the old woman loved him. And the Queen, who knew a man when she saw one, though not, it is said, in the usual way, plotted for him a splendid ambitious career. Lands were given him, houses assigned him. He was to be the son of her old age; the limb of her infirmity; the oak tree on which she leant her degradation. She croaked out these promises and strange domineering tendernesses (they were at Richmond* now) sitting bolt upright in her stiff brocades by the fire which, however high they piled it, never kept her warm.

Meanwhile, the long winter months drew on. Every tree in the Park was lined with frost. The river ran sluggishly. One day when the snow was on the ground and the dark panelled rooms were full of shadows and the stags were barking in the Park, she saw in the mirror, which she kept for fear of spies always by her, through the door, which she kept for fear of murderers always open, a boy—could it be Orlando?—kissing a girl—who in the Devil's name was the brazen hussy? Snatching at her golden-hilted sword she struck violently at the mirror.* The glass crashed; people came running; she was lifted and set in her chair again; but she was stricken after that and groaned much, as her days wore to an end, of man's treachery.

It was Orlando's fault perhaps; yet, after all, are we to blame Orlando? The age was the Elizabethan; their morals were not ours; nor their poets; nor their climate; nor their vegetables even. Everything was different. The weather itself, the heat and cold of summer and winter, was, we may believe, of another temper altogether. The brilliant amorous day was divided as sheerly from the night as land from water. Sunsets were redder and more intense; dawns were whiter and more auroral. Of our crepuscular half-lights and lingering twilights they knew nothing. The rain fell vehemently, or not at all. The sun blazed or there was darkness. Translating this to the spiritual regions as their wont is, the poets sang beautifully how roses fade and petals fall. The moment is brief they sang; the moment is over; one long night is then to be slept by all. As for using the artifices of the greenhouse or conservatory to prolong or preserve these fresh pinks and roses, that was not their way. The withered intricacies and ambiguities of our more gradual and doubtful age were unknown to them. Violence was all. The flower bloomed and faded. The sun rose and sank. The lover loved and went. And what the poets said in rhyme, the young translated into practice. Girls were roses, and their seasons were short as the flowers'. Plucked they must be before nightfall;* for the day was brief and the day was all. Thus, if Orlando followed the leading of the climate, of the poets, of the age itself, and plucked his flower in the window-seat even with the snow on the ground and the Queen vigilant in the corridor, we can scarcely bring ourselves to blame him. He was young; he was boyish; he did but as nature bade him do. As for the girl, we know no more than Queen Elizabeth herself did what her name was. It may have been Doris, Chloris, Delia, or Diana,* for he made rhymes to them all in turn; equally, she may have been a court lady, or some serving maid. For Orlando's taste was broad; he was no lover of garden flowers only; the wild and the weeds even had always a fascination for him.

Here, indeed, we lay bare rudely, as a biographer may, a curious trait in him, to be accounted for, perhaps, by the fact that a certain grandmother of his had worn a smock and carried milkpails. Some grains of the Kentish or Sussex earth were mixed with the thin, fine fluid which came to him from Normandy. He held that the mixture of brown earth and blue blood was a good one. Certain it is that he had always a liking for low company, especially for that of lettered people whose wits so often keep them under, as if there were the sympathy of blood between them. At this season of his life, when his head brimmed with rhymes and he never went to bed without striking off some conceit, the cheek of an innkeeper's daughter seemed fresher and the wit of a gamekeeper's niece seemed quicker than those of the ladies at Court. Hence, he began going frequently to Wapping Old Stairs* and the beer gardens at night, wrapped in a grey cloak to hide the star at his neck and the garter at his knee. There, with a mug before him, among the sanded alleys and bowling greens and all the simple architecture of such places, he listened to sailors' stories of hardship and horror and cruelty on the Spanish main; how some had lost their toes, others their noses—for the spoken story was never so rounded or so finely coloured as the written. Especially he loved to hear them volley forth their songs of the Azores,* while the parrakeets, which they had brought from those parts, pecked at the rings in their ears, tapped with their hard acquisitive beaks at the rubies on their fingers, and swore as vilely as their masters. The women were scarcely less bold in their speech and less free in their manner than the birds. They perched on his knee, flung their arms round his neck and, guessing that something out of the common lay hid beneath his duffle cloak, were quite as eager to come at the truth of the matter as Orlando himself.

Nor was opportunity lacking. The river was astir early and late with barges, wherries, and craft of all description. Every day sailed to sea some fine ship bound for the Indies;* now and again another blackened and ragged with hairy unknown men on board crept painfully to anchor. No one missed a boy or girl if they dallied a little on the water after sunset; or raised an eyebrow if gossip had seen them sleeping soundly among the treasure sacks safe in each other's arms. Such indeed was the adventure that befel Orlando, Sukey, and the Earl of Cumberland.* The day was hot; their loves had been active; they had fallen asleep among the rubies. Late that night the Earl, whose fortunes were much bound up in the Spanish ventures, came to check the booty alone with a lantern. He flashed the light on a barrel. He started back with an oath. Twined about the cask two spirits lay sleeping. Superstitious by nature, and his conscience laden with many a crime, the Earl took the couple—they were wrapped in a red cloak, and Sukey's bosom was almost as white as the eternal snows of Orlando's poetry—for a phantom sprung from the graves of drowned sailors to upbraid him. He crossed himself. He vowed repentance. The row of alms houses still standing in the Sheen Road* is the visible fruit of that moment's panic. Twelve poor old women of the parish today drink tea and tonight bless his Lordship for a roof above their heads; so that illicit love in a treasure ship—but we omit the moral.

Soon, however, Orlando grew tired, not only of the discomfort of this way of life, and of the crabbed streets of the neighbourhood, but of the primitive manner of the people. For it has to be remembered that crime and poverty had none of the attraction for the Elizabethans that they have for us. They had none of our modern shame of book learning; none of our belief that to be born the son of a butcher is a blessing and to be unable to read a virtue; no fancy that what we call 'life' and 'reality' are somehow connected with ignorance and brutality; nor, indeed, any equivalent for these two words at all. It was not to seek 'life' that Orlando went among them; not in quest of 'reality' that he left them. But when he had heard a score of times how Jakes had lost his nose and Sukey her honour—and they told the stories admirably, it must be admitted—he began to be a little weary of the repetition, for a nose can only be cut off in one way and maidenhood lost in another—or so it seemed to him—whereas the arts and the sciences had a diversity about them which stirred his curiosity profoundly. So, always keeping them in happy memory, he left off frequenting the beer gardens and the skittle alleys, hung his grey cloak in his wardrobe, let his star shine at his neck and his garter twinkle at his knee, and appeared once more at the Court of King James.* He was young, he was rich, he was handsome. No one could have been received with greater acclamation than he was.

It is certain indeed that many ladies were ready to show him their favours. The names of three at least were freely coupled with his in marriage—Clorinda, Favilla, Euphrosyne*—so he called them in his sonnets.

To take them in order; Clorinda was a sweet-mannered gentle lady enough;—indeed Orlando was greatly taken with her for six months and a half, but she had white eyelashes and could not bear the sight of blood. A hare brought up roasted at her father's table turned her faint. She was much under the influence of the Priests too, and stinted her underlinen in order to give to the poor. She took it on her to reform Orlando of his sins, which sickened him, so that he drew back from the marriage, and did not much regret it when she died soon after of the smallpox.

Favilla, who comes next, was of a different sort altogether. She was the daughter of a poor Somersetshire gentleman; who, by sheer assiduity and the use of her eyes had worked her way up at court, where her address in horsemanship,* her fine instep, and her grace in dancing won the admiration of all. Once, however, she was so ill-advised as to whip a spaniel that had torn one of her silk stockings (and it must be said in justice that Favilla had few stockings and those for the most part of drugget*) within an inch of its life beneath Orlando's window. Orlando, who was a passionate lover of animals, now noticed that her teeth were crooked, and the two front turned inward, which, he said, is a sure sign of a perverse and cruel disposition in woman, and so broke the engagement that very night for ever.

The third, Euphrosyne, was by far the most serious of his flames. She was by birth one of the Irish Desmonds* and had therefore a family tree of her own as old and deeply rooted as Orlando's itself. She was fair, florid, and a trifle phlegmatic. She spoke Italian well, had a perfect set of teeth in the upper jaw, though those on the lower were slightly discoloured. She was never without a whippet or spaniel at her knee; fed them with white bread from her own plate; sang sweetly to the virginals; and was never dressed before mid-day owing to the extreme care she took of her person. In short, she would have made a perfect wife for such a nobleman as Orlando, and matters had gone so far that the lawyers on both sides were busy with covenants, jointures, settlements, messuages, tenements, and whatever is needed before one great fortune can mate with another when, with the suddenness and severity that then marked the English climate, came the Great Frost.*

The Great Frost was, historians tell us, the most severe that has ever visited these islands. Birds froze in mid-air and fell like stones to the ground. At Norwich a young countrywoman started to cross the road in her usual robust health and was seen by the onlookers to turn visibly to powder and be blown in a puff of dust over the roofs as the icy blast struck her at the street corner. The mortality among sheep and cattle was enormous. Corpses froze and could not be drawn from the sheets. It was no uncommon sight to come upon a whole herd of swine frozen immovable upon the road. The fields were full of shepherds, ploughmen, teams of horses, and little bird-scaring boys all struck stark in the act of the moment, one with his hand to his nose, another with the bottle to his lips, a third with a stone raised to throw at the raven who sat, as if stuffed, upon the hedge within a yard of him. The severity of the frost was so extraordinary that a kind of petrifaction sometimes ensued; and it was commonly supposed that the great increase of rocks in some parts of Derbyshire was due to no eruption, for there was none, but to the solidification of unfortunate wayfarers who had been turned literally to stone where they stood. The Church could give little help in the matter, and though some landowners had these relics blessed, the most part preferred to use them either as landmarks, scratching-posts for sheep, or, when the form of the stone allowed, drinking troughs for cattle, which purposes they serve, admirably for the most part, to this day.

But while the country people suffered the extremity of want, and the trade of the country was at a standstill, London enjoyed a carnival of the utmost brilliancy. The Court was at Greenwich, and the new King seized the opportunity that his coronation gave him to curry favour with the citizens. He directed that the river, which was frozen to a depth of twenty feet and more for six or seven miles on either side, should be swept, decorated and given all the semblance of a park or pleasure ground, with arbours, mazes, alleys, drinking booths, etc., at his expense. For himself and the courtiers, he reserved a certain space immediately opposite the Palace gates; which, railed off from the public only by a silken rope, became at once the centre of the most brilliant society in England. Great statesmen, in their beards and ruffs, despatched affairs of state under the crimson awning of the Royal Pagoda. Soldiers planned the conquest of the Moor and the downfall of the Turk in striped arbours surmounted by plumes of ostrich feathers. Admirals strode up and down the narrow pathways, glass in hand, sweeping the horizon and telling stories of the north-west passage and the Spanish Armada.* Lovers dallied upon divans spread with sables. Frozen roses fell in showers when the Queen and her ladies walked abroad. Coloured balloons hovered motionless in the air. Here and there burnt vast bonfires of cedar and oak wood, lavishly salted, so that the flames were of green, orange, and purple fire. But however fiercely they burnt, the heat was not enough to melt the ice which, though of singular transparency, was yet of the hardness of steel. So clear indeed was it that there could be seen, congealed at a depth of several feet, here a porpoise, there a flounder. Shoals of eels lay motionless in a trance, but whether their state was one of death or merely of suspended animation which the warmth would revive puzzled the philosophers. Near London Bridge, where the river had frozen to a depth of some twenty fathoms, a wrecked wherry boat was plainly visible, lying on the bed of the river where it had sunk last autumn, overladen with apples. The old bumboat woman, who was carrying her fruit to market on the Surrey side, sat there in her plaids and farthingales with her lap full of apples, for all the world as if she were about to serve a customer, though a certain blueness about the lips hinted the truth. 'Twas a sight King James specially liked to look upon, and he would bring a troupe of courtiers to gaze with him. In short, nothing could exceed the brilliancy and gaiety of the scene by day. But it was at night that the carnival was at its merriest. For the frost continued unbroken; the nights were of perfect stillness; the moon and stars blazed with the hard fixity of diamonds, and to the fine music of flute and trumpet the courtiers danced.

Orlando, it is true, was none of those who tread lightly the corantoe and lavolta;* he was clumsy and a little absent-minded. He much preferred the plain dances of his own country, which he danced as a child to these fantastic foreign measures. He had indeed just brought

his feet together about six in the evening of the seventh of January at
the finish of some such quadrille or minuet* when he beheld, coming
from the pavilion of the Muscovite Embassy, a figure, which, whether
boy's or woman's, for the loose tunic and trousers of the Russian fashion served to disguise the sex, filled him with the highest curiosity.
The person, whatever the name or sex, was about middle height, very
slenderly fashioned, and dressed entirely in oyster-coloured velvet,
trimmed with some unfamiliar greenish-coloured fur. But these
details were obscured by the extraordinary seductiveness which issued
from the whole person. Images, metaphors of the most extreme and
extravagant twined and twisted in his mind. He called her a melon,
a pineapple, an olive tree, an emerald, and a fox in the snow all in the
space of three seconds;* he did not know whether he had heard her,
tasted her, seen her, or all three together. (For though we must pause
not a moment in the narrative we may here hastily note that all his
images at this time were simple in the extreme to match his senses
and were mostly taken from things he had liked the taste of as a boy.
But if his senses were simple they were at the same time extremely
strong. To pause therefore and seek the reasons of things is out of the
question.) . . . A melon, an emerald, a fox in the snow—so he raved,
so he stared. When the boy, for alas, a boy it must be—no woman
could skate with such speed and vigour—swept almost on tiptoe past
him, Orlando was ready to tear his hair with vexation that the person
was of his own sex, and thus all embraces were out of the question.
But the skater came closer. Legs, hands, carriage, were a boy's, but
no boy ever had a mouth like that; no boy had those breasts; no boy
had eyes which looked as if they had been fished from the bottom of
the sea. Finally, coming to a stop and sweeping a curtsey with the
utmost grace to the King, who was shuffling past on the arm of some
Lord-in-waiting, the unknown skater came to a standstill. She was
not a handsbreadth off. She was a woman. Orlando stared; trembled;
turned hot; turned cold; longed to hurl himself through the summer
air; to crush acorns beneath his feet; to toss his arms with the beech
trees and the oaks. As it was, he drew his lips up over his small white
teeth; opened them perhaps half an inch as if to bite; shut them as if
he had bitten. The Lady Euphrosyne hung upon his arm.

The stranger's name, he found, was the Princess Marousha
Stanilovska Dagmar Natasha Iliana Romanovitch, and she had come
in the train of the Muscovite Ambassador, who was her uncle perhaps,

or perhaps her father, to attend the coronation. Very little was known of the Muscovites. In their great beards and furred hats they sat almost silent; drinking some black liquid which they spat out now and then upon the ice. None spoke English, and French with which some at least were familiar was then little spoken at the English Court.

It was through this accident that Orlando and the Princess became acquainted. They were seated opposite each other at the great table spread under a huge awning for the entertainment of the notables. The Princess was placed between two young Lords, one Lord Francis Vere and the other the young Earl of Moray.* It was laughable to see the predicament she soon had them in, for though both were fine lads in their way, the babe unborn had as much knowledge of the French tongue as they had. When at the beginning of dinner the Princess turned to the Earl and said, with a grace which ravished his heart, 'Je crois avoir fait la connaissance d'un gentilhomme qui vous était apparenté en Pologne l'été dernier', or 'La beauté des dames de la cour d'Angleterre me met dans le ravissement. On ne peut voir une dame plus gracieuse que votre reine, ni une coiffure plus belle que la sienne,'* both Lord Francis and the Earl showed the highest embarrassment. The one helped her largely to horse-radish sauce, the other whistled to his dog and made him beg for a marrow bone. At this the Princess could no longer contain her laughter, and Orlando, catching her eyes across the boars' heads and stuffed peacocks, laughed too. He laughed, but the laugh on his lips froze in wonder. Whom had he loved, what had he loved, he asked himself in a tumult of emotion, until now? An old woman, he answered, all skin and bone. Red-cheeked trulls* too many to mention. A puling nun. A hard-bitten cruel-mouthed adventuress. A nodding mass of lace and ceremony. Love had meant to him nothing but sawdust and cinders. The joys he had had of it tasted insipid in the extreme. He marvelled how he could have gone through with it without yawning. For as he looked the thickness of his blood melted; the ice turned to wine in his veins; he heard the waters flowing and the birds singing; spring broke over the hard wintry landscape; his manhood woke; he grasped a sword in his hand; he charged a more daring foe than Pole or Moor; he dived in deep water; he saw the flower of danger growing in a crevice; he stretched his hand—in fact he was rattling off one of his most impassioned sonnets when the Princess addressed him, 'Would you have the goodness to pass the salt?'

He blushed deeply.

'With all the pleasure in the world, Madame,' he replied, speaking French with a perfect accent. For, heaven be praised, he spoke the tongue as his own; his mother's maid had taught him. Yet perhaps it would have been better for him had he never learnt that tongue; never answered that voice; never followed the light of those eyes. . . .

The Princess continued. Who were those bumpkins, she asked him, who sat beside her with the manners of stablemen? What was the nauseating mixture they had poured on her plate? Did the dogs eat at the same table with the men in England? Was that figure of fun at the end of the table with her hair rigged up like a Maypole (comme une grande perche mal fagotée)* really the Queen? And did the King always slobber like that? And which of those popinjays was George Villiers?* Though these questions rather discomposed Orlando at first, they were put with such archness and drollery that he could not help but laugh; and he saw from the blank faces of the company that nobody understood a word, he answered her as freely as she asked him, speaking, as she did, in perfect French.

Thus began an intimacy between the two which soon became the scandal of the Court.

Soon it was observed Orlando paid the Muscovite far more attention than mere civility demanded. He was seldom far from her side, and their conversation, though unintelligible to the rest, was carried on with such animation, provoked such blushes and laughter, that the dullest could guess the subject. Moreover, the change in Orlando himself was extraordinary. Nobody had ever seen him so animated. In one night he had thrown off his boyish clumsiness; he was changed from a sulky stripling, who could not enter a ladies' room without sweeping half the ornaments from the table, to a nobleman, full of grace and manly courtesy. To see him hand the Muscovite (as she was called) to her sledge, or offer her his hand for the dance, or catch the spotted kerchief which she had let drop, or discharge any other of those manifold duties which the supreme lady exacts and the lover hastens to anticipate was a sight to kindle the dull eyes of age, and to make the quick pulse of youth beat faster. Yet over it all hung a cloud. The old men shrugged their shoulders. The young tittered between their fingers. All knew that Orlando was betrothed to another. The Lady Margaret O'Brien O'Dare O'Reilly Tyrconnel (for that was the proper name of Euphrosyne of the Sonnets) wore Orlando's splendid sapphire on the second finger of her left hand. It was she who had the supreme right to his attentions. Yet she might drop all the handker-chiefs in her wardrobe (of which she had many scores) upon the ice and Orlando never stooped to pick them up. She might wait twenty minutes for him to hand her to her sledge, and in the end have to be content with the services of her Blackamoor. When she skated, which she did rather clumsily, no one was at her elbow to encourage her, and, if she fell, which she did rather heavily, no one raised her to her feet and dusted the snow from her petticoats. Although she was natur-ally phlegmatic, slow to take offence, and more reluctant than most people to believe that a mere foreigner could oust her from Orlando's affections, still even the Lady Margaret herself was brought at last to suspect that something was brewing against her peace of mind.

Indeed, as the days passed, Orlando took less and less care to hide his feelings. Making some excuse or other, he would leave the com-pany as soon as they had dined, or steal away from the skaters, who were forming sets for a quadrille. Next moment it would be seen that the Muscovite was missing too. But what most outraged the Court, and stung it in its tenderest part, which is its vanity, was that the couple was often seen to slip under the silken rope, which railed off the Royal enclosure from the public part of the river and to disap-pear among the crowd of common people. For suddenly the Princess would stamp her foot and cry, 'Take me away. I detest your English mob,' by which she meant the English Court itself. She could stand it no longer. It was full of prying old women, she said, who stared in one's face, and of bumptious young men who trod on one's toes. They smelt bad. Their dogs ran between her legs. It was like being in a cage. In Russia they had rivers ten miles broad on which one could gallop six horses abreast all day long without meeting a soul. Besides, she wanted to see the Tower, the Beefeaters, the Heads on Temple Bar,* and the jewellers' shops in the city. Thus, it came about that Orlando took her into the city, showed her the Beefeaters and the rebels' heads, and bought her whatever took her fancy in the Royal Exchange.* But this was not enough. Each increasingly desired the other's company in privacy all day long where there were none to marvel or to stare. Instead of taking the road to London, therefore, they turned the other way about and were soon beyond the crowd among the frozen reaches of the Thames where, save for sea birds and some old country woman hacking at the ice in a vain attempt to draw

a pailful of water or gathering what sticks or dead leaves she could find
for firing, not a living soul ever came their way. The poor kept closely
to their cottages, and the better sort, who could afford it, crowded for
warmth and merriment to the city.

Hence, Orlando and Sasha, as he called her for short, and because
it was the name of a white Russian fox he had had as a boy—a creature soft as snow, but with teeth of steel, which bit him so savagely
that his father had it killed—hence, they had the river to themselves.
Hot with skating and with love they would throw themselves down
in some solitary reach, where the yellow osiers fringed the bank, and
wrapped in a great fur cloak Orlando would take her in his arms, and
know, for the first time, he murmured, the delights of love. Then,
when the ecstasy was over and they lay lulled in a swoon on the ice,
he would tell her of his other loves, and how, compared with her, they
had been of wood, of sackcloth, and of cinders.* And laughing at his
vehemence, she would turn once more in his arms and give him, for
love's sake, one more embrace. And then they would marvel that the
ice did not melt with their heat, and pity the poor old woman who
had no such natural means of thawing it, but must hack at it with
a chopper of cold steel. And then, wrapped in their sables, they would
talk of everything under the sun; of sights and travels; of Moor and
Pagan; of this man's beard and that woman's skin; of a rat that fed
from her hand at table; of the arras that moved always in the hall at
home; of a face; of a feather. Nothing was too small for such converse,
nothing was too great.

Then, suddenly Orlando would fall into one of his moods of melancholy; the sight of the old woman hobbling over the ice might be
the cause of it, or nothing; and would fling himself face downwards
on the ice and look into the frozen waters and think of death. For
the philosopher* is right who says that nothing thicker than a knife's
blade separates happiness from melancholy; and he goes on to opine
that one is twin fellow to the other; and draws from this the conclusion that all extremes of feeling are allied to madness; and so bids us
take refuge in the true Church (in his view the Anabaptist), which is
the only harbour, port, anchorage, etc., he said, for those tossed on
this sea.

'All ends in death,' Orlando would say, sitting upright, his face
clouded with gloom. (For that was the way his mind worked now, in
violent see-saws from life to death, stopping at nothing in between, so

that the biographer must not stop either, but must fly as fast as he can
and so keep pace with the unthinking passionate foolish actions and
sudden extravagant words in which, it is impossible to deny, Orlando
at this time of his life indulged.)

'All ends in death,' Orlando would say, sitting upright on the ice.
But Sasha who after all had no English blood in her but was from
Russia where the sunsets are longer, the dawns less sudden, and sentences often left unfinished from doubt as to how best to end them—
Sasha stared at him, perhaps sneered at him, for he must have seemed
a child to her, and said nothing. But at length the ice grew cold
beneath them, which she disliked, so pulling him to his feet again, she
talked so enchantingly, so wittily, so wisely (but unfortunately always
in French, which notoriously loses its flavour in translation) that he
forgot the frozen waters or night coming or the old woman or whatever it was, and would try to tell her—plunging and splashing among
a thousand images which had gone as stale as the women who inspired
them—what she was like. Snow, cream, marble, cherries, alabaster,
golden wire? None of these. She was like a fox, or an olive tree; like
the waves of the sea when you look down upon them from a height;
like an emerald; like the sun on a green hill which is yet clouded—like
nothing he had seen or known in England. Ransack the language as he
might, words failed him. He wanted another landscape, and another
tongue. English was too frank, too candid, too honeyed a speech for
Sasha. For in all she said, however open she seemed and voluptuous,
there was something hidden; in all she did, however daring, there was
something concealed. So the green flame seems hidden in the emerald, or the sun prisoned in a hill. The clearness was only outward;
within was a wandering flame. It came; it went; she never shone with
the steady beam of an Englishwoman—here, however, remembering
the Lady Margaret and her petticoats, Orlando ran wild in his trans-
ports and swept her over the ice, faster, faster, vowing that he would
chase the flame, dive for the gem, and so on and so on, the words
coming on the pants of his breath with the passion of a poet whose
poetry is half pressed out of him by pain.

But Sasha was silent. When Orlando had done telling her that
she was a fox, an olive tree, or a green hill-top, and had given her
the whole history of his family; how their house was one of the most
ancient in Britain; how they had come from Rome with the Caesars
and had the right to walk down the Corso (which is the chief street

in Rome) under a tasselled palanquin,* which he said is a privilege
reserved only for those of imperial blood (for there was an orgulous*
credulity about him which was pleasant enough), he would pause and
ask her, Where was her own house? What was her father? Had she
brothers? Why was she here alone with her uncle? Then, somehow,
though she answered readily enough, an awkwardness would come
between them. He suspected at first that her rank was not as high
as she would like; or that she was ashamed of the savage ways of her
people, for he had heard that the women in Muscovy wear beards and
the men are covered with fur from the waist down; that both sexes are
smeared with tallow to keep the cold out, tear meat with their fingers
and live in huts where an English noble would scruple to keep his
cattle; so that he forbore to press her. But on reflection, he concluded
that her silence could not be for that reason; she herself was entirely
free from hair on the chin; she dressed in velvet and pearls, and her
manners were certainly not those of a woman bred in a cattle-shed.

What, then, did she hide from him? The doubt underlying the tremendous force of his feelings was like a quicksand beneath a monument which shifts suddenly and makes the whole pile shake. The
agony would seize him suddenly. Then he would blaze out in such
wrath that she did not know how to quiet him. Perhaps she did not
want to quiet him; perhaps his rages pleased her and she provoked
them purposely—such is the curious obliquity of the Muscovitish
temperament.

To continue the story—skating farther than their wont that day
they reached that part of the river where the ships had anchored
and been frozen in midstream. Among them was the ship of the
Muscovite Embassy flying its double-headed black eagle from the
main mast, which was hung with many-coloured icicles several yards
in length. Sasha had left some of her clothing on board, and supposing the ship to be empty they climbed on deck and went in search
of it. Remembering certain passages in his own past, Orlando would
not have marvelled had some good citizens sought this refuge before
them; and so it turned out. They had not ventured far when a fine
young man started up from some business of his own behind a coil
of rope and saying, apparently, for he spoke Russian, that he was one
of the crew and would help the Princess to find what she wanted, lit
a lump of candle and disappeared with her into the lower parts of
the ship.

Time went by, and Orlando, wrapped in his own dreams, thought only of the pleasures of life; of his jewel—of her rarity; of means for making her irrevocably and indissolubly his own. Obstacles there were and hardships to be overcome. She was determined to live in Russia, where there were frozen rivers and wild horses and men, she said, who gashed each other's throats open. It is true that a landscape of pine and snow, habits of lust and slaughter, did not entice him. Nor was he anxious to cease his pleasant country ways of sport and tree-planting; relinquish his office; ruin his career; shoot the reindeer instead of the rabbit; drink vodka instead of canary, and slip a knife up his sleeve—for what purpose, he knew not. Still, all this and more than all this he would do for her sake. As for his marriage with the Lady Margaret, fixed though it was for this day sennight,* the thing was so palpably absurd that he scarcely gave it a thought. Her kinsmen would abuse him for deserting a great lady; his friends would deride him for ruining the finest career in the world for a Cossack woman and a waste of snow—it weighed not a straw in the balance compared with Sasha herself. On the first dark night they would fly. They would take ship to Russia. So he pondered; so he plotted as he walked up and down the deck.

He was recalled, turning westward, by the sight of the sun, slung like an orange on the cross of St Paul's. It was blood-red and sinking rapidly. It must be almost evening. Sasha had been gone this hour and more. Seized instantly with those dark forebodings which shadowed even his most confident thoughts of her, he plunged the way he had seen them go into the hold of the ship; and, after stumbling among chests and barrels in the darkness, was made aware by a faint glimmer in a corner that they were seated there. For one second, he had a vision of them; saw Sasha seated on the sailor's knee; saw her bend towards him; saw them embrace before the light was blotted out in a red cloud by his rage. He blazed into such a howl of anguish that the whole ship echoed. Sasha threw herself between them, or the sailor would have been stifled before he could draw his cutlass. Then a deadly sickness came over Orlando, and they had to lay him on the floor and give him brandy to drink before he revived. And then, when he had recovered and was sat upon a heap of sacking on deck, Sasha hung over him, passing before his dizzied eyes softly, sinuously, like the fox that had bit him, now cajoling, now denouncing, so that he came to doubt what he had seen. Had not the candle guttered; had not the shadows moved? The box was heavy, she said; the man was helping her to move it. Orlando believed her one moment—for who can be sure that his rage has not painted what he most dreads to find?—the next was the more violent with anger at her deceit. Then Sasha herself turned white; stamped her foot on deck; said she would go that night, and called upon her Gods to destroy her, if she, a Romanovitch, had lain in the arms of a common seaman. Indeed, looking at them together (which he could hardly bring himself to do) Orlando was outraged by the foulness of his imagination that could have painted so frail a creature in the paws of that hairy sea brute. The man was huge; stood six feet four in his stockings; wore common wire rings in his ears; and looked like a dray horse upon which some wren or robin has perched in its flight. So he yielded; believed her; and asked her pardon. Yet, when they were going down the ship's side, lovingly again, Sasha paused with her hand on the ladder, and called back to this tawny wide-cheeked monster a volley of Russian greetings, jests, or endearments, not a word of which Orlando could understand. But there was something in her tone (it might be the fault of the Russian consonants) that reminded Orlando of a scene some nights since, when he had come upon her in secret gnawing a candle-end in a corner, which she had picked from the floor. True, it was pink; it was gilt; and it was from the King's table; but it was tallow, and she gnawed it. Was there not, he thought, handing her on to the ice, something rank in her, something coarse flavoured, something peasant born? And he fancied her at forty grown unwieldy though she was now slim as a reed, and lethargic though she was now blithe as a lark. But again as they skated towards London such suspicions melted in his breast, and he felt as if he had been hooked by a great fish through the nose and rushed through the waters unwillingly, yet with his own consent.

It was an evening of astonishing beauty. As the sun sank, all the domes, spires, turrets, and pinnacles of London rose in inky blackness against the furious red sunset clouds. Here was the fretted cross at Charing; there the dome of St Paul's;* there the massy* square of the Tower buildings; there like a grove of trees stripped of all leaves save a knob at the end were the heads on the pikes at Temple Bar.* Now the Abbey windows were lit up and burnt like a heavenly, many-coloured shield (in Orlando's fancy); now all the west seemed a golden window with troops of angels (in Orlando's fancy again) passing up and down the heavenly stairs perpetually. All the time they seemed to be skating

THE RUSSIAN PRINCESS AS A CHILD

on fathomless depths of air, so blue the ice had become; and so glassy smooth was it that they sped quicker and quicker to the city with the white gulls circling about them, and cutting in the air with their wings the very same sweeps that they cut on the ice with their skates.

Sasha, as if to reassure him, was tenderer than usual and even more delightful. Seldom would she talk about her past life, but now she told him how, in winter in Russia, she would listen to the wolves howling across the steppes, and thrice, to show him, she barked like a wolf. Upon which he told her of the stags in the snow at home, and how they would stray into the great hall* for warmth and be fed by an old man with porridge from a bucket. And then she praised him; for his love of beasts; for his gallantry; for his legs. Ravished with her praises and shamed to think how he had maligned her by fancying her on the knees of a common sailor and grown fat and lethargic at forty, he told her that he could find no words to praise her; yet instantly bethought him how she was like the spring and green grass and rushing waters, and seizing her more tightly than ever, he swung her with him half across the river so that the gulls and the cormorants swung too. And halting at length, out of breath, she said, panting slightly, that he was like a million-candled Christmas tree (such as they have in Russia) hung with yellow globes; incandescent; enough to light a whole street by; (so one might translate it) for what with his glowing cheeks, his dark curls, his black and crimson cloak, he looked as if he were burning with his own radiance, from a lamp lit within.

All the colour, save the red of Orlando's cheeks, soon faded. Night came on. As the orange light of sunset vanished it was succeeded by an astonishing white glare from the torches, bonfires, flaming cressets,* and other devices by which the river was lit up and the strangest transformation took place. Various churches and noblemen's palaces, whose fronts were of white stone showed in streaks and patches as if floating on the air. Of St Paul's, in particular, nothing was left but a gilt cross. The Abbey appeared like the grey skeleton of a leaf. Everything suffered emaciation and transformation. As they approached the carnival, they heard a deep note like that struck on a tuning-fork which boomed louder and louder until it became an uproar. Every now and then a great shout followed a rocket into the air. Gradually they could discern little figures breaking off from the vast crowd and spinning hither and thither like gnats on the surface of a river. Above and around this brilliant circle like a bowl of darkness pressed the deep black of a winter's night. And then into this darkness there began to rise with pauses, which kept the expectation alert and the mouth open, flowering rockets; crescents; serpents; a crown. At one moment the woods and distant hills showed green as on a summer's day; the next all was winter and blackness again.

By this time Orlando and the Princess were close to the Royal enclosure and found their way barred by a great crowd of the common people, who were pressing as near to the silken rope as they dared. Loth to end their privacy and encounter the sharp eyes that were on the watch for them, the couple lingered there, shouldered by apprentices; tailors; fishwives; horse dealers; cony catchers;* starving scholars; maid-servants in their whimples; orange girls; ostlers;* sober citizens; bawdy tapsters; and a crowd of little ragamuffins such as always haunt the outskirts of a crowd, screaming and scrambling among people's feet—all the riff-raff of the London streets indeed was there, jesting and jostling, here casting dice, telling fortunes, shoving, tickling, pinching; here uproarious, there glum; some of them with mouths gaping a yard wide; others as little reverent as daws on a house-top; all as variously rigged out as their purse or stations allowed; here in fur and broadcloth; there in tatters with their feet kept from the ice only by a dishclout* bound about them. The main press of people, it appeared, stood opposite a booth or stage something like our Punch and Judy show upon which some kind of theatrical performance was going forward. A black man was waving his arms and vociferating. There was a woman in white* laid upon a bed. Rough though the staging was, the actors running up and down a pair of steps and sometimes tripping, and the crowd stamping their feet and whistling, or when they were bored, tossing a piece of orange peel on to the ice which a dog would scramble for, still the astonishing, sinuous melody of the words stirred Orlando like music. Spoken with extreme speed and a daring agility of tongue which reminded him of the sailors singing in the beer gardens at Wapping, the words even without meaning were as wine to him. But now and again a single phrase would come to him over the ice which was as if torn from the depths of his heart. The frenzy of the Moor seemed to him his own frenzy, and when the Moor suffocated the woman in her bed it was Sasha he killed with his own hands.

At last the play was ended. All had grown dark. The tears streamed down his face. Looking up into the sky there was nothing but blackness

there too. Ruin and death, he thought, cover all. The life of man ends
in the grave. Worms devour us.

> Methinks it should be now a huge eclipse
> Of sun and moon, and that the affrighted globe
> Should yawn——*

Even as he said this a star of some pallor rose in his memory. The night
was dark; it was pitch dark; but it was such a night as this that they
had waited for; it was on such a night as this that they had planned
to fly. He remembered everything. The time had come. With a burst
of passion he snatched Sasha to him, and hissed in her ear 'Jour de
ma vie!'* It was their signal. At midnight they would meet at an inn
near Blackfriars. Horses waited there. Everything was in readiness for
their flight. So they parted, she to her tent, he to his. It still wanted
an hour of the time.

Long before midnight Orlando was in waiting. The night was of
so inky a blackness that a man was on you before he could be seen,
which was all to the good, but it was also of the most solemn stillness
so that a horse's hoof, or a child's cry, could be heard at a distance
of half a mile. Many a time did Orlando, pacing the little courtyard,
hold his heart at the sound of some nag's steady footfall on the cobbles, or at the rustle of a woman's dress. But the traveller was only
some merchant, making home belated; or some woman of the quarter
whose errand was nothing so innocent. They passed, and the street
was quieter than before. Then those lights which burnt downstairs in
the small, huddled quarters where the poor of the city lived moved up
to the sleeping-rooms, and then, one by one, were extinguished. The
street lanterns in these purlieus were few at most; and the negligence
of the night watchman often suffered them to expire long before dawn.
The darkness then became even deeper than before. Orlando looked
to the wicks of his lantern, saw to the saddle girths; primed his pistols;
examined his holsters; and did all these things a dozen times at least
till he could find nothing more needing his attention. Though it still
lacked some twenty minutes to midnight, he could not bring himself
to go indoors to the inn parlour, where the hostess was still serving
sack and the cheaper sort of canary wine to a few seafaring men, who
would sit there trolling their ditties, and telling their stories of Drake,
Hawkins, and Grenville,* till they toppled off the benches and rolled
asleep on the sanded floor. The darkness was more compassionate to

his swollen and violent heart. He listened to every footfall; speculated on every sound. Each drunken shout and each wail from some poor wretch laid in the straw or in other distress cut his heart to the quick, as if it boded ill omen to his venture. Yet, he had no fear for Sasha. Her courage made nothing of the adventure. She would come alone, in her cloak and trousers, booted like a man. Light as her footfall was, it would hardly be heard, even in this silence.

So he waited in the darkness. Suddenly he was struck in the face by a blow, soft, yet heavy, on the side of his cheek. So strung with expectation was he, that he started and put his hand to his sword. The blow was repeated a dozen times on forehead and cheek. The dry frost had lasted so long that it took him a minute to realize that these were rain-drops falling; the blows were the blows of the rain. At first, they fell slowly, deliberately, one by one. But soon the six drops became sixty; then six hundred; then ran themselves together in a steady spout of water. It was as if the hard and consolidated sky poured itself forth in one profuse fountain. In the space of five minutes Orlando was soaked to the skin.

Hastily putting the horses under cover, he sought shelter beneath the lintel of the door whence he could still observe the courtyard. The air was thicker now than ever, and such a steaming and dron-ing rose from the downpour that no footfall of man or beast could be heard above it. The roads, pitted as they were with great holes, would be under water and perhaps impassable. But of what effect this would have upon their flight he scarcely thought. All his senses were bent upon gazing along the cobbled pathway—gleaming in the light of the lantern—for Sasha's coming. Sometimes, in the darkness, he seemed to see her wrapped about with rain strokes. But the phantom vanished. Suddenly, with an awful and ominous voice, a voice full of horror and alarm which raised every hair of anguish in Orlando's soul, St Paul's struck the first stroke of midnight. Four times more it struck remorselessly. With the superstition of a lover, Orlando had made out that it was on the sixth stroke that she would come. But the sixth stroke echoed away, and the seventh came and the eighth, and to his apprehensive mind they seemed notes first heralding and then proclaiming death and disaster. When the twelfth struck he knew that his doom was sealed. It was useless for the rational part of him to reason; she might be late; she might be prevented; she might have missed her way. The passionate and feeling heart of Orlando knew

the truth. Other clocks struck, jangling one after another. The whole
world seemed to ring with the news of her deceit and his derision.
The old suspicions subterraneously at work in him rushed forth from
concealment openly. He was bitten by a swarm of snakes, each more
poisonous than the last. He stood in the doorway in the tremendous
rain without moving. As the minutes passed, he sagged a little at the
knees. The downpour rushed on. In the thick of it, great guns seemed
to boom. Huge noises as of the tearing and rending of oak trees could
be heard. There were also wild cries and terrible inhuman groanings.
But Orlando stood there immovable till Paul's clock struck two, and
then, crying aloud with an awful irony, and all his teeth showing, 'Jour
de ma vie!' he dashed the lantern to the ground, mounted his horse
and galloped he knew not where.

  Some blind instinct, for he was past reasoning, must have driven
him to take the river bank in the direction of the sea. For when the
dawn broke, which it did with unusual suddenness, the sky turning
a pale yellow and the rain almost ceasing, he found himself on the
banks of the Thames off Wapping. Now a sight of the most extraordinary nature met his eyes. Where, for three months and more, there
had been solid ice of such thickness that it seemed permanent as
stone, and a whole gay city had been stood on its pavement, was now
a race of turbulent yellow waters. The river had gained its freedom
in the night. It was as if a sulphur spring (to which view many philosophers inclined) had risen from the volcanic regions beneath and
burst the ice asunder with such vehemence that it swept the huge
and massy fragments furiously apart. The mere look of the water was
enough to turn one giddy. All was riot and confusion. The river was
strewn with icebergs. Some of these were as broad as a bowling green
and as high as a house; others no bigger than a man's hat, but most
fantastically twisted. Now would come down a whole convoy of ice
blocks sinking everything that stood in their way. Now, eddying and
swirling like a tortured serpent, the river would seem to be hurtling
itself between the fragments and tossing them from bank to bank, so
that they could be heard smashing against the piers and pillars. But
what was the most awful and inspiring of terror was the sight of the
human creatures who had been trapped in the night and now paced
their twisting and precarious islands in the utmost agony of spirit.
Whether they jumped into the flood or stayed on the ice their doom
was certain. Sometimes quite a cluster of these poor creatures would

come down together, some on their knees, others suckling their babies. One old man seemed to be reading aloud from a holy book. At other times, and his fate perhaps was the most dreadful, a solitary wretch would stride his narrow tenement alone. As they swept out to sea, some could be heard crying vainly for help, making wild promises to amend their ways, confessing their sins and vowing altars and wealth if God would hear their prayers. Others were so dazed with terror that they sat immovable and silent looking steadfastly before them. One crew of young watermen or post-boys, to judge by their liveries, roared and shouted the lewdest tavern songs, as if in bravado, and were dashed against a tree and sunk with blasphemies on their lips. An old nobleman—for such his furred gown and golden chain proclaimed him—went down not far from where Orlando stood, calling vengeance upon the Irish rebels,* who, he cried with his last breath, had plotted this devilry. Many perished clasping some silver pot or other treasure to their breasts; and at least a score of poor wretches were drowned by their own cupidity, hurling themselves from the bank into the flood rather than let a gold goblet escape them, or see before their eyes the disappearance of some furred gown. For furniture, valuables, possessions of all sorts were carried away on the icebergs. Among other strange sights was to be seen a cat suckling its young; a table laid sumptuously for a supper of twenty; a couple in bed; together with an extraordinary number of cooking utensils.

Dazed and astounded, Orlando could do nothing for some time but watch the appalling race of waters as it hurled itself past him. At last, seeming to recollect himself, he clapped spurs to his horse and galloped hard along the river bank in the direction of the sea. Rounding a bend of the river, he came opposite that reach where, not two days ago, the ships of the Ambassadors had seemed immovably frozen. Hastily, he made count of them all: the French; the Spanish; the Austrian; the Turk. All still floated, though the French had broken loose from her moorings, and the Turkish vessel had taken a great rent in her side and was fast filling with water. But the Russian ship was nowhere to be seen. For one moment Orlando thought it must have foundered; but, raising himself in his stirrups and shading his eyes, which had the sight of a hawk's, he could just make out the shape of a ship on the horizon. The black eagles were flying from the masthead. The ship of the Muscovite Embassy was standing out to sea.

Flinging himself from his horse, he made, in his rage, as if he would breast the flood. Standing knee-deep in water he hurled at the faithless woman all the insults that have ever been the lot of her sex. Faithless, mutable, fickle, he called her; devil, adulteress, deceiver; and the swirling waters took his words, and tossed at his feet a broken pot and a little straw.

CHAPTER II

THE biographer is now faced with a difficulty which it is better perhaps to confess than to gloss over. Up to this point in telling the story of Orlando's life, documents, both private and historical, have made it possible to fulfil the first duty of a biographer, which is to plod, without looking to right or left, in the indelible footprints of truth; unenticed by flowers; regardless of shade; on and on methodically till we fall plump into the grave and write *finis* on the tombstone above our heads. But now we come to an episode which lies right across our path, so that there is no ignoring it. Yet it is dark, mysterious, and undocumented; so that there is no explaining it. Volumes might be written in interpretation of it; whole religious systems founded upon the signification of it. Our simple duty is to state the facts as far as they are known, and so let the reader make of them what he may.

In the summer of that disastrous winter which saw the frost, the flood, the deaths of many thousands, and the complete downfall of Orlando's hopes—for he was exiled from Court; in deep disgrace with the most powerful nobles of his time; the Irish house of Desmond was justly enraged; the King had already trouble enough with the Irish not to relish this further addition—in that summer Orlando retired to his great house in the country and there lived in complete solitude. One June morning—it was Saturday the 18th—he failed to rise at his usual hour, and when his groom went to call him he was found fast asleep. Nor could he be awakened. He lay as if in a trance, without perceptible breathing; and though dogs were set to bark under his window; cymbals, drums, bones beaten perpetually in his room; a gorse bush put under his pillow; and mustard plasters applied to his feet, still he did not wake, take food, or show any sign of life for seven whole days. On the seventh day he woke at his usual time (a quarter before eight, precisely) and turned the whole posse of caterwauling wives and village soothsayers out of his room; which was natural enough; but what was strange was that he showed no consciousness of any such trance, but dressed himself and sent for his horse as if he had woken from a single night's slumber. Yet some change, it was suspected, must have taken place in the chambers of his brain, for though he was perfectly rational and seemed graver and more sedate in his ways than before, he appeared to have an imperfect recollection of his past life. He would listen when people spoke of the great frost or the skating or the carnival, but he never gave any sign, except by passing his hand across his brow as if to wipe away some cloud, of having witnessed them himself. When the events of the past six months were discussed, he seemed not so much distressed as puzzled, as if he were troubled by confused memories of some time long gone or were trying to recall stories told him by another. It was observed that if Russia was mentioned or Princesses or ships, he would fall into a gloom of an uneasy kind and get up and look out of the window or call one of the dogs to him, or take a knife and carve a piece of cedar wood. But the doctors were hardly wiser then than they are now, and after prescribing rest and exercise, starvation and nourishment, society and solitude, that he should lie in bed all day and ride forty miles between lunch and dinner, together with the usual sedatives and irritants, diversified, as the fancy took them, with possets of newt's slobber on rising, and draughts of peacock's gall on going to bed, they left him to himself, and gave it as their opinion that he had been asleep for a week.

But if sleep it was, of what nature, we can scarcely refrain from asking, are such sleeps as these? Are they remedial measures—trances in which the most galling memories, events that seem likely to cripple life for ever, are brushed with a dark wing which rubs their harshness off and gilds them, even the ugliest and basest, with a lustre, an incandescence? Has the finger of death to be laid on the tumult of life from time to time lest it rend us asunder? Are we so made that we have to take death in small doses daily or we could not go on with the business of living? And then what strange powers are these that penetrate our most secret ways and change our most treasured possessions without our willing it? Had Orlando, worn out by the extremity of his suffering, died for a week, and then come to life again? And if so, of what nature is death and of what nature life? Having waited well over half an hour for an answer to these questions, and none coming, let us get on with the story.

Now Orlando gave himself up to a life of extreme solitude. His disgrace at Court and the violence of his grief were partly the reason of it, but as he made no effort to defend himself and seldom invited anyone to visit him (though he had many friends who would willingly have done so) it appeared as if to be alone in the great house of his fathers suited his temper. Solitude was his choice. How he spent his time, nobody quite knew. The servants, of whom he kept a full retinue, though much of their business was to dust empty rooms and to smooth the coverlets of beds that were never slept in, watched, in the dark of the evening, as they sat over their cakes and ale, a light passing along the galleries, through the banqueting-halls, up the staircase, into the bedrooms, and knew that their master was perambulating the house alone. None dared follow him, for the house was haunted by a great variety of ghosts, and the extent of it made it easy to lose one's way and either fall down some hidden staircase or open a door which, should the wind blow it to, would shut upon one for ever—accidents of no uncommon occurrence, as the frequent discovery of the skeletons of men and animals in attitudes of great agony made evident. Then the light would be lost altogether, and Mrs Grimsditch, the housekeeper, would say to Mr Dupper,* the chaplain, how she hoped his Lordship had not met with some bad accident. Mr Dupper would opine that his Lordship was on his knees, no doubt, among the tombs of his ancestors in the Chapel, which was in the Billiard Table Court, half a mile away on the south side. For he had sins on his conscience, Mr Dupper was afraid; upon which Mrs Grimsditch would retort, rather sharply, that so had most of us; and Mrs Stewkley and Mrs Field and old Nurse Carpenter* would all raise their voices in his Lordship's praise; and the grooms and the stewards would swear that it was a thousand pities to see so fine a nobleman moping about the house when he might be hunting the fox or chasing the deer; and even the little laundry maids and scullery maids, the Judys and the Faiths,* who were handing round the tankards and cakes, would pipe up their testimony to his Lordship's gallantry; for never was there a kinder gentleman, or one more free with those little pieces of silver which serve to buy a knot of ribbon or put a posy in one's hair; until even the Blackamoor whom they called Grace Robinson* by way of making a Christian woman of her, understood what they were at, and agreed that his Lordship was a handsome, pleasant, darling gentleman in the only way she could, that is to say by showing all her teeth at once in a broad grin. In short, all his serving men and women held him in high respect, and cursed the foreign Princess (but they called her by a coarser name than that) who had brought him to this pass.

But though it was probably cowardice, or love of hot ale, that led Mr Dupper to imagine his Lordship safe among the tombs so that he need not go in search of him, it may well have been that Mr Dupper was right. Orlando now took a strange delight in thoughts of death and decay, and, after pacing the long galleries and ballrooms with a taper in his hand, looking at picture after picture as if he sought the likeness of somebody whom he could not find, would mount into the family pew and sit for hours watching the banners stir and the moonlight waver with a bat or death's head moth to keep him company. Even this was not enough for him, but he must descend into the crypt where his ancestors lay, coffin piled upon coffin, for ten generations together. The place was so seldom visited that the rats had made free with the lead work, and now a thigh bone would catch at his cloak as he passed, or he would crack the skull of some old Sir Malise* as it rolled beneath his foot. It was a ghastly sepulchre; dug deep beneath the foundations of the house as if the first Lord of the family, who had come from France with the Conqueror,* had wished to testify how all pomp is built upon corruption; how the skeleton lies beneath the flesh; how we that dance and sing above must lie below; how the crimson velvet turns to dust; how the ring (here Orlando, stooping his lantern, would pick up a gold circle lacking a stone, that had rolled into a corner) loses its ruby and the eye which was so lustrous shines no more. 'Nothing remains of all these Princes', Orlando would say, indulging in some pardonable exaggeration of their rank, 'except one digit,' and he would take a skeleton hand in his and bend the joints this way and that. 'Whose hand was it?' he went on to ask. 'The right or the left? The hand of man or woman, of age or youth? Had it urged the war horse, or plied the needle? Had it plucked the rose, or grasped cold steel? Had it——' but here either his invention failed him or, what is more likely, provided him with so many instances of what a hand can do that he shrank, as his wont was, from the cardinal labour of composition, which is excision, and he put it with the other bones, thinking how there was a writer called Thomas Browne, a Doctor of Norwich, whose writing upon such subjects took his fancy amazingly.*

So, taking his lantern and seeing that the bones were in order, for though romantic, he was singularly methodical and detested nothing so much as a ball of string on the floor, let alone the skull of an ancestor, he returned to that curious, moody pacing down the galleries, looking for something among the pictures, which was interrupted at length by a veritable spasm of sobbing, at the sight of a Dutch snow scene by an unknown artist. Then it seemed to him that life was not worth living any more. Forgetting the bones of his ancestors and how life is founded on a grave, he stood there shaken with sobs, all for the desire of a woman in Russian trousers, with slanting eyes, a pouting mouth and pearls about her neck. She had gone. She had left him. He was never to see her again. And so he sobbed. And so he found his way back to his own rooms; and Mrs Grimsditch, seeing the light in the window, put the tankard from her lips and said Praise be to God, his Lordship was safe in his room again; for she had been thinking all this while that he was foully murdered.*

Orlando now drew his chair up to the table; opened the works of Sir Thomas Browne and proceeded to investigate the delicate articulation of one of the doctor's longest and most marvellously contorted cogitations.

For though these are not matters on which a biographer can profitably enlarge it is plain enough to those who have done a reader's part in making up from bare hints dropped here and there the whole boundary and circumference of a living person; can hear in what we only whisper a living voice; can see, often when we say nothing about it, exactly what he looked like; know without a word to guide them precisely what he thought—and it is for readers such as these that we write—it is plain then to such a reader that Orlando was strangely compounded of many humours—of melancholy, of indolence, of passion, of love of solitude, to say nothing of all those contortions and subtleties of temper which were indicated on the first page, when he slashed at a dead nigger's head; cut it down; hung it chivalrously out of his reach again and then betook himself to the window-seat with a book. The taste for books was an early one. As a child he was sometimes found at midnight by a page still reading. They took his taper away, and he bred glow-worms to serve his purpose. They took the glow-worms away, and he almost burnt the house down with a tinder. To put it in a nutshell, leaving the novelist to smooth out the crumpled silk and all its implications, he was a nobleman afflicted with a love of literature. Many people of his time, still more of his rank, escaped the infection and were thus free to run or ride or make love at their own sweet will. But some were early infected by a germ said to be bred of the pollen of the asphodel and to be blown out of Greece and Italy, which was of so deadly a nature that it would shake the hand as it was raised to strike, and cloud the eye as it sought its prey, and make the tongue stammer as it declared its love. It was the fatal nature of this disease to substitute a phantom for reality, so that Orlando, to whom fortune had given every gift—plate, linen, houses, men-servants, carpets, beds in profusion—had only to open a book for the whole vast accumulation to turn to mist. The nine acres of stone which were his house vanished; one hundred and fifty indoor servants disappeared; his eighty riding horses became invisible; it would take too long to count the carpets, sofas, trappings, china, plate, cruets, chafing dishes and other movables often of beaten gold, which evaporated like so much sea mist under the miasma. So it was, and Orlando would sit by himself, reading, a naked man.

The disease gained rapidly upon him now in his solitude. He would read often six hours into the night; and when they came to him for orders about the slaughtering of cattle or the harvesting of wheat, he would push away his folio and look as if he did not understand what was said to him. This was bad enough and wrung the hearts of Hall, the falconer, of Giles, the groom,* of Mrs Grimsditch, the housekeeper, of Mr Dupper, the chaplain. A fine gentleman like that, they said, had no need of books. Let him leave books, they said, to the palsied or the dying. But worse was to come. For once the disease of reading has laid upon the system it weakens it so that it falls an easy prey to that other scourge which dwells in the inkpot and festers in the quill. The wretch takes to writing. And while this is bad enough in a poor man, whose only property is a chair and a table set beneath a leaky roof—for he has not much to lose, after all—the plight of a rich man, who has houses and cattle, maid-servants, asses and linen, and yet writes books, is pitiable in the extreme. The flavour of it all goes out of him; he is riddled by hot irons; gnawed by vermin. He would give every penny he has (such is the malignity of the germ) to write one little book and become famous; yet all the gold in Peru will not buy him the treasure of a well-turned line. So he falls into consumption and sickness, blows his brains out, turns his face to the wall. It matters not in what attitude they find him. He has passed through the gates of Death and known the flames of Hell.

Happily, Orlando was of a strong constitution and the disease (for reasons presently to be given) never broke him down as it has broken many of his peers. But he was deeply smitten with it, as the sequel shows. For when he had read for an hour or so in Sir Thomas Browne, and the bark of the stag and the call of the night watchman showed that it was the dead of night and all safe asleep, he crossed the room, took a silver key from his pocket and unlocked the doors of a great inlaid cabinet* which stood in the corner. Within were some fifty drawers of cedar wood and upon each was a paper neatly written in Orlando's hand. He paused, as if hesitating which to open. One was inscribed 'The Death of Ajax', another 'The Birth of Pyramus', another 'Iphigenia in Aulis', another 'The Death of Hippolytus', another 'Meleager', another 'The Return of Odysseus',*—in fact there was scarcely a single drawer that lacked the name of some mythological personage at a crisis of his career. In each drawer lay a document of considerable size all written over in Orlando's hand. The truth was that Orlando had been afflicted thus for many years. Never had any boy begged apples as Orlando begged paper; nor sweetmeats as he begged ink. Stealing away from talk and games, he had hidden himself behind curtains, in priest's holes,* or in the cupboard behind his mother's bedroom which had a great hole in the floor and smelt horribly of starling's dung, with an inkhorn in one hand, a pen in another, and on his knee a roll of paper. Thus had been written, before he was turned twenty-five, some forty-seven plays, histories, romances, poems; some in prose, some in verse; some in French, some in Italian; all romantic, and all long. One he had had printed by John Ball of the Feathers and Coronet opposite St Paul's Cross, Cheapside;* but though the sight of it gave him extreme delight, he had never dared show it even to his mother, since to write, much more to publish, was, he knew, for a nobleman an inexpiable disgrace.

Now, however, that it was the dead of night and he was alone, he chose from this repository one thick document called 'Xenophila a Tragedy'* or some such title, and one thin one, called simply 'The Oak Tree' (this was the only monosyllabic title among the lot), and then he approached the inkhorn, fingered the quill, and made other such passes as those addicted to this vice begin their rites with. But he paused.

As this pause was of extreme significance in his history, more so, indeed, than many acts which bring men to their knees and make rivers run with blood, it behoves us to ask why he paused; and to reply, after due reflection, that it was for some such reason as this. Nature, who has played so many queer tricks upon us, making us so unequally of clay and diamonds, of rainbow and granite,* and stuffed them into a case, often of the most incongruous, for the poet has a butcher's face and the butcher a poet's; nature, who delights in muddle and mystery, so that even now (the first of November 1927)* we know not why we go upstairs, or why we come down again, our most daily movements are like the passage of a ship on an unknown sea, and the sailors at the masthead ask, pointing their glasses to the horizon; Is there land or is there none? to which, if we are prophets, we make answer 'Yes'; if we are truthful we say 'No'; nature, who has so much to answer for besides the perhaps unwieldy length of this sentence, has further complicated her task and added to our confusion by providing not only a perfect rag-bag of odds and ends within us—a piece of a policeman's trousers lying cheek by jowl with Queen Alexandra's* wedding veil—but has contrived that the whole assortment shall be lightly stitched together by a single thread. Memory is the seamstress, and a capricious one at that. Memory runs her needle in and out, up and down, hither and thither. We know not what comes next, or what follows after. Thus, the most ordinary movement in the world, such as sitting down at a table and pulling the inkstand towards one, may agitate a thousand odd, disconnected fragments, now bright, now dim, hanging and bobbing and dipping and flaunting, like the underlinen of a family of fourteen on a line in a gale of wind. Instead of being a single, downright, bluff piece of work of which no man need feel ashamed, our commonest deeds are set about with a fluttering and flickering of wings, a rising and falling of lights. Thus it was that Orlando, dipping his pen in the ink, saw the mocking face of the lost Princess and asked himself a million questions instantly which were as arrows dipped in gall. Where was she; and why had she left him? Was the Ambassador her uncle or her lover? Had they plotted? Was she forced? Was she married? Was she dead?—all of which so drove their venom into him that, as if to vent his agony somewhere, he plunged his quill so deep into the inkhorn that the ink spirted over the table, which act, explain it how one may (and no explanation perhaps is possible—Memory is inexplicable), at once substituted for the face of the Princess a face of a very different sort. But whose was it, he asked himself? And he had to wait, perhaps half a minute, looking at the new picture which lay on top of the old, as one lantern slide is half seen through the next,* before he could say to himself, 'This is the face of that rather fat, shabby man who sat in Twitchett's room ever so many years ago when old Queen Bess* came here to dine; and I saw him,' Orlando continued, catching at another of those little coloured

rags, 'sitting at the table, as I peeped in on my way downstairs, and he
had the most amazing eyes,' said Orlando, 'that ever were, but who the
devil was he?' Orlando asked, for here Memory added to the forehead
and eyes, first, a coarse, grease-stained ruffle, then a brown doublet,
and finally a pair of thick boots such as citizens wear in Cheapside.*
'Not a Nobleman; not one of us,' said Orlando (which he would not
have said aloud, for he was the most courteous of gentlemen; but it
shows what an effect noble birth has upon the mind and incidentally
how difficult it is for a nobleman to be a writer), 'a poet, I dare say.'
By all the laws, Memory, having disturbed him sufficiently, should
now have blotted the whole thing out completely, or have fetched up
something so idiotic and out of keeping—like a dog chasing a cat or
an old woman blowing her nose into a red cotton handkerchief—that,
in despair of keeping pace with her vagaries, Orlando should have
struck his pen in earnest against his paper. (For we can, if we have
the resolution, turn the hussy, Memory, and all her ragtag and bob-
tail out of the house.) But Orlando paused. Memory still held before
him the image of a shabby man with big, bright eyes. Still he looked,
still he paused. It is these pauses that are our undoing. It is then that
sedition enters the fortress and our troops rise in insurrection. Once
before he had paused, and love with its horrid rout, its shawms,* its
cymbals, and its heads with gory locks torn from the shoulders had
burst in. From love he had suffered the tortures of the damned. Now,
again, he paused, and into the breach thus made, leapt Ambition,
the harridan, and Poetry, the witch, and Desire of Fame, the strum-
pet; all joined hands and made of his heart their dancing ground.
Standing upright in the solitude of his room, he vowed that he would
be the first poet of his race and bring immortal lustre upon his name.
He said (reciting the names and exploits of his ancestors) that Sir
Boris had fought and killed the Paynim;* Sir Gawain,* the Turk; Sir
Miles, the Pole; Sir Andrew, the Frank; Sir Richard, the Austrian;
Sir Jordan, the Frenchman; and Sir Herbert, the Spaniard. But of
all that killing and campaigning, that drinking and love-making, that
spending and hunting and riding and eating, what remained? A skull;
a finger. Whereas, he said, turning to the page of Sir Thomas Browne,
which lay open upon the table—and again he paused. Like an incantation rising from all parts of the room, from the night wind and the
moonlight, rolled the divine melody of those words which, lest they
should outstare this page, we will leave where they lie entombed,

not dead, embalmed rather, so fresh is their colour, so sound their breathing—and Orlando, comparing that achievement with those of his ancestors, cried out that they and their deeds were dust and ashes, but this man and his words were immortal.

He soon perceived, however, that the battles which Sir Miles and the rest had waged against armed knights to win a kingdom, were not half so arduous as this which he now undertook to win immortality against the English language. Anyone moderately familiar with the rigours of composition will not need to be told the story in detail; how he wrote and it seemed good; read and it seemed vile; corrected and tore up; cut out; put in; was in ecstasy; in despair; had his good nights and bad mornings; snatched at ideas and lost them; saw his book plain before him and it vanished; acted his people's parts as he ate; mouthed them as he walked; now cried; now laughed; vacillated between this style and that; now preferred the heroic and pompous; next the plain and simple; now the vales of Tempe;* then the fields of Kent or Cornwall; and could not decide whether he was the divinest genius or the greatest fool in the world.

It was to settle this last question that he decided after many months of such feverish labour, to break the solitude of years and communicate with the outer world. He had a friend in London, one Giles Isham of Norfolk,* who, though of gentle birth, was acquainted with writers and could doubtless put him in touch with some member of that blessed, indeed sacred, fraternity. For, to Orlando in the state he was now in, there was a glory about a man who had written a book and had it printed, which outshone all the glories of blood and state. To his imagination it seemed as if even the bodies of those instinct with such divine thoughts must be transfigured. They must have aureoles for hair, incense for breath, and roses must grow between their lips—which was certainly not true either of himself or Mr Dupper. He could think of no greater happiness than to be allowed to sit behind a curtain and hear them talk. Even the imagination of that bold and various discourse made the memory of what he and his courtier friends used to talk about—a dog, a horse, a woman, a game of cards—seem brutish in the extreme. He bethought him with pride that he had always been called a scholar, and sneered at for his love of solitude and books. He had never been apt at pretty phrases. He would stand stock still, blush, and stride like a grenadier in a ladies' drawing-room. He had twice fallen, in sheer abstraction, from his horse. He had broken Lady Winchilsea's fan* once while making a rhyme. Eagerly recalling these and other instances of his unfitness for the life of society, an ineffable hope, that all the turbulence of his youth, his clumsiness, his blushes, his long walks, and his love of the country proved that he himself belonged to the sacred race rather than to the noble—was by birth a writer, rather than an aristocrat—possessed him. For the first time since the night of the great flood he was happy.

He now commissioned Mr Isham of Norfolk to deliver to Mr Nicholas Greene* of Clifford's Inn a document which set forth Orlando's admiration for his works (for Nick Greene was a very famous writer at that time) and his desire to make his acquaintance; which he scarcely dared ask; for he had nothing to offer in return; but if Mr Nicholas Greene would condescend to visit him, a coach and four would be at the corner of Fetter Lane at whatever hour Mr Greene chose to appoint, and bring him safely to Orlando's house. One may fill up the phrases which then followed; and figure Orlando's delight when, in no long time, Mr Greene signified his acceptance of the Noble Lord's invitation; took his place in the coach and was set down in the hall to the south of the main building punctually at seven o'clock on Monday, April the twenty-first.

Many Kings, Queens, and Ambassadors had been received there; Judges had stood there in their ermine. The loveliest ladies of the land had come there; and the sternest warriors. Banners hung there which had been at Flodden and at Agincourt.* There were displayed the painted coats of arms with their lions and their leopards and their coronets. There were the long tables where the gold and silver plate was stood; and there the vast fireplaces of wrought Italian marble where nightly a whole oak tree, with its million leaves and its nests of rook and wren, was burnt to ashes. Nicholas Greene, the poet stood there now, plainly dressed in his slouched hat and black doublet, carrying in one hand a small bag.

That Orlando as he hastened to greet him was slightly disappointed was inevitable. The poet was not above middle height; was of a mean figure; was lean and stooped somewhat, and, stumbling over the mastiff on entering, the dog bit him. Moreover, Orlando for all his knowledge of mankind was puzzled where to place him. There was something about him which belonged neither to servant, squire, or noble. The head with its rounded forehead and beaked nose was fine, but the chin receded. The eyes were brilliant, but the lips hung loose and slobbered. It was the expression of the face as a whole, however, that was disquieting. There was none of that stately composure which makes the faces of the nobility so pleasing to look at; nor had it anything of the dignified servility of a well-trained domestic's face; it was a face seamed, puckered, and drawn together. Poet though he was, it seemed as if he were more used to scold than to flatter; to quarrel than to coo; to scramble than to ride; to struggle than to rest; to hate than to love. This, too, was shown by the quickness of his movements; and by something fiery and suspicious in his glance. Orlando was somewhat taken aback. But they went to dinner.

Here, Orlando, who usually took such things for granted, was, for the first time, unaccountably ashamed of the number of his servants and of the splendour of his table. Stranger still, he bethought him with pride—for the thought was generally distasteful—of that great grandmother Moll who had milked the cows. He was about somehow to allude to this humble woman and her milk-pails, when the poet forestalled him by saying that it was odd, seeing how common the name of Greene was, that the family had come over with the Conqueror and was of the highest nobility in France. Unfortunately, they had come down in the world and done little more than leave their name to the royal borough of Greenwich. Further talk of the same sort, about lost castles, coats of arms, cousins who were baronets in the north, intermarriage with noble families in the west, how some Greens spelt the name with an e at the end, and others without, lasted till the venison was on the table. Then Orlando contrived to say something of Grandmother Moll and her cows, and had eased his heart a little of its burden by the time the wild-fowl were before them. But it was not until the Malmsey* was passing freely that Orlando dared mention what he could not help thinking a more important matter than the Greens or the cows; that is to say the sacred subject of poetry. At the first mention of the word, the poet's eyes flashed fire; he dropped the fine gentleman airs he had worn; thumped his glass on the table, and launched into one of the longest, most intricate, most passionate, and bitterest stories that Orlando had ever heard, save from the lips of a jilted woman, about a play of his; another poet; and a critic. Of the nature of poetry itself, Orlando only gathered that it was harder to sell than prose, and though the lines were shorter took longer in the writing. So the talk went on with ramifications interminable, until Orlando ventured to hint that he had himself been so rash as to write—but here the poet leapt from his chair. A mouse had squeaked in the wainscot, he said. The truth was, he explained, that his nerves were in a state where a mouse's squeak upset them for a fortnight. Doubtless the house was full of vermin, but Orlando had not heard them. The poet then gave Orlando the full story of his health for the past ten years or so. It had been so bad that one could only marvel that he still lived. He had had the palsy, the gout, the ague, the dropsy, and the three sorts of fever in succession; added to which he had an enlarged heart, a great spleen, and a diseased liver. But, above all, he had, he told Orlando, sensations in his spine which defied description. There was one knob about the third from the top which burnt like fire; another about the second from the bottom which was cold as ice. Sometimes he woke with a brain like lead; at others it was as if a thousand wax tapers were alight and people were throwing fireworks inside him. He could feel a rose leaf through his mattress, he said; and knew his way almost about London by the feel of the cobbles. Altogether he was a piece of machinery so finely made and curiously put together (here he raised his hand as if unconsciously, and indeed it was of the finest shape imaginable) that it confounded him to think that he had only sold five hundred copies of his poem, but that of course was largely due to the conspiracy against him. All he could say, he concluded, banging his fist upon the table, was that the art of poetry was dead in England.

How that could be with Shakespeare, Marlowe, Ben Jonson, Browne, Donne,* all now writing or just having written, Orlando, reeling off the names of his favourite heroes, could not think.

Greene laughed sardonically. Shakespeare, he admitted, had written some scenes that were well enough; but he had taken them chiefly from Marlowe. Marlowe was a likely boy, but what could you say of a lad who died before he was thirty? As for Browne, he was for writing poetry in prose, and people soon got tired of such conceits as that. Donne was a mountebank who wrapped up his lack of meaning in hard words. The gulls were taken in; but the style would be out of fashion twelve months hence. As for Ben Jonson—Ben Jonson was a friend of his and he never spoke ill of his friends.

No, he concluded, the great age of literature is past; the great age of literature was the Greek; the Elizabethan age was inferior in every respect to the Greek. In such ages men cherished a divine

ambition which he might call La Gloire* (he pronounced it Glawr,
so that Orlando did not at first catch his meaning). Now all young
writers were in the pay of the booksellers and poured out any trash
that would sell.* Shakespeare was the chief offender in this way and
Shakespeare was already paying the penalty. Their own age, he said,
was marked by precious conceits and wild experiments—neither of
which the Greeks would have tolerated for a moment. Much though
it hurt him to say it—for he loved literature as he loved his life—he
could see no good in the present and had no hope of the future. Here
he poured himself out another glass of wine.

Orlando was shocked by these doctrines; yet could not help observing that the critic himself seemed by no means downcast. On the contrary, the more he denounced his own time, the more complacent he
became. He could remember, he said, a night at the Cock Tavern in
Fleet Street* when Kit Marlowe was there and some others. Kit was
in high feather, rather drunk, which he easily became, and in a mood
to say silly things. He could see him now, brandishing his glass at
the company and hiccoughing out, 'Stap my vitals, Bill' (this was to
Shakespeare), 'there's a great wave coming and you're on the top of
it,' by which he meant, Greene explained, that they were trembling
on the verge of a great age in English literature,* and that Shakespeare
was to be a poet of some importance. Happily for himself, he was
killed two nights later in a drunken brawl, and so did not live to see
how this prediction turned out. 'Poor foolish fellow,' said Greene, 'to
go and say a thing like that. A great age, forsooth—the Elizabethan
a great age!'

'So, my dear Lord,' he continued, settling himself comfortably in
his chair and rubbing the wine-glass between his fingers, 'we must
make the best of it, cherish the past and honour those writers—there
are still a few left of 'em—who take antiquity for their model and
write, not for pay but for Glawr.' (Orlando could have wished him
a better accent.) 'Glawr', said Greene, 'is the spur of noble minds.
Had I a pension of three hundred pounds a year paid quarterly,
I would live for Glawr alone. I would lie in bed every morning reading
Cicero.* I would imitate his style so that you couldn't tell the difference between us. That's what I call fine writing,' said Greene; 'that's
what I call Glawr. But it's necessary to have a pension to do it.'

By this time Orlando had abandoned all hope of discussing his own
work with the poet; but this mattered the less as the talk now got

upon the lives and characters of Shakespeare, Ben Jonson, and the rest, all of whom Greene had known intimately and about whom he had a thousand anecdotes of the most amusing kind to tell. Orlando had never laughed so much in his life. These, then, were his gods! Half were drunken and all were amorous. Most of them quarrelled with their wives; not one of them was above a lie or an intrigue of the most paltry kind. Their poetry was scribbled down on the backs of washing bills held to the heads of printer's devils* at the street door. Thus Hamlet went to press; thus Lear; thus Othello. No wonder, as Greene said, that these plays show the faults they do. The rest of the time was spent in carousings and junketings in taverns and in beer gardens, when things were said that passed belief for wit, and things were done that made the utmost frolic of the courtiers seem pale in comparison. All this Greene told with a spirit that roused Orlando to the highest pitch of delight. He had a power of mimicry that brought the dead to life, and could say the finest things of books provided they were written three hundred years ago.

So time passed, and Orlando felt for his guest a strange mixture of liking and contempt, of admiration and pity, as well as something too indefinite to be called by any one name, but had something of fear in it and something of fascination. He talked incessantly about himself, yet was such good company that one could listen to the story of his ague for ever. Then he was so witty; then he was so irreverent; then he made so free with the names of God and Woman; then he was so full of queer crafts and had such strange lore in his head; could make salad in three hundred different ways; knew all that could be known of the mixing of wines; played half-a-dozen musical instruments, and was the first person, and perhaps the last, to toast cheese in the great Italian fireplace. That he did not know a geranium from a carnation, an oak from a birch tree, a mastiff from a greyhound, a teg* from a ewe, wheat from barley, plough land from fallow; was ignorant of the rotation of the crops;* thought oranges grew underground and turnips on trees; preferred any townscape to any landscape;—all this and much more amazed Orlando, who had never met anybody of his kind before. Even the maids, who despised him, tittered at his jokes, and the men-servants, who loathed him, hung about to hear his stories. Indeed, the house had never been so lively as now that he was there—all of which gave Orlando a great deal to think about, and caused him to compare this way of life with the old. He recalled the sort of talk he had been used to about the King of Spain's apoplexy or the mating of a bitch; he bethought him how the day passed between the stables and the dressing closet; he remembered how the Lords snored over their wine and hated anybody who woke them up. He bethought him how active and valiant they were in body; how slothful and timid in mind. Worried by these thoughts, and unable to strike a proper balance, he came to the conclusion that he had admitted to his house a plaguey spirit of unrest that would never suffer him to sleep sound again.

At the same moment, Nick Greene came to precisely the opposite conclusion. Lying in bed of a morning on the softest pillows between the smoothest sheets and looking out of his oriel window upon turf which for centuries had known neither dandelion nor dock weed, he thought that unless he could somehow make his escape, he should be smothered alive. Getting up and hearing the pigeons coo, dressing and hearing the fountains fall, he thought that unless he could hear the drays roar upon the cobbles of Fleet Street, he would never write another line. If this goes on much longer, he thought, hearing the footman mend the fire and spread the table with silver dishes next door, I shall fall asleep and (here he gave a prodigious yawn) sleeping die.

So he sought Orlando in his room, and explained that he had not been able to sleep a wink all night because of the silence. (Indeed, the house was surrounded by a park fifteen miles in circumference and a wall ten feet high.) Silence, he said, was of all things the most oppressive to his nerves. He would end his visit, by Orlando's leave, that very morning. Orlando felt some relief at this, yet also a great reluctance to let him go. The house, he thought, would seem very dull without him. On parting (for he had never yet liked to mention the subject), he had the temerity to press his play upon the Death of Hercules upon the poet and ask his opinion of it. The poet took it; muttered something about Glawr and Cicero, which Orlando cut short by promising to pay the pension quarterly; whereupon Greene, with many protestations of affection, jumped into the coach and was gone.

The great hall had never seemed so large, so splendid, or so empty as the chariot rolled away. Orlando knew that he would never have the heart to make toasted cheese in the Italian fireplace again. He would never have the wit to crack jokes about Italian pictures; never have the skill to mix punch as it should be mixed; a thousand good quips and cranks would be lost to him. Yet what a relief to be out of the sound of that querulous voice, what a luxury to be alone once more, so he could not help reflecting, as he unloosed the mastiff which had been tied up these six weeks because it never saw the poet without biting him.

Nick Greene was set down at the corner of Fetter Lane* that same afternoon, and found things going on much as he had left them. Mrs Greene, that is to say, was giving birth to a baby in one room; Tom Fletcher* was drinking gin in another. Books were tumbled all about the floor; dinner—such as it was—was set on a dressing-table where the children had been making mud pies. But this, Greene felt, was the atmosphere for writing; here he could write, and write he did. The subject was made for him. A noble Lord at home. A visit to a Nobleman in the country—his new poem was to have some such title as that. Seizing the pen with which his little boy was tickling the cat's ears, and dipping it in the egg-cup which served for ink-pot, Greene dashed off a very spirited satire there and then. It was so done to a turn that no one could doubt that the young Lord who was roasted was Orlando; his most private sayings and doings, his enthusiasms and follies, down to the very colour of his hair and the foreign way he had of rolling his r's, were there to the life. And if there had been any doubt about it, Greene clinched the matter by introducing, with scarcely any disguise, passages from that aristocratic tragedy, the Death of Hercules, which he found as he expected, wordy and bombastic in the extreme.

The pamphlet, which ran at once into several editions, and paid the expenses of Mrs Greene's tenth lying-in, was soon sent by friends who take care of such matters to Orlando himself. When he had read it, which he did with deadly composure from start to finish, he rang for the footman; delivered the document to him at the end of a pair of tongs; bade him drop it in the filthiest heart of the foulest midden* on the estate. Then, when the man was turning to go he stopped him, 'Take the swiftest horse in the stable,' he said, 'ride for dear life to Harwich.* There embark upon a ship which you will find bound for Norway. Buy for me from the King's own kennels the finest elk-hounds of the Royal strain, male and female. Bring them back without delay. For', he murmured, scarcely above his breath as he turned to his books, 'I have done with men.'

The footman, who was perfectly trained in his duties, bowed and disappeared. He fulfilled his task so efficiently that he was back that day three weeks, leading in his hand a leash of the finest elk-hounds, one of whom, a female, gave birth that very night under the dinner-table to a litter of eight fine puppies. Orlando had them brought to his bedchamber.

'For', he said, 'I have done with men.'

Nevertheless, he paid the pension quarterly.

Thus, at the age of thirty, or thereabouts, this young Nobleman had not only had every experience that life has to offer, but had seen the worthlessness of them all. Love and ambition, women and poets were all equally vain. Literature was a farce. The night after reading Greene's Visit to a Nobleman in the Country, he burnt in a great conflagration fifty-seven poetical works, only retaining 'The Oak Tree', which was his boyish dream and very short. Two things alone remained to him in which he now put any trust: dogs and nature; an elk-hound and a rose bush. The world, in all its variety, life in all its complexity, had shrunk to that. Dogs and a bush were the whole of it. So feeling quit of a vast mountain of illusion, and very naked in consequence, he called his hounds to him and strode through the Park.

So long had he been secluded, writing and reading, that he had half forgotten the amenities of nature, which in June can be great. When he reached that high mound whence on fine days half of England with a slice of Wales and Scotland thrown in can be seen, he flung himself under his favourite oak tree and felt that if he need never speak to another man or woman so long as he lived; if his dogs did not develop the faculty of speech; if he never met a poet or a Princess again, he might make out what years remained to him in tolerable content.

Here he came then, day after day, week after week, month after month, year after year. He saw the beech trees turn golden and the young ferns unfurl; he saw the moon sickle and then circular; he saw—but probably the reader can imagine the passage which should follow and how every tree and plant in the neighbourhood is described first green, then golden; how moons rise and suns set; how spring follows winter and autumn summer; how night succeeds day and day night; how there is first a storm and then fine weather; how things remain much as they are for two or three hundred years or so, except for a little dust and a few cobwebs which one old woman can sweep up in half an hour; a conclusion which, one cannot help feeling, might have been reached more quickly by the simple statement that 'Time passed'* (here the exact amount could be indicated in brackets) and nothing whatever happened.

But Time, unfortunately, though it makes animals and vegetables bloom and fade with amazing punctuality, has no such simple effect upon the mind of man. The mind of man, moreover, works with equal strangeness upon the body of time. An hour, once it lodges in the queer element of the human spirit, may be stretched to fifty or a hundred times its clock length; on the other hand, an hour may be accurately represented on the timepiece of the mind by one second. This extraordinary discrepancy between time on the clock and time in the mind is less known than it should be and deserves fuller investigation. But the biographer, whose interests are, as we have said, highly restricted, must confine himself to one simple statement: when a man has reached the age of thirty, as Orlando now had, time when he is thinking becomes inordinately long; time when he is doing becomes inordinately short. Thus Orlando gave his orders and did the business of his vast estates in a flash; but directly he was alone on the mound under the oak tree, the seconds began to round and fill until it seemed as if they would never fall. They filled themselves, moreover, with the strangest variety of objects. For not only did he find himself confronted by problems which have puzzled the wisest of men, such as What is love? What friendship? What truth? but directly he came to think about them, his whole past, which seemed to him of extreme length and variety, rushed into the falling second, swelled it a dozen times its natural size, coloured it a thousand tints, and filled it with all the odds and ends in the universe.

In such thinking (or by whatever name it should be called) he spent months and years of his life. It would be no exaggeration to say that he would go out after breakfast a man of thirty and come home to dinner a man of fifty-five at least. Some weeks added a century to his age, others no more than three seconds at most. Altogether, the task of estimating the length of human life (of the animals' we presume not to speak) is beyond our capacity, for directly we say that it is ages long, we are reminded that it is briefer than the fall of a rose leaf to the ground. Of the two forces which alternately, and what is more confusing still, at the same moment, dominate our unfortunate numbskulls—brevity and diuturnity*—Orlando was sometimes under the influence of the elephant-footed deity, then of the gnat-winged fly. Life seemed to him of prodigious length. Yet even so, it went like a flash. But even when it stretched longest and the moments swelled biggest and he seemed to wander alone in deserts of vast eternity,* there was no time for the smoothing out and deciphering of those thickly scored parchments which thirty years among men and women had rolled tight in his heart and brain. Long before he had done thinking about Love (the oak tree had put forth its leaves and shaken them to the ground a dozen times in the process) Ambition would jostle it off the field, to be replaced by Friendship or Literature. And as the first question had not been settled—What is Love?—back it would come at the least provocation or none, and hustle Books or Metaphors or What one lives for into the margin, there to wait till they saw their chance to rush into the field again. What made the process still longer was that it was profusely illustrated, not only with pictures, as that of old Queen Elizabeth, laid on her tapestry couch in rose-coloured brocade with an ivory snuff-box in her hand and a gold-hilted sword by her side, but with scents—she was strongly perfumed—and with sounds; the stags were barking in Richmond Park that winter's day. And so, the thought of love would be all ambered over with snow and winter; with log fires burning; with Russian women, gold swords, and the bark of stags; with old King James' slobbering and fireworks and sacks of treasure in the holds of Elizabethan sailing ships. Every single thing, once he tried to dislodge it from its place in his mind, he found thus cumbered with other matter like the lump of glass which, after a year at the bottom of the sea, is grown about with bones and dragon-flies, and coins and the tresses of drowned women.

'Another metaphor by Jupiter!' he would exclaim as he said this (which will show the disorderly and circuitous way in which his mind worked and explain why the oak tree flowered and faded so often before he came to any conclusion about Love). 'And what's the point of it?' he would ask himself. 'Why not say simply in so many words——' and then he would try to think for half an hour,—or was it two years and a half?—how to say simply in so many words what love is. 'A figure like that is manifestly untruthful,' he argued, 'for no dragon-fly, unless under very exceptional circumstances, could live at the bottom of the sea. And if literature is not the Bride and Bedfellow of Truth, what is she? Confound it all,' he cried, 'why say Bedfellow when one's already said Bride? Why not simply say what one means and leave it?'

So then he tried saying the grass is green and the sky is blue and so to propitiate the austere spirit of poetry whom still, though at a great distance, he could not help reverencing. 'The sky is blue,' he said, 'the grass is green.' Looking up, he saw that, on the contrary, the sky is like the veils which a thousand Madonnas have let fall from their hair; and the grass fleets and darkens like a flight of girls fleeing the embraces of hairy satyrs from enchanted woods. 'Upon my word,' he said (for he had fallen into the bad habit of speaking aloud), 'I don't see that one's more true than another. Both are utterly false.' And he despaired of being able to solve the problem of what poetry is and what truth is and fell into a deep dejection.

And here we may profit by a pause in his soliloquy to reflect how odd it was to see Orlando stretched there on his elbow on a June day and to reflect that this fine fellow with all his faculties about him and a healthy body, witness cheeks and limbs—a man who never thought twice about heading a charge or fighting a duel—should be so subject to the lethargy of thought, and rendered so susceptible by it, that when it came to a question of poetry, or his own competence in it, he was as shy as a little girl behind her mother's cottage door. In our belief, Greene's ridicule of his tragedy hurt him as much as the Princess' ridicule of his love. But to return——

Orlando went on thinking. He kept looking at the grass and at the sky and trying to bethink him what a true poet, who has his verses published in London, would say about them. Memory meanwhile (whose habits have already been described) kept steady before his eyes the face of Nicholas Greene, as if that sardonic loose-lipped man, treacherous as he had proved himself, were the Muse in person, and it was to him that Orlando must do homage. So Orlando, that summer morning, offered him a variety of phrases, some plain, others figured, and Nick Greene kept shaking his head and sneering and muttering something about Glawr and Cicero and the death of poetry in our time. At length, starting to his feet (it was now winter and very cold) Orlando swore one of the most remarkable oaths of his lifetime, for it bound him to a servitude than which none is stricter. 'I'll be blasted', he said, 'if I ever write another word, or try to write another word, to please Nick Greene or the Muse. Bad, good, or indifferent, I'll write, from this day forward, to please myself'; and here he made as if he were tearing a whole budget of papers across and tossing them in the face of that sneering loose-lipped man. Upon which, as a cur ducks if you stoop to shy a stone at him, Memory ducked her effigy of Nick Greene out of sight; and substituted for it—nothing whatever.

But Orlando, all the same, went on thinking. He had indeed much to think of. For when he tore the parchment across, he tore, in one rending, the scrolloping,* emblazoned scroll which he had made out in his own favour in the solitude of his room appointing himself, as the King appoints Ambassadors, the first poet of his race, the first writer of his age, conferring eternal immortality upon his soul and granting his body a grave among laurels and the intangible banners of a people's reverence perpetually. Eloquent as this all was, he now tore it up and threw it in the dustbin. 'Fame', he said, 'is like' (and since there was no Nick Greene to stop him, he went on to revel in images of which we will choose only one or two of the quietest) 'a braided coat which hampers the limbs; a jacket of silver which curbs the heart; a painted shield which covers a scarecrow,' etc. etc. The pith of his phrases was that while fame impedes and constricts, obscurity wraps about a man like a mist; obscurity is dark, ample, and free; obscurity lets the mind take its way unimpeded. Over the obscure man is poured the merciful suffusion of darkness. None knows where he goes or comes. He may seek the truth and speak it; he alone is free; he alone is truthful; he alone is at peace. And so he sank into a quiet mood, under the oak tree, the hardness of whose roots, exposed above the ground, seemed to him rather comfortable than otherwise.

Sunk for a long time in profound thoughts as to the value of obscurity, and the delight of having no name, but being like a wave which returns to the deep body of the sea; thinking how obscurity rids the mind of the irk of envy and spite; how it sets running in the veins the free waters of generosity and magnanimity; and allows giving and taking without thanks offered or praise given; which must have been the way of all great poets, he supposed (though his knowledge of Greek was not enough to bear him out), for, he thought, Shakespeare must have written like that, and the church builders built like that, anonymously, needing no thanking or naming, but only their work in the daytime and a little ale perhaps at night— 'What an admirable life this is,' he thought, stretching his limbs out under the oak tree. 'And why not enjoy it this very moment?' The thought struck him like a bullet. Ambition dropped like a plummet. Rid of the heart-burn of rejected love, and of vanity rebuked, and all the other stings and pricks which the nettle-bed of life had burnt upon him when ambitious of fame, but could no longer inflict upon one careless of glory, he opened his eyes, which had been wide open all the time, but had seen only thoughts, and saw, lying in the hollow beneath him, his house.

There it lay in the early sunshine of spring. It looked a town rather than a house, but a town built, not hither and thither, as this man wished or that, but circumspectly, by a single architect with one idea in his head. Courts and buildings, grey, red, plum colour, lay orderly and symmetrical; the courts were some of them oblong and some square; in this was a fountain; in that a statue; the buildings were some of them low, some pointed; here was a chapel, there a belfry; spaces of the greenest grass lay in between and clumps of cedar trees and beds of bright flowers; all were clasped—yet so well set out was it that it seemed that every part had room to spread itself fittingly—by the roll of a massive wall; while smoke from innumerable chimneys curled perpetually into the air. This vast, yet ordered building, which could house a thousand men and perhaps two thousand horses, was built, Orlando thought, by workmen whose names are unknown. Here have lived, for more centuries than I can count, the obscure generations of my own obscure family. Not one of these Richards, Johns, Annes, Elizabeths has left a token of himself behind him, yet all, working together with their spades and their needles, their love-making and their child-bearing, have left this.

Never had the house looked more noble and humane.

Why, then, had he wished to raise himself above them? For it seemed vain and arrogant in the extreme to try to better that anonymous work of creation; the labours of those vanished hands. Better was it to go unknown and leave behind you an arch, a potting shed, a wall where peaches ripen, than to burn like a meteor and leave no dust. For after all, he said, kindling as he looked at the great house on the greensward below, the unknown lords and ladies who lived there never forgot to set aside something for those who come after; for the roof that will leak; for the tree that will fall. There was always a warm corner for the old shepherd in the kitchen; always food for the hungry; always their goblets were polished, though they lay sick;

and their windows were lit though they lay dying. Lords though they were, they were content to go down into obscurity with the molecatcher and the stone-mason. Obscure noblemen, forgotten builders—thus he apostrophized them with a warmth that entirely gainsaid such critics as called him cold, indifferent, slothful (the truth being that a quality often lies just on the other side of the wall from where we seek it)—thus he apostrophized his house and race in terms of the most moving eloquence; but when it came to the peroration—and what is eloquence that lacks a peroration?—he fumbled. He would have liked to have ended with a flourish to the effect that he would follow in their footsteps and add another stone to their building. Since, however, the building already covered nine acres, to add even a single stone seemed superfluous. Could one mention furniture in a peroration? Could one speak of chairs and tables and mats to lie beside people's beds? For whatever the peroration wanted, that was what the house stood in need of. Leaving his speech unfinished for the moment, he strode downhill again resolved henceforward to devote himself to the furnishing of the mansion. The news—that she was to attend him instantly—brought tears to the eyes of good old Mrs Grimsditch, now grown somewhat old. Together they perambulated the house.

The towel horse in the King's bedroom ('and that was King Jamie, my Lord,' she said, hinting that it was many a day since a King had slept under their roof; but the odious Parliament days were over* and there was now a Crown in England again) lacked a leg; there were no stands to the ewers in the little closet leading into the waiting room of the Duchess's page; Mr Greene had made a stain on the carpet with his nasty pipe smoking, which she and Judy, for all their scrubbing, had never been able to wash out. Indeed, when Orlando came to reckon up the matter of furnishing with rosewood chairs and cedarwood cabinets, with silver basins, china bowls, and Persian carpets, every one of the three hundred and sixty-five bedrooms* which the house contained, he saw that it would be no light one; and if some thousands of pounds of his estate remained over, these would do little more than hang a few galleries with tapestry, set the dining hall with fine, carved chairs and provide mirrors of solid silver and chairs of the same metal (for which he had an inordinate passion) for the furnishing of the royal bedchambers.

He now set to work in earnest, as we can prove beyond a doubt if we look at his ledgers. Let us glance at an inventory of what he bought at this time, with the expenses totted up in the margin—but these we omit.

'To fifty pairs of Spanish blankets, ditto curtains of crimson and white taffeta; the valence to them of white satin embroidered with crimson and white silk. . . .

'To seventy yellow satin chairs and sixty stools, suitable with their buckram covers to them all. . . .

'To sixty seven walnut tree tables. . . .

'To seventeen dozen boxes containing each dozen five dozen of Venice glasses. . . .

'To one hundred and two mats, each thirty yards long. . . .

'To ninety seven cushions of crimson damask laid with silver parchment lace and footstools of cloth of tissue and chairs suitable. . . .

'To fifty branches for a dozen lights apiece. . . .'*

Already—it is an effect lists have upon us—we are beginning to yawn. But if we stop, it is only that the catalogue is tedious, not that it is finished. There are ninety-nine pages more of it and the total sum disbursed ran into many thousands—that is to say millions of our money. And if his day was spent like this, at night again, Lord Orlando might be found reckoning out what it would cost to level a million molehills,* if the men were paid tenpence an hour; and again, how many hundredweight of nails at 5½d. a gill were needed to repair the fence* round the park, which was fifteen miles in circumference. And so on and so on.

The tale, we say, is tedious, for one cupboard is much like another, and one molehill not much different from a million. Some pleasant journeys it cost him; and some fine adventures. As, for instance, when he set a whole city of blind women near Bruges to stitch hangings for a silver canopied bed; and the story of his adventure with a Moor in Venice of whom he bought (but only at the sword's point) his lacquered cabinet, might, in other hands, prove worth the telling. Nor did the work lack variety; for here would come, drawn by teams from Sussex, great trees, to be sawn across and laid along the gallery for flooring;* and then a chest from Persia, stuffed with wool and sawdust, from which, at last, he would take a single plate, or one topaz ring.

At length, however, there was no room in the galleries for another table; no room on the tables for another cabinet; no room in the cabinet for another rose-bowl; no room in the bowl for another handful of potpourri; there was no room for anything anywhere; in short the house was furnished. In the garden snowdrops, crocuses, hyacinths, magnolias, roses, lilies, asters, the dahlia in all its varieties, pear trees and apple trees and cherry trees and mulberry trees, with an enormous quantity of rare and flowering shrubs, of trees evergreen and perennial, grew so thick on each other's roots that there was no plot of earth without its bloom, and no stretch of sward without its shade. In addition, he had imported wild fowl with gay plumage; and two Malay bears, the surliness of whose manners concealed, he was certain, trusty hearts.

All now was ready; and when it was evening and the innumerable silver sconces were lit and the light airs which for ever moved about the galleries stirred the blue and green arras, so that it looked as if the huntsmen were riding and Daphne flying;* when the silver shone and lacquer glowed and wood kindled; when the carved chairs held their arms out and dolphins swam upon the walls* with mermaids on their backs; when all this and much more than all this was complete and to his liking, Orlando walked through the house with his elk-hounds following and felt content. He had matter now, he thought, to fill out his peroration. Perhaps it would be well to begin the speech all over again. Yet, as he paraded the galleries he felt that still something was lacking. Chairs and tables, however richly gilt and carved, sofas, resting on lions' paws with swans' necks curving under them, beds even of the softest swansdown are not by themselves enough. People sitting in them, people lying in them improve them amazingly. Accordingly Orlando now began a series of very splendid entertainments to the nobility and gentry of the neighbourhood. The three hundred and sixty-five bedrooms were full for a month at a time. Guests jostled each other on the fifty-two staircases. Three hundred servants bustled about the pantries. Banquets took place almost nightly. Thus, in a very few years, Orlando had worn the nap off his velvet, and spent the half of his fortune; but he had earned the good opinion of his neighbours, held a score of offices in the county, and was annually presented with perhaps a dozen volumes dedicated to his Lordship in rather fulsome terms by grateful poets. For though he was careful not to consort with writers at that time and kept himself always aloof from ladies of foreign blood, still, he was excessively generous both to women and to poets, and both adored him.

But when the feasting was at its height and his guests were at their revels, he was apt to take himself off to his private room alone.* There when the door was shut, and he was certain of privacy, he would have out an old writing book, stitched together with silk stolen from his mother's workbox, and labelled in a round schoolboy hand, 'The Oak Tree, A Poem'. In this he would write till midnight chimed and long after. But as he scratched out as many lines as he wrote in, the sum of them was often, at the end of the year, rather less than at the beginning, and it looked as if in the process of writing the poem would be completely unwritten. For it is for the historian of letters to remark that he had changed his style amazingly. His floridity was chastened; his abundance curbed; the age of prose was congealing those warm fountains. The very landscape outside was less stuck about with garlands and the briars themselves were less thorned and intricate. Perhaps the senses were a little duller and honey and cream less seductive to the palate. Also that the streets were better drained and the houses better lit had its effect upon the style, it cannot be doubted.

One day he was adding a line or two with enormous labour to 'The Oak Tree, A Poem', when a shadow crossed the tail of his eye. It was no shadow, he soon saw, but the figure of a very tall lady in riding hood and mantle crossing the quadrangle on which his room looked out. As this was the most private of the courts, and the lady was a stranger to him, Orlando marvelled how she had got there. Three days later the same apparition appeared again; and on Wednesday noon appeared once more. This time, Orlando was determined to follow her, nor apparently was she afraid to be found, for she slackened her steps as he came up and looked him full in the face. Any other woman thus caught in a Lord's private grounds would have been afraid; any other woman with that face, headdress, and aspect would have thrown her mantilla across her shoulders to hide it. For this lady resembled nothing so much as a hare; a hare startled, but obdurate; a hare whose timidity is overcome by an immense and foolish audacity; a hare that sits upright and glowers at its pursuer with great, bulging eyes; with ears erect but quivering, with nose pointed, but twitching. This hare, moreover, was six feet high and wore a headdress into the bargain of some antiquated kind which made her look still taller. Thus confronted, she stared at Orlando with a stare in which timidity and audacity were most strangely combined.

First, she asked him, with a proper, but somewhat clumsy curtsey, to forgive her her intrusion. Then, rising to her full height again, which must have been something over six feet two, she went on to say—but with such a cackle of nervous laughter, so much tee-heeing and haw-hawing that Orlando thought she must have escaped from a lunatic asylum—that she was the Archduchess Harriet Griselda of Finster-Aarhorn and Scand-op-Boom in the Roumanian territory.* She desired above all things to make his acquaintance, she said. She had taken lodging over a baker's shop at the Park Gates. She had seen his picture and it was the image of a sister of hers who was—here she guffawed—long since dead. She was visiting the English court. The Queen was her Cousin. The King was a very good fellow but seldom went to bed sober. Here she tee-heed and haw-hawed again. In short, there was nothing for it but to ask her in and give her a glass of wine.

Indoors, her manners regained the hauteur natural to a Roumanian Archduchess; and had she not shown a knowledge of wines rare in a lady, and made some observations upon firearms and the customs of sportsmen in her country, which were sensible enough, the talk would have lacked spontaneity. Jumping to her feet at last, she announced that she would call the following day, swept another prodigious curt-sey and departed. The following day, Orlando rode out. The next, he turned his back; on the third he drew his curtain. On the fourth it rained, and as he could not keep a lady in the wet, nor was alto-gether averse to company, he invited her in and asked her opinion whether a suit of armour, which belonged to an ancestor of his, was the work of Jacobi or of Topp.* He inclined to Topp. She held another opinion—it matters very little which. But it is of some importance to the course of our story that, in illustrating her argument, which had to do with the working of the tie pieces, the Archduchess Harriet took the golden shin case and fitted it to Orlando's leg.

That he had a pair of the shapeliest legs that any Nobleman has ever stood upright upon has already been said.

Perhaps something in the way she fastened the ankle buckle; or her stooping posture; or Orlando's long seclusion; or the natural sym-pathy which is between the sexes; or the Burgundy; or the fire—any of these causes may have been to blame; for certainly blame there is on one side or another, when a Nobleman of Orlando's breeding, entertaining a lady in his house, and she his elder by many years, with a face a yard long and staring eyes, dressed somewhat ridiculously

THE ARCHDUCHESS HARRIET

too, in a mantle and riding cloak though the season was warm—blame there is when such a Nobleman is so suddenly and violently overcome by passion of some sort that he has to leave the room.

But what sort of passion, it may well be asked, could this be? And the answer is double faced as Love herself. For Love—but leaving Love out of the argument for a moment, the actual event was this:

When the Archduchess Harriet Griselda stooped to fasten the buckle, Orlando heard, suddenly and unaccountably, far off the beating of Love's wings. The distant stir of that soft plumage roused in him a thousand memories of rushing waters, of loveliness in the snow and faithlessness in the flood; and the sound came nearer; and he blushed and trembled; and he was moved as he had thought never to be moved again; and he was ready to raise his hands and let the bird of beauty alight upon his shoulders, when—horror!—a creaking sound like that the crows make tumbling over the trees began to reverberate; the air seemed dark with coarse black wings; voices croaked; bits of straw, twigs, and feathers dropped; and there pitched down upon his shoulders the heaviest and foulest of the birds; which is the vulture. Thus he rushed from the room and sent the footman to see the Archduchess Harriet to her carriage.

For Love, to which we may now return, has two faces; one white, the other black; two bodies; one smooth, the other hairy. It has two hands, two feet, two tails, two, indeed, of every member and each one is the exact opposite of the other. Yet, so strictly are they joined together that you cannot separate them. In this case, Orlando's love began her flight towards him with her white face turned, and her smooth and lovely body outwards. Nearer and nearer she came wafting before her airs of pure delight. All of a sudden (at the sight of the Archduchess presumably) she wheeled about, turned the other way round; showed herself black, hairy, brutish; and it was Lust the vulture, not Love, the Bird of Paradise, that flopped, foully and disgustingly, upon his shoulders. Hence he ran; hence he fetched the footman.

But the harpy is not so easily banished as all that. Not only did the Archduchess continue to lodge at the Baker's, but Orlando was haunted every day and night by phantoms of the foulest kind. Vainly, it seemed, had he furnished his house with silver and hung the walls with arras, when at any moment a dung-bedraggled fowl could settle upon his writing table. There she was, flopping about among the chairs; he saw her waddling ungracefully across the galleries. Now, she perched, top heavy upon a fire screen. When he chased her out, back she came and pecked at the glass till she broke it.

Thus realizing that his home was uninhabitable, and that steps must be taken to end the matter instantly, he did what any other young man would have done in his place, and asked King Charles* to send him as Ambassador Extraordinary to Constantinople.* The King was walking in Whitehall. Nell Gwyn* was on his arm. She was pelting him with hazel nuts. 'Twas a thousand pities, that amorous lady sighed, that such a pair of legs should leave the country.

Howbeit, the Fates were hard; she could do no more than toss one kiss over her shoulder before Orlando sailed.

CHAPTER III

IT is, indeed, highly unfortunate, and much to be regretted that at this stage of Orlando's career, when he played a most important part in the public life of his country, we have least information to go upon. We know that he discharged his duties to admiration—witness his Bath and his Dukedom.* We know that he had a finger in some of the most delicate negotiations between King Charles and the Turks—to that, treaties in the vault of the Record Office bear testimony. But the revolution which broke out during his period of office, and the fire which followed, have so damaged or destroyed all those papers from which any trustworthy record could be drawn, that what we can give is lamentably incomplete. Often the paper was scorched a deep brown in the middle of the most important sentence. Just when we thought to elucidate a secret that has puzzled historians for a hundred years, there was a hole in the manuscript big enough to put your finger through. We have done our best to piece out a meagre summary from the charred fragments that remain; but often it has been necessary to speculate, to surmise, and even to use the imagination.

Orlando's day was passed, it would seem, somewhat in this fashion. About seven, he would rise, wrap himself in a long Turkish cloak, light a cheroot, and lean his elbows on the parapet. Thus he would stand, gazing at the city beneath him, apparently entranced. At this hour the mist would lie so thick that the domes of Santa Sofia* and the rest would seem to be afloat; gradually the mist would uncover them; the bubbles would be seen to be firmly fixed; there would be the river; there the Galata Bridge;* there the green-turbaned pilgrims without eyes or noses, begging alms; there the pariah dogs picking up offal; there the shawled women; there the innumerable donkeys; there men on horses carrying long poles. Soon, the whole town would be astir with the cracking of whips, the beating of gongs, cryings to prayer, lashing of mules, and rattle of brass-bound wheels, while sour odours, made from bread fermenting and incense, and spice, rose even to the heights of Pera* itself and seemed the very breath of the strident multicoloured and barbaric population.

Nothing, he reflected, gazing at the view which was now sparkling in the sun, could well be less like the counties of Surrey and Kent or

the towns of London and Tunbridge Wells.* To the right and left rose
in bald and stony prominence the inhospitable Asian mountains, to
which the arid castle of a robber chief or two might hang; but par-
sonage there was none, nor manor house, nor cottage, nor oak, elm,
violet, ivy, or wild eglantine. There were no hedges for ferns to grow
on, and no fields for sheep to graze. The houses were white as egg-
shells and as bald. That he, who was English root and fibre, should
yet exult to the depths of his heart in this wild panorama, and gaze
and gaze at those passes and far heights planning journeys there alone
on foot where only the goat and shepherd had gone before; should
feel a passion of affection for the bright, unseasonable flowers, love
the unkempt, pariah dogs beyond even his elk-hounds at home, and
snuff the acrid, sharp smell of the streets eagerly into his nostrils, surprised him. He wondered if, in the season of the Crusades, one of his
ancestors had taken up with a Circassian* peasant woman; thought
it possible; fancied a certain darkness in his complexion; and, going
indoors again, withdrew to his bath.

An hour later, properly scented, curled, and anointed, he would
receive visits from secretaries and other high officials carrying, one
after another, red boxes which yielded only to his own golden key.
Within were papers of the highest importance, of which only fragments, here a flourish, there a seal firmly attached to a piece of burnt
silk, now remain. Of their contents then, we cannot speak, but can
only testify that Orlando was kept busy, what with his wax and seals,
his various coloured ribbons which had to be diversely attached, his
engrossing of titles and making of flourishes round capital letters, till
luncheon came—a splendid meal of perhaps thirty courses.

After luncheon, lackeys announced that his coach and six was at
the door, and he went, preceded by purple Janissaries* running on
foot and waving great ostrich feather fans above their heads, to call
upon the other ambassadors and dignitaries of state. The ceremony
was always the same. On reaching the courtyard, the Janissaries
struck with their fans upon the main portal, which immediately flew
open revealing a large chamber, splendidly furnished. Here were
seated two figures, generally of the opposite sexes. Profound bows
and curtseys were exchanged. In the first room, it was permissible
only to mention the weather. Having said that it was fine or wet, hot
or cold, the Ambassador then passed on to the next chamber, where
again, two figures rose to greet him. Here it was only permissible to

compare Constantinople as a place of residence with London; and the Ambassador naturally said that he preferred Constantinople, and his hosts naturally said, though they had not seen it, that they preferred London. In the next chamber, King Charles's and the Sultan's healths had to be discussed at some length. In the next were discussed the Ambassador's health and that of his host's wife, but more briefly. In the next the Ambassador complimented his host upon his furniture, and the host complimented the Ambassador upon his dress. In the next, sweet meats were offered, the host deploring their badness, the Ambassador extolling their goodness. The ceremony ended at length with the smoking of a hookah and the drinking of a glass of coffee; but though the motions of smoking and drinking were gone through punctiliously there was neither tobacco in the pipe nor coffee in the glass, as, had either smoke or drink been real, the human frame would have sunk beneath the surfeit. For, no sooner had the Ambassador despatched one such visit, than another had to be undertaken. The same ceremonies were gone through in precisely the same order six or seven times over at the houses of the other great officials, so that it was often late at night before the Ambassador reached home. Though Orlando performed these tasks to admiration and never denied that they are, perhaps, the most important part of a diplomatist's duties, he was undoubtedly fatigued by them, and often depressed to such a pitch of gloom that he preferred to take his dinner alone with his dogs. To them, indeed, he might be heard talking in his own tongue. And sometimes, it is said, he would pass out of his own gates late at night so disguised that the sentries did not know him. Then he would mingle with the crowd on the Galata Bridge; or stroll through the bazaars; or throw aside his shoes and join the worshippers in the Mosques. Once, when it was given out that he was ill of a fever, shepherds, bringing their goats to market, reported that they had met an English Lord on the mountain top and heard him praying to his God. This was thought to be Orlando himself, and his prayer was, no doubt, a poem said aloud, for it was known that he still carried about with him, in the bosom of his cloak, a much scored manuscript; and servants, listening at the door, heard the Ambassador chanting something* in an odd, sing-song voice when he was alone.

It is with fragments such as these that we must do our best to make up a picture of Orlando's life and character at this time. There exist, even to this day, rumours, legends, anecdotes of a floating and

ORLANDO AS AMBASSADOR

unauthenticated kind about Orlando's life in Constantinople—(we have quoted but a few of them) which go to prove that he possessed, now that he was in the prime of life, the power to stir the fancy and rivet the eye which will keep a memory green long after all that more durable qualities can do to preserve it is forgotten. The power is a mysterious one compounded of beauty, birth, and some rarer gift, which we may call glamour and have done with it. 'A million candles', as Sasha had said, burnt in him without his being at the trouble of lighting a single one. He moved like a stag, without any need to think about his legs. He spoke in his ordinary voice and echo beat a silver gong. Hence rumours gathered round him. He became the adored of many women and some men. It was not necessary that they should speak to him or even that they should see him; they conjured up before them especially when the scenery was romantic, or the sun was setting, the figure of a noble gentleman in silk stockings. Upon the poor and uneducated, he had the same power as upon the rich. Shepherds, gipsies, donkey drivers, still sing songs about the English Lord 'who dropped his emeralds in the well', which undoubtedly refer to Orlando, who once, it seems, tore his jewels from him in a moment of rage or intoxication and flung them in a fountain; whence they were fished by a page boy. But this romantic power, it is well known, is often associated with a nature of extreme reserve. Orlando seems to have made no friends. As far as is known, he formed no attachments. A certain great lady came all the way from England in order to be near him, and pestered him with her attentions, but he continued to discharge his duties so indefatigably that he had not been Ambassador at the Horn more than two years and a half before King Charles signified his intention of raising him to the highest rank in the peerage. The envious said that this was Nell Gwyn's tribute to the memory of a leg. But, as she had seen him once only, and was then busily engaged in pelting her royal master with nutshells, it is likely that it was his merits that won him his Dukedom, not his calves.

Here we must pause, for we have reached a moment of great significance in his career. For the conferring of the Dukedom was the occasion of a very famous, and indeed, much disputed incident, which we must now describe, picking our way among burnt papers and little bits of tape as best we may. It was at the end of the great fast of Ramadan that the Order of the Bath and the patent of nobility

arrived in a frigate commanded by Sir Adrian Scrope;* and Orlando
made this the occasion for an entertainment more splendid than any
that has been known before or since in Constantinople. The night was
fine; the crowd immense, and the windows of the Embassy brilliantly
illuminated. Again, details are lacking, for the fire had its way with
all such records, and has left only tantalizing fragments which leave
the most important points obscure. From the diary of John Fenner
Brigge,* however, an English naval officer, who was among the guests,
we gather that people of all nationalities 'were packed like herrings in
a barrel' in the courtyard. The crowd pressed so unpleasantly close
that Brigge soon climbed into a Judas tree, the better to observe the
proceedings. The rumour had got about among the natives (and here
is additional proof of Orlando's mysterious power over the imagination) that some kind of miracle was to be performed. 'Thus,' writes
Brigge (but his manuscript is full of burns and holes, some sentences
being quite illegible), 'when the rockets began to soar into the air,
there was considerable uneasiness among us lest the native population should be seized . . . fraught with unpleasant consequences to
all . . . English ladies in the company, I own that my hand went to my
cutlass. Happily,' he continues in his somewhat long-winded style,
'these fears seemed, for the moment, groundless and, observing the
demeanour of the natives . . . I came to the conclusion that this demonstration of our skill in the art of pyrotechny was valuable, if only
because it impressed upon them . . . the superiority of the British.
. . . Indeed, the sight was one of indescribable magnificence. I found
myself alternately praising the Lord that he had permitted . . . and
wishing that my poor, dear mother. . . . By the Ambassador's orders,
the long windows, which are so imposing a feature of Eastern architecture, for though ignorant in many ways . . . were thrown wide; and
within, we could see a tableau vivant or theatrical display in which
English ladies and gentlemen . . . represented a masque the work
of one . . . The words were inaudible, but the sight of so many of
our countrymen and women, dressed with the highest elegance and
distinction . . . moved me to emotions of which I am certainly not
ashamed, though unable. . . . I was intent upon observing the astonishing conduct of Lady —— which was of a nature to fasten the eyes
of all upon her, and to bring discredit upon her sex and country,
when'—unfortunately a branch of the Judas tree broke, Lieutenant
Brigge fell to the ground, and the rest of the entry records only his

gratitude to Providence (who plays a very large part in the diary) and the exact nature of his injuries.

Happily, Miss Penelope Hartopp,* daughter of the General of that name, saw the scene from inside and carries on the tale in a letter, much defaced too, which ultimately reached a female friend at Tunbridge Wells. Miss Penelope was no less lavish in her enthusiasm than the gallant officer. 'Ravishing,' she exclaims ten times on one page, 'wondrous . . . utterly beyond description . . . gold plate . . . candelabras . . . negroes in plush breeches . . . pyramids of ice . . . fountains of negus* . . . jellies made to represent His Majesty's ships . . . swans made to represent water lilies . . . birds in golden cages . . . gentlemen in slashed crimson velvet . . . Ladies' headdresses *at least* six foot high . . . musical boxes . . . Mr Peregrine said I looked *quite* lovely which I only repeat to you, my dearest, because I know. . . . Oh! how I longed for you all! . . . surpassing anything we have seen at the Pantiles* . . . oceans to drink . . . some gentlemen overcome . . . Lady Betty ravishing . . . Poor Lady Bonham made the unfortunate mistake of sitting down without a chair beneath her. . . . Gentlemen all very gallant . . . wished a thousand times for you and dearest Betsy. . . . But the sight of all others, the cynosure of all eyes . . . as all admitted, for none could be so vile as to deny it, was the Ambassador himself. Such a leg! Such a countenance!! Such princely manners!!! To see him come into the room! To see him go out again! And something *interesting* in the expression, which makes one feel, one scarcely knows why, that he has *suffered*! They say a lady was the cause of it. The heartless monster!!! How can one of our *reputed tender sex* have had the effrontery!!! He is unmarried, and half the ladies in the place are wild for love of him. . . . A thousand, thousand kisses to Tom, Gerry, Peter, and dearest Mew' [presumably her cat].

From the Gazette of the time, we gather that 'as the clock struck twelve, the Ambassador appeared on the centre Balcony which was hung with priceless rugs. Six Turks of the Imperial Body Guard, each over six foot in height, held torches to his right and left. Rockets rose into the air at his appearance, and a great shout went up from the people, which the Ambassador acknowledged, bowing deeply, and speaking a few words of thanks in the Turkish language, which it was one of his accomplishments to speak with fluency. Next, Sir Adrian Scrope, in the full dress of a British Admiral, advanced; the Ambassador knelt on one knee; the Admiral placed the Collar of the

Most Noble Order of the Bath round his neck, then pinned the Star to his breast; after which another gentleman of the diplomatic corps advancing in a stately manner placed on his shoulders the ducal robes, and handed him on a crimson cushion, the ducal coronet.'

At length, with a gesture of extraordinary majesty and grace, first bowing profoundly, then raising himself proudly erect, Orlando took the golden circlet of strawberry leaves and placed it, with a gesture which none that saw it ever forgot, upon his brows. It was at this point that the first disturbance began. Either the people had expected a miracle—some say a shower of gold was prophesied to fall from the skies—which did not happen, or this was the signal chosen for the attack to begin; nobody seems to know; but as the coronet settled on Orlando's brows a great uproar rose. Bells began ringing; the harsh cries of the prophets were heard above the shouts of the people; many Turks fell flat to the ground and touched the earth with their foreheads. A door burst open. The natives pressed into the banqueting rooms. Women shrieked. A certain lady, who was said to be dying for love of Orlando, seized a candelabra and dashed it to the ground. What might not have happened, had it not been for the presence of Sir Adrian Scrope and a squad of British blue-jackets, nobody can say. But the Admiral ordered the bugles to be sounded; a hundred blue-jackets* stood instantly at attention; the disorder was quelled, and quiet, at least for the time being, fell upon the scene.

So far, we are on the firm, if rather narrow, ground of ascertained truth. But nobody has ever known exactly what took place later that night. The testimony of the sentries and others seems, however, to prove that the Embassy was empty of company, and shut up for the night in the usual way by two A.M. The Ambassador was seen to go to his room, still wearing the insignia of his rank, and shut the door. Some say he locked it, which was against his custom. Others maintain that they heard music of a rustic kind, such as shepherds play, later that night in the courtyard under the Ambassador's window. A washer-woman, who was kept awake by toothache, said that she saw a man's figure, wrapped in a cloak or dressing gown, come out upon the balcony. Then, she said, a woman, much muffled, but apparently of the peasant class, was drawn up by means of a rope which the man let down to her on to the balcony. There, the washer-woman said, they embraced passionately 'like lovers', and went into the room together, drawing the curtains so that no more could be seen.

Next morning, the Duke, as we must now call him, was found by his secretaries sunk in profound slumber amid bed clothes that were much tumbled. The room was in some disorder, his coronet having rolled on the floor, and his cloak and garter being flung all of a heap on a chair. The table was littered with papers. No suspicion was felt at first, as the fatigues of the night had been great. But when afternoon came and he still slept, a doctor was summoned. He applied remedies which had been used on the previous occasion, plasters, nettles, emetics, etc., but without success. Orlando slept on. His secretaries then thought it their duty to examine the papers on the table. Many were scribbled over with poetry, in which frequent mention was made of an oak tree. There were also various state papers and others of a private nature concerning the management of his estates in England. But at length they came upon a document of far greater significance. It was nothing less, indeed, than a deed of marriage, drawn up, signed, and witnessed between his Lordship, Orlando, Knight of the Garter, etc., etc., etc., and Rosina Pepita,* a dancer, father unknown, but reputed a gipsy, mother also unknown but reputed a seller of old iron in the market-place over against the Galata Bridge. The secretaries looked at each other in dismay. And still Orlando slept. Morning and evening they watched him, but, save that his breathing was regular and his cheeks still flushed their habitual deep rose, he gave no sign of life. Whatever science or ingenuity could do to waken him they did. But still he slept.

On the seventh day of his trance (Thursday, May the 10th) the first shot was fired of that terrible and bloody insurrection of which Lieutenant Brigge had detected the first symptoms. The Turks rose against the Sultan, set fire to the town, and put every foreigner they could find, either to the sword or to the bastinado.* A few English managed to escape; but, as might have been expected, the gentlemen of the British Embassy preferred to die in defence of their red boxes, or, in extreme cases, to swallow bunches of keys rather than let them fall into the hands of the Infidel. The rioters broke into Orlando's room, but seeing him stretched to all appearances dead they left him untouched, and only robbed him of his coronet and the robes of the Garter.

And now again obscurity descends, and would indeed that it were deeper! Would, we almost have it in our hearts to exclaim, that it were so deep that we could see nothing whatever through its opacity!

Would that we might here take the pen and write Finis to our work! Would that we might spare the reader what is to come and say to him in so many words, Orlando died and was buried. But here, alas, Truth, Candour, and Honesty, the austere Gods who keep watch and ward by the inkpot of the biographer, cry No! Putting their silver trumpets to their lips they demand in one blast, Truth! And again they cry Truth! and sounding yet a third time in concert they peal forth, The Truth and nothing but the Truth!

At which—Heaven be praised! for it affords us a breathing space— the doors gently open, as if a breath of the gentlest and holiest zephyr had wafted them apart, and three figures enter. First, comes our Lady of Purity; whose brows are bound with fillets of the whitest lamb's wool; whose hair is as an avalanche of the driven snow; and in whose hand reposes the white quill of a virgin goose. Following her, but with a statelier step, comes our Lady of Chastity; on whose brow is set like a turret of burning but unwasting fire a diadem of icicles; her eyes are pure stars, and her fingers, if they touch you, freeze you to the bone. Close behind her, sheltering indeed in the shadow of her more stately sisters, comes our Lady of Modesty, frailest and fairest of the three; whose face is only shown as the young moon shows when it is thin and sickle shaped and half hidden among clouds. Each advances towards the centre of the room where Orlando still lies sleeping; and with gestures at once appealing and commanding, *Our Lady of Purity* speaks first:

'I am the guardian of the sleeping fawn; the snow is dear to me; and the moon rising; and the silver sea. With my robes I cover the speckled hen's eggs and the brindled sea shell; I cover vice and poverty. On all things frail or dark or doubtful, my veil descends. Wherefore, speak not, reveal not. Spare, O spare!'

Here the trumpets peal forth.

'Purity Avaunt! Begone Purity!'

Then *Our Lady of Chastity* speaks:

'I am she whose touch freezes and whose glance turns to stone. I have stayed the star in its dancing, and the wave as it falls. The highest Alps are my dwelling place; and when I walk, the lightnings flash in my hair; where my eyes fall, they kill. Rather than let Orlando wake, I will freeze him to the bone. Spare, O spare!'

Here the trumpets peal forth.

'Chastity Avaunt! Begone Chastity!'

Then *Our Lady of Modesty* speaks, so low that one can hardly hear:
'I am she that men call Modesty. Virgin I am and ever shall be. Not
for me the fruitful fields and the fertile vineyard. Increase is odious
to me; and when the apples burgeon or the flocks breed, I run, I run;
I let my mantle fall. My hair covers my eyes. I do not see. Spare,
O spare!'

Again the trumpets peal forth:
'Modesty Avaunt! Begone Modesty!'

With gestures of grief and lamentation the three sisters now join
hands and dance slowly, tossing their veils and singing as they go:

'Truth come not out from your horrid den. Hide deeper, fearful
Truth. For you flaunt in the brutal gaze of the sun things that were
better unknown and undone; you unveil the shameful; the dark you
make clear, Hide! Hide! Hide!'

Here they make as if to cover Orlando with their draperies. The
trumpets, meanwhile, still blare forth,
'The Truth and nothing but the Truth.'

At this the Sisters try to cast their veils over the mouths of the
trumpets so as to muffle them, but in vain, for now all the trumpets
blare forth together,
'Horrid Sisters, go!'

The sisters become distracted and wail in unison, still circling and
flinging their veils up and down.

'It has not always been so! But men want us no longer; the women
detest us. We go; we go. I (*Purity says this*) to the hen roost. I (*Chastity
says this*) to the still unravished heights* of Surrey. I (*Modesty says
this*) to any cosy nook where there are ivy and curtains in plenty.'

'For there, not here (all speak together joining hands and making
gestures of farewell and despair towards the bed where Orlando lies
sleeping) dwell still in nest and boudoir, office and lawcourt those
who love us; those who honour us, virgins and city men; lawyers and
doctors; those who prohibit; those who deny; those who reverence
without knowing why; those who praise without understanding; the
still very numerous (Heaven be praised) tribe of the respectable; who
prefer to see not; desire to know not; love the darkness; those still worship us, and with reason; for we have given them Wealth, Prosperity,
Comfort, Ease. To them we go, you we leave. Come, Sisters, come!
This is no place for us here.'

They retire in haste, waving their draperies over their heads, as if to shut out something that they dare not look upon and close the door behind them.

We are, therefore, now left entirely alone in the room with the sleeping Orlando and the trumpeters. The trumpeters, ranging themselves side by side in order, blow one terrific blast:—

'THE TRUTH!'

at which Orlando woke.

He stretched himself. He rose. He stood upright in complete nakedness before us, and while the trumpets pealed Truth! Truth! Truth! we have no choice left but confess—he was a woman.

* * * * *

The sound of the trumpets died away and Orlando stood stark naked. No human being, since the world began, has ever looked more ravishing. His form combined in one the strength of a man and a woman's grace. As he stood there, the silver trumpets prolonged their note, as if reluctant to leave the lovely sight which their blast had called forth; and Chastity, Purity, and Modesty, inspired, no doubt, by Curiosity, peeped in at the door and threw a garment like a towel at the naked form which, unfortunately, fell short by several inches. Orlando looked himself up and down in a long looking-glass, without showing any signs of discomposure, and went, presumably, to his bath.

We may take advantage of this pause in the narrative to make certain statements. Orlando had become a woman—there is no denying it. But in every other respect, Orlando remained precisely as he had been. The change of sex, though it altered their future, did nothing whatever to alter their identity. Their faces remained, as their portraits prove, practically the same. His memory—but in future we must, for convention's sake, say 'her' for 'his', and 'she' for 'he'—her memory then, went back through all the events of her past life without encountering any obstacle. Some slight haziness there may have been, as if a few dark drops had fallen into the clear pool of memory; certain things had become a little dimmed; but that was all. The change seemed to have been accomplished painlessly and completely and in such a way that Orlando herself showed no surprise at it. Many people, taking this into account, and holding that such a change of sex is against nature, have been at great pains to prove (1) that Orlando had always been a woman, (2) that Orlando is at this moment a man.

Let biologists and psychologists determine. It is enough for us to state the simple fact; Orlando was a man till the age of thirty; when he became a woman and has remained so ever since.

But let other pens treat of sex and sexuality;* we quit such odious subjects as soon as we can. Orlando had now washed, and dressed herself in those Turkish coats and trousers which can be worn indifferently by either sex; and was forced to consider her position. That it was precarious and embarrassing in the extreme must be the first thought of every reader who has followed her story with sympathy. Young, noble, beautiful, she had woken to find herself in a position than which we can conceive none more delicate for a young lady of rank. We should not have blamed her had she rung the bell, screamed, or fainted. But Orlando showed no such signs of perturbation. All her actions were deliberate in the extreme, and might indeed have been thought to show tokens of premeditation. First, she carefully examined the papers on the table; took such as seemed to be written in poetry, and secreted them in her bosom; next she called her Seleuchi hound,* which had never left her bed all these days, though half famished with hunger, fed and combed him; then stuck a pair of pistols in her belt; finally wound about her person several strings of emeralds and pearls of the finest orient* which had formed part of her Ambassadorial wardrobe. This done, she leant out of the window, gave one low whistle, and descended the shattered and blood-stained staircase, now strewn with the litter of waste-paper baskets, treaties, despatches, seals, sealing wax, etc., and so entered the court-yard. There, in the shadow of a giant fig tree, waited an old gipsy on a donkey. He led another by the bridle. Orlando swung her leg over it; and thus, attended by a lean dog, riding a donkey, in company of a gipsy, the Ambassador of Great Britain at the Court of the Sultan left Constantinople.

They rode for several days and nights and met with a variety of adventures, some at the hands of men, some at the hands of nature, in all of which Orlando acquitted herself with courage. Within a week they reached the high ground outside Broussa,* which was then the chief camping ground of the gipsy tribe to which Orlando had allied herself. Often she had looked at those mountains from her balcony at the Embassy; often had longed to be there; and to find oneself where one has longed to be always, to a reflective mind, gives food for thought. For some time, however, she was too well pleased with the change to spoil it by thinking. The pleasure of having no documents to seal or sign, no flourishes to make, no calls to pay, was enough. The gipsies followed the grass; when it was grazed down, on they moved again. She washed in streams if she washed at all; no boxes, red, blue, or green, were presented to her; there was not a key, let alone a golden key, in the whole camp; as for 'visiting', the word was unknown. She milked the goats; she collected brushwood; she stole a hen's egg now and then, but always put a coin or a pearl in place of it; she herded cattle; she stripped vines; she trod the grape; she filled the goat-skin and drank from it; and when she remembered how, at about this time of day, she should have been making the motions of drinking and smoking over an empty coffee-cup and a pipe which lacked tobacco, she laughed aloud, cut herself another hunch of bread, and begged for a puff from old Rustum's pipe,* filled though it was with cow dung.

The gipsies, with whom it is obvious that she must have been in secret communication before the revolution, seem to have looked upon her as one of themselves (which is always the highest compliment a people can pay), and her dark hair and dark complexion bore out the belief that she was, by birth, one of them and had been snatched by an English Duke from a nut tree when she was a baby and taken to that barbarous land where people live in houses because they are too feeble and diseased to stand the open air. Thus, though in many ways inferior to them, they were willing to help her to become more like them; taught her their arts of cheese-making and basket-weaving, their science of stealing and bird-snaring, and were even prepared to consider letting her marry among them.

But Orlando had contracted in England some of the customs or diseases (whatever you choose to consider them) which cannot, it seems, be expelled. One evening, when they were all sitting round the camp fire and the sunset was blazing over the Thessalian hills,* Orlando exclaimed:

'How good to eat!'

(The gipsies have no word for 'beautiful'.* This is the nearest.)

All the young men and women burst out laughing uproariously. The sky good to eat, indeed! The elders, however, who had seen more of foreigners than they had, became suspicious. They noticed that Orlando often sat for whole hours doing nothing whatever, except look here and then there; they would come upon her on some hill-top staring straight in front of her, no matter whether the goats were grazing or straying.

They began to suspect that she had other beliefs than their own, and the older men and women thought it probable that she had fallen into the clutches of the vilest and cruellest among all the Gods, which is Nature. Nor were they far wrong. The English disease, a love of Nature, was inborn in her, and here, where Nature was so much larger and more powerful than in England, she fell into its hands as she had never done before. The malady is too well known, and has been, alas, too often described to need describing afresh, save very briefly. There were mountains; there were valleys; there were streams. She climbed the mountains; roamed the valleys; sat on the banks of the streams. She likened the hills to ramparts, to the breasts of doves, and the flanks of kine. She compared the flowers to enamel and the turf to Turkey rugs worn thin. Trees were withered hags, and sheep were grey boulders. Everything, in fact, was something else. She found the tarn on the mountain-top and almost threw herself in to seek the wisdom she thought lay hid there; and when, from the mountain-top, she beheld far off, across the Sea of Marmara, the plains of Greece, and made out (her eyes were admirable) the Acropolis* with a white streak or two which must, she thought, be the Parthenon, her soul expanded with her eyeballs, and she prayed that she might share the majesty of the hills, know the serenity of the plains, etc., etc., as all such believers do. Then, looking down, the red hyacinth, the purple iris wrought her to cry out in ecstasy at the goodness, the beauty of nature; raising her eyes again, she beheld the eagle soaring, and imagined its raptures and made them her own. Returning home, she saluted each star, each peak, and each watch-fire as if they signalled to her alone; and at last, when she flung herself upon her mat in the gipsies' tent, she could not help bursting out again, How good to eat! How good to eat! (For it is a curious fact that though human beings have such imperfect means of communication, that they can only say 'good to eat' when they mean 'beautiful' and the other way about, they will yet endure ridicule and misunderstanding rather than keep any experience to themselves.) All the young gipsies laughed. But Rustum el Sadi, the old man who had brought Orlando out of Constantinople on his donkey, sat silent. He had a nose like a scimitar; his cheeks were furrowed as if from the age-long descent of iron hail; he was brown and keen-eyed, and as he sat tugging at his hookah he observed Orlando narrowly. He had the deepest suspicion that her God was Nature. One day he found her in tears. Interpreting this to mean that her God had punished her, he told her that he was not surprised.

He showed her the fingers of his left hand, withered by the frost; he showed her his right foot, crushed where a rock had fallen. This, he said, was what her God did to men. When she said, 'But so beautiful', using the English word, he shook his head; and when she repeated it he was angry. He saw that she did not believe what he believed, and that was enough, wise and ancient as he was, to enrage him.

This difference of opinion disturbed Orlando, who had been perfectly happy until now. She began to think, was Nature beautiful or cruel; and then she asked herself what this beauty was; whether it was in things themselves, or only in herself; so she went on to the nature of reality, which led her to truth, which in its turn led to Love, Friendship, Poetry (as in the days on the high mound at home); which meditations, since she could impart no word of them, made her long, as she had never longed before, for pen and ink.

'Oh! if only I could write!' she cried (for she had the odd conceit of those who write that words written are shared). She had no ink; and but little paper. But she made ink from berries and wine; and finding a few margins and blank spaces in the manuscript of 'The Oak Tree', managed, by writing a kind of shorthand, to describe the scenery in a long, blank version poem, and to carry on a dialogue with herself about this Beauty and Truth concisely enough. This kept her extremely happy for hours on end. But the gipsies became suspicious. First, they noticed that she was less adept than before at milking and cheese-making; next, she often hesitated before replying; and once a gipsy boy who had been asleep, woke in a terror feeling her eyes upon him. Sometimes this constraint would be felt by the whole tribe, numbering some dozens of grown men and women. It sprang from the sense they had (and their senses are very sharp and much in advance of their vocabulary) that whatever they were doing crumbled like ashes in their hands. An old woman making a basket, a boy skinning a sheep, would be singing or crooning contentedly at their work, when Orlando would come into the camp, fling herself down by the fire and gaze into the flames. She need not even look at them, and yet they felt, here is someone who doubts; (we make a rough-and-ready translation from the gipsy language) here is someone who does not do the thing for the sake of doing; nor looks for looking's sake; here is someone who believes neither in sheep-skin nor basket; but sees (here they looked apprehensively about the tent) something else. Then a vague but most unpleasant feeling would begin to work in the boy

and in the old woman. They broke their withys; they cut their fingers.
A great rage filled them. They wished Orlando would leave the tent
and never come near them again. Yet she was of a cheerful and willing
disposition, they owned; and one of her pearls was enough to buy the
finest herd of goats in Broussa.

Slowly, she began to feel that there was some difference between
her and the gipsies which made her hesitate sometimes to marry and
settle down among them for ever. At first she tried to account for it by
saying that she came of an ancient and civilized race, whereas these
gipsies were an ignorant people, not much better than savages. One
night when they were questioning her about England she could not
help with some pride describing the house where she was born, how
it had 365 bedrooms and had been in the possession of her family for
four or five hundred years. Her ancestors were earls, or even dukes,
she added. At this she noticed again that the gipsies were uneasy; but
not angry as before when she had praised the beauty of nature. Now
they were courteous, but concerned as people of fine breeding are
when a stranger has been made to reveal his low birth or poverty.
Rustum followed her out of the tent alone and said that she need
not mind if her father were a Duke, and possessed all the bedrooms
and furniture that she described. They would none of them think
the worse of her for that. Then she was seized with a shame that she
had never felt before. It was clear that Rustum and the other gipsies
thought a descent of four or five hundred years only* the meanest
possible. Their own families went back at least two or three thousand
years. To the gipsy whose ancestors had built the Pyramids centuries
before Christ was born, the genealogy of Howards and Plantagenets*
was no better and no worse than that of the Smiths and the Joneses;
both were negligible. Moreover, where the shepherd boy had a lin-
eage of such antiquity, there was nothing specially memorable or
desirable in ancient birth; vagabonds and beggars all shared it. And
then, though he was too courteous to speak openly, it was clear that
the gipsy thought that there was no more vulgar ambition than to
possess bedrooms by the hundred (they were on top of a hill as they
spoke; it was night; the mountains rose around them) when the whole
earth is ours. Looked at from the gipsy point of view, a Duke, Orlando
understood, was nothing but a profiteer or robber who snatched land
and money from people who rated these things of little worth, and
could think of nothing better to do than to build three hundred and

sixty-five bedrooms when one was enough, and none was even better than one. She could not deny that her ancestors had accumulated field after field; house after house; honour after honour; yet had none of them been saints or heroes, or great benefactors of the human race. Nor could she counter the argument (Rustum was too much of a gentleman to press it, but she understood) that any man who did now what her ancestors had done three or four hundred years ago would be denounced—and by her own family most loudly—for a vulgar upstart, an adventurer, a *nouveau riche*.

She sought to answer such arguments by the familiar if oblique method of finding the gipsy life itself rude and barbarous; and so, in a short time, much bad blood was bred between them. Indeed, such differences of opinion are enough to cause bloodshed and revolution. Towns have been sacked for less, and a million martyrs have suffered at the stake rather than yield an inch upon any of the points here debated. No passion is stronger in the breast of man than the desire to make others believe as he believes. Nothing so cuts at the root of his happiness and fills him with rage as the sense that another rates low what he prizes high. Whigs and Tories, Liberal party and Labour party*—for what do they battle except their own prestige? It is not love of truth but desire to prevail that sets quarter against quarter and makes parish desire the downfall of parish. Each seeks peace of mind and subserviency rather than the triumph of truth and the exaltation of virtue—but these moralities belong, and should be left to the historian, since they are as dull as ditch water.

'Four hundred and seventy-six bedrooms mean nothing to them,' sighed Orlando.

'She prefers a sunset to a flock of goats,' said the gipsies.

What was to be done, Orlando could not think. To leave the gipsies and become once more an Ambassador seemed to her intolerable. But it was equally impossible to remain for ever where there was neither ink nor writing paper, neither reverence for the Talbots nor respect for a multiplicity of bedrooms. So she was thinking, one fine morning on the slopes of Mount Athos,* when minding her goats. And then Nature, in whom she trusted, either played her a trick or worked a miracle—again, opinions differ too much for it to be possible to say which. Orlando was gazing rather disconsolately at the steep hill-side in front of her. It was now midsummer, and if we must compare the landscape to anything, it would have been to a dry bone; to a sheep's skeleton; to a gigantic skull picked white by a thousand vultures. The heat was intense, and the little fig tree under which Orlando lay only served to print patterns of fig-leaves upon her light burnous.*

Suddenly a shadow, though there was nothing to cast a shadow, appeared on the bald mountain-side opposite. It deepened quickly and soon a green hollow showed where there had been barren rock before. As she looked, the hollow deepened and widened, and a great park-like space opened in the flank of the hill. Within, she could see an undulating and grassy lawn; she could see oak trees dotted here and there; she could see the thrushes hopping among the branches. She could see the deer stepping delicately from shade to shade, and could even hear the hum of insects and the gentle sighs and shivers of a summer's day in England. After she had gazed entranced for some time, snow began falling; soon the whole landscape was covered and marked with violet shades instead of yellow sunlight. Now she saw heavy carts coming along the roads, laden with tree trunks, which they were taking, she knew, to be sawn for firewood; and then appeared the roofs and belfries and towers and courtyards of her own home. The snow was falling steadily, and she could now hear the slither and flop which it made as it slid down the roof and fell to the ground. The smoke went up from a thousand chimneys. All was so clear and minute that she could see a daw pecking for worms in the snow. Then, gradually, the violet shadows deepened and closed over the carts and the lawns and the great house itself. All was swallowed up. Now there was nothing left of the grassy hollow, and instead of the green lawns was only the blazing hill-side which a thousand vultures seemed to have picked bare. At this, she burst into a passion of tears, and striding back to the gipsies' camp, told them that she must sail for England the very next day.

It was happy for her that she did so. Already the young men had plotted her death. Honour, they said, demanded it, for she did not think as they did. Yet they would have been sorry to cut her throat; and welcomed the news of her departure. An English merchant ship, as luck would have it, was already under sail in the harbour about to return to England; and Orlando, by breaking off another pearl from her necklace, not only paid her passage but had some bank-notes left over in her wallet. These she would have liked to present to the gipsies. But they despised wealth she knew; and she had to content herself with embraces, which on her part were sincere.

CHAPTER IV

WITH some of the guineas left from the sale of the tenth pearl of her string, Orlando bought herself a complete outfit of such clothes as women then wore, and it was in the dress of a young Englishwoman of rank that she now sat on the deck of the *Enamoured Lady*. It is a strange fact, but a true one, that up to this moment she had scarcely given her sex a thought. Perhaps the Turkish trousers which she had hitherto worn had done something to distract her thoughts; and the gipsy women, except in one or two important particulars, differ very little from the gipsy men. At any rate, it was not until she felt the coil of skirts about her legs and the Captain offered, with the greatest politeness, to have an awning spread for her on deck, that she realized with a start the penalties and the privileges of her position. But that start was not of the kind that might have been expected.

It was not caused, that is to say, simply and solely by the thought of her chastity and how she could preserve it. In normal circumstances a lovely young woman alone would have thought of nothing else; the whole edifice of female government is based on that foundation stone; chastity is their jewel, their centre-piece, which they run mad to protect, and die when ravished of. But if one has been a man for thirty years or so, and an Ambassador into the bargain, if one has held a Queen in one's arms and one or two other ladies, if report be true, of less exalted rank, if one has married a Rosina Pepita, and so on, one does not perhaps give such a very great start about that. Orlando's start was of a very complicated kind, and not to be summed up in a trice. Nobody, indeed, ever accused her of being one of those quick wits who run to the end of things in a minute. It took her the entire length of the voyage to moralize out the meaning of her start, and so, at her own pace, we will follow her.

'Lord,' she thought, when she had recovered from her start, stretching herself out at length under her awning, 'this is a pleasant, lazy way of life, to be sure. But', she thought, giving her legs a kick, 'these skirts are plaguey things to have about one's heels. Yet the stuff (flowered paduasoy*) is the loveliest in the world. Never have I seen my own skin (here she laid her hand on her knee) look to such advantage as now. Could I, however, leap overboard and swim in clothes like these? No! Therefore, I should have to trust to the protection of a blue-jacket. Do I object to that? Now do I?' she wondered, here encountering the first knot in the smooth skein of her argument.

Dinner came before she had untied it, and then it was the Captain himself—Captain Nicholas Benedict Bartolus, a sea-captain of distinguished aspect, who did it for her as he helped her to a slice of corned beef.

'A little of the fat, Ma'am?' he asked. 'Let me cut you just the tiniest little slice the size of your finger nail.' At those words a delicious tremor ran through her frame. Birds sang; the torrents rushed. It recalled the feeling of indescribable pleasure with which she had first seen Sasha, hundreds of years ago. Then she had pursued, now she fled. Which is the greater ecstasy? The man's or the woman's?* And are they not perhaps the same? No, she thought, this is the most delicious (thanking the Captain but refusing), to refuse, and see him frown. Well, she would, if he wished it, have the very thinnest, smallest shiver* in the world. This was the most delicious of all, to yield and see him smile. 'For nothing', she thought, regaining her couch on deck, and continuing the argument, 'is more heavenly than to resist and to yield; to yield and to resist. Surely it throws the spirit into such a rapture as nothing else can. So that I'm not sure', she continued, 'that I won't throw myself overboard, for the mere pleasure of being rescued by a blue-jacket after all.'

(It must be remembered that she was like a child entering into possession of a pleasaunce* or toy cupboard; her arguments would not commend themselves to mature women, who have had the run of it all their lives.)

'But what used we young fellows in the cockpit of the *Marie Rose** to say about a woman who threw herself overboard for the pleasure of being rescued by a blue-jacket?' she said. 'We had a word for them. Ah! I have it. . . .' (But we must omit that word; it was disrespectful in the extreme and passing strange on a lady's lips.) 'Lord! Lord!' she cried again at the conclusion of her thoughts, 'must I then begin to respect the opinion of the other sex, however monstrous I think it? If I wear skirts, if I can't swim, if I have to be rescued by a blue-jacket, by God!' she cried, 'I must!' Upon which a gloom fell over her. Candid by nature, and averse to all kinds of equivocation, to tell lies bored her. It seemed to her a roundabout way of going to work. Yet, she reflected, the flowered paduasoy—the pleasure of being rescued by a blue-jacket—if these were only to be obtained by roundabout ways, roundabout one must go, she supposed. She remembered how, as a young man, she had insisted that women must be obedient, chaste, scented, and exquisitely apparelled. 'Now I shall have to pay in my own person for those desires,' she reflected; 'for women are not (judging by my own short experience of the sex) obedient, chaste, scented, and exquisitely apparelled by nature. They can only attain these graces, without which they may enjoy none of the delights of life, by the most tedious discipline. There's the hairdressing,' she thought, 'that alone will take an hour of my morning; there's looking in the looking-glass, another hour; there's staying* and lacing; there's washing and powdering; there's changing from silk to lace and from lace to paduasoy; there's being chaste year in year out. . . .' Here she tossed her foot impatiently, and showed an inch or two of calf. A sailor on the mast, who happened to look down at the moment, started so violently that he missed his footing and only saved himself by the skin of his teeth. 'If the sight of my ankles means death to an honest fellow who, no doubt, has a wife and family to support, I must, in all humanity, keep them covered,' Orlando thought. Yet her legs were among her chiefest beauties. And she fell to thinking what an odd pass we have come to when all a woman's beauty has to be kept covered lest a sailor may fall from a mast-head. 'A pox on them!' she said, realizing for the first time what, in other circumstances, she would have been taught as a child, that is to say, the sacred responsibilities of womanhood.

'And that's the last oath I shall ever be able to swear,' she thought, 'once I set foot on English soil. And I shall never be able to crack a man over the head, or tell him he lies in his teeth, or draw my sword and run him through the body, or sit among my peers, or wear a coronet, or walk in procession, or sentence a man to death, or lead an army, or prance down Whitehall on a charger, or wear seventy-two different medals on my breast. All I can do, once I set foot on English soil, is to pour out tea and ask my lords how they like it. D'you take sugar?* D'you take cream?' And mincing out the words, she was horrified to perceive how low an opinion she was forming of the other sex, the manly, to which it had once been her pride to belong. 'To fall from a masthead', she thought, 'because you see a woman's ankles; to dress up like a Guy Fawkes* and parade the streets, so that women may praise you; to deny a woman teaching lest she may laugh at you; to be the slave of the frailest chit in petticoats, and yet to go about as if you

ORLANDO ON HER RETURN TO ENGLAND

were the Lords of creation.—Heavens!' she thought, 'what fools they
make of us—what fools we are!' And here it would seem from some
ambiguity in her terms that she was censuring both sexes equally, as if
she belonged to neither; and indeed, for the time being, she seemed to
vacillate; she was man; she was woman; she knew the secrets, shared
the weaknesses of each. It was a most bewildering and whirligig state
of mind to be in. The comforts of ignorance seemed utterly denied
her. She was a feather blown on the gale. Thus it is no great wonder,
as she pitted one sex against the other, and found each alternately
full of the most deplorable infirmities, and was not sure to which
she belonged—it was no great wonder that she was about to cry out
that she would return to Turkey and become a gipsy again when the
anchor fell with a great splash into the sea; the sails came tumbling on
deck, and she perceived (so sunk had she been in thought that she had
seen nothing for several days) that the ship was anchored off the coast
of Italy. The Captain at once sent to ask the honour of her company
ashore with him in the long-boat.

When she returned the next morning, she stretched herself on her
couch under the awning and arranged her draperies with the greatest
decorum about her ankles.

'Ignorant and poor as we are compared with the other sex,' she
thought, continuing the sentence which she had left unfinished the
other day, 'armoured with every weapon as they are, while they debar
us even from a knowledge of the alphabet' (and from these opening
words it is plain that something had happened during the night to
give her a push towards the female sex, for she was speaking more as
a woman speaks than as a man, yet with a sort of content after all),
'still—they fall from the mast-head.' Here she gave a great yawn and
fell asleep. When she woke, the ship was sailing before a fair breeze so
near the shore that towns on the cliffs' edge seemed only kept from
slipping into the water by the interposition of some great rock or the
twisted roots of some ancient olive tree. The scent of oranges wafted
from a million trees, heavy with the fruit, reached her on deck.
A score of blue dolphins, twisting their tails, leapt high now and again
into the air. Stretching her arms out (arms, she had learnt already,
have no such fatal effects as legs), she thanked Heaven that she was
not prancing down Whitehall on a war-horse, nor even sentencing
a man to death. 'Better is it', she thought, 'to be clothed with poverty
and ignorance, which are the dark garments of the female sex; better

to leave the rule and discipline of the world to others; better be quit of martial ambition, the love of power, and all the other manly desires if so one can more fully enjoy the most exalted raptures known to the human spirit, which are', she said aloud, as her habit was when deeply moved, 'contemplation, solitude, love.'

'Praise God that I'm a woman!' she cried, and was about to run into the extreme folly—than which none is more distressing in woman or man either—of being proud of her sex, when she paused over the singular word, which, for all we can do to put it in its place, has crept in at the end of the last sentence: Love. 'Love,' said Orlando. Instantly—such is its impetuosity—love took a human shape—such is its pride. For where other thoughts are content to remain abstract, nothing will satisfy this one but to put on flesh and blood, mantilla* and petticoats, hose and jerkin. And as all Orlando's loves had been women, now, through the culpable laggardry of the human frame to adapt itself to convention, though she herself was a woman, it was still a woman she loved; and if the consciousness of being of the same sex had any effect at all, it was to quicken and deepen those feelings which she had had as a man. For now a thousand hints and mysteries became plain to her that were then dark. Now, the obscurity, which divides the sexes and lets linger innumerable impurities in its gloom, was removed, and if there is anything in what the poet says about truth and beauty,* this affection gained in beauty what it lost in falsity. At last, she cried, she knew Sasha as she was, and in the ardour of this discovery, and in the pursuit of all those treasures which were now revealed, she was so rapt and enchanted that it was as if a cannon ball had exploded at her ear when a man's voice said, 'Permit me, Madam,' a man's hand raised her to her feet; and the fingers of a man with a three-masted sailing ship tattooed on the middle finger pointed to the horizon.

'The cliffs of England, Ma'am,' said the Captain, and he raised the hand which had pointed at the sky to the salute. Orlando now gave a second start, even more violent than the first.

'Christ Jesus!' she cried.

Happily, the sight of her native land after long absence excused both start and exclamation, or she would have been hard put to it to explain to Captain Bartolus the raging and conflicting emotions which now boiled within her. How tell him that she, who now trembled on his arm, had been a Duke and an Ambassador? How explain to him that she, who had been lapped like a lily in folds of paduasoy, had hacked heads off, and lain with loose women among treasure sacks in the holds of pirate ships on summer nights when the tulips were abloom and the bees buzzing off Wapping Old Stairs? Not even to herself could she explain the giant start she gave, as the resolute right hand of the sea-captain indicated the cliffs of the British Islands.

'To refuse and to yield,' she murmured, 'how delightful; to pursue and conquer, how august; to perceive and to reason, how sublime.' Not one of these words so coupled together seemed to her wrong; nevertheless, as the chalky cliffs loomed nearer, she felt culpable; dishonoured; unchaste, which, for one who had never given the matter a thought, was strange. Closer and closer they drew, till the samphire gatherers, hanging half-way down the cliff,* were plain to the naked eye. And watching them, she felt, scampering up and down within her, like some derisive ghost who in another instant will pick up her skirts and flaunt out of sight, Sasha the lost, Sasha the memory, whose reality she had proved just now so surprisingly—Sasha, she felt, mopping and mowing and making all sorts of disrespectful gestures towards the cliffs and the samphire gatherers; and when the sailors began chanting, 'So good-bye and adieu to you, Ladies of Spain',* the words echoed in Orlando's sad heart, and she felt that however much landing there meant comfort, meant opulence, meant consequence and state (for she would doubtless pick up some noble Prince and reign, his consort, over half Yorkshire), still, if it meant conventionality, meant slavery, meant deceit, meant denying her love, fettering her limbs, pursing her lips, and restraining her tongue, then she would turn about with the ship and set sail once more for the gipsies.

Among the hurry of these thoughts, however, there now rose, like a dome of smooth, white marble, something which, whether fact or fancy, was so impressive to her fevered imagination that she settled upon it as one has seen a swarm of vibrant dragon-flies alight, with apparent satisfaction, upon the glass bell which shelters some tender vegetable. The form of it, by the hazard of fancy, recalled that earliest, most persistent memory—the man with the big forehead in Twitchett's sitting-room, the man who sat writing, or rather looking, but certainly not at her, for he never seemed to see her poised there in all her finery, lovely boy though she must have been, she could not deny it—and whenever she thought of him, the thought spread round it, like the risen moon on turbulent waters, a sheet of silver

calm. Now her hand went to her bosom (the other was still in the
Captain's keeping), where the pages of her poem were hidden safe. It
might have been a talisman that she kept there. The distraction of sex,
which hers was, and what it meant, subsided; she thought now only
of the glory of poetry, and the great lines of Marlowe, Shakespeare,
Ben Jonson, Milton began booming and reverberating, as if a golden
clapper beat against a golden bell in the cathedral tower which was
her mind. The truth was that the image of the marble dome which her
eyes had first discovered so faintly that it suggested a poet's forehead
and thus started a flock of irrelevant ideas, was no figment, but a reality; and as the ship advanced down the Thames before a favouring
gale, the image with all its associations gave place to the truth, and
revealed itself as nothing more and nothing less than the dome of
a vast cathedral rising among a fretwork of white spires.

'St Paul's,'* said Captain Bartolus, who stood by her side. 'The
Tower of London,' he continued. 'Greenwich Hospital, erected in
memory of Queen Mary by her husband, his late majesty, William
the Third.* Westminster Abbey. The Houses of Parliament.' As
he spoke, each of these famous buildings rose to view. It was a fine
September morning. A myriad of little watercraft plied from bank
to bank. Rarely has a gayer, or more interesting, spectacle presented
itself to the gaze of a returned traveller. Orlando hung over the prow,
absorbed in wonder. Her eyes had been used too long to savages and
nature not to be entranced by these urban glories. That, then, was
the dome of St Paul's which Mr Wren had built during her absence.
Near by, a shock of golden hair burst from a pillar—Captain Bartolus
was at her side to inform her that that was the Monument; there had
been a plague and a fire* during her absence, he said. Do what she
could to restrain them, the tears came to her eyes, until, remembering that it is becoming in a woman to weep, she let them flow. Here,
she thought, had been the great carnival. Here, where the waves
slapped briskly, had stood the Royal Pavilion. Here she had first met
Sasha. About here (she looked down into the sparkling waters) one
had been used to see the frozen bumboat woman with her apples on
her lap. All that splendour and corruption was gone. Gone, too, was
the dark night, the monstrous downpour, the violent surges of the
flood. Here, where yellow icebergs had raced circling with a crew of
terror-stricken wretches on top, a covey of swans floated, orgulous,
undulant, superb. London itself had completely changed since she

had last seen it. Then, she remembered, it had been a huddle of little black, beetle-browed houses. The heads of rebels had grinned on
pikes at Temple Bar. The cobbled pavements had reeked of garbage
and ordure. Now, as the ship sailed past Wapping, she caught glimpses
of broad and orderly thoroughfares. Stately coaches drawn by teams
of well-fed horses stood at the doors of houses whose bow windows,
whose plate glass, whose polished knockers, testified to the wealth and
modest dignity of the dwellers within. Ladies in flowered silk (she put
the Captain's glass to her eye) walked on raised footpaths. Citizens in
broidered coats took snuff at street corners under lamp-posts. She
caught sight of a variety of painted signs swinging in the breeze and
could form a rapid notion from what was painted on them of the
tobacco, of the stuff, of the silk, of the gold, of the silver ware, of the
gloves, of the perfumes, and of a thousand other articles which were
sold within. Nor could she do more as the ship sailed to its anchorage by London Bridge* than glance at coffee-house windows where,
on balconies, since the weather was fine, a great number of decent
citizens sat at ease, with china dishes in front of them, clay pipes by
their sides, while one among them read from a news sheet, and was
frequently interrupted by the laughter or the comments of the others.
Were these taverns, were these wits, were these poets? she asked of
Captain Bartolus, who obligingly informed her that even now—if she
turned her head a little to the left and looked along the line of his
first finger—so—they were passing the Cocoa Tree,* where,—yes,
there he was—one might see Mr Addison taking his coffee; the other
two gentlemen—'there, Ma'am, a little to the right of the lamp-post,
one of 'em humped, t'other much the same as you or me'—were
Mr Dryden and Mr Pope.[1]* 'Sad dogs,' said the Captain, by which
he meant that they were Papists,* 'but men of parts,* none the less,'
he added, hurrying aft to superintend the arrangements for landing.

'Addison, Dryden, Pope,' Orlando repeated as if the words were
an incantation. For one moment she saw the high mountains above
Broussa, the next, she had set her foot upon her native shore.

But now Orlando was to learn how little the most tempestuous flutter of excitement avails against the iron countenance of the law; how
harder than the stones of London Bridge it is, and than the lips of

[1] The Captain must have been mistaken, as a reference to any textbook of literature
will show; but the mistake was a kindly one, and so we let it stand.*

a cannon more severe. No sooner had she returned to her home in
Blackfriars* than she was made aware by a succession of Bow Street
runners* and other grave emissaries from the Law Courts that she
was a party to three major suits which had been preferred against her
during her absence, as well as innumerable minor litigations, some
arising out of, others depending on them. The chief charges against
her were (1) that she was dead, and therefore could not hold any property whatsoever; (2) that she was a woman, which amounts to much
the same thing; (3) that she was an English Duke who had married
one Rosina Pepita, a dancer; and had had by her three sons, which
sons now declaring that their father was deceased, claimed that all
his property descended to them. Such grave charges as these would,
of course, take time and money to dispose of. All her estates were put
in Chancery* and her titles pronounced in abeyance while the suits
were under litigation. Thus it was in a highly ambiguous condition,
uncertain whether she was alive or dead, man or woman, Duke or
nonentity, that she posted down to her country seat, where, pending
the legal judgement, she had the Law's permission to reside in a state
of incognito or incognita, as the case might turn out to be.

It was a fine evening in December when she arrived and the snow
was falling and the violet shadows were slanting much as she had seen
them from the hill-top at Broussa. The great house lay more like
a town than a house, brown and blue, rose and purple in the snow,
with all its chimneys smoking busily as if inspired with a life of their
own. She could not restrain a cry as she saw it there tranquil and
massive, couched upon the meadows. As the yellow coach entered the
park and came bowling along the drive between the trees, the red deer
raised their heads as if expectantly, and it was observed that instead
of showing the timidity natural to their kind, they followed the
coach and stood about the courtyard when it drew up. Some tossed
their antlers, others pawed the ground as the step was let down and
Orlando alighted. One, it is said, actually knelt in the snow before her.
She had not time to reach her hand towards the knocker before both
wings of the great door were flung open, and there, with lights and
torches held above their heads, were Mrs Grimsditch, Mr Dupper,
and a whole retinue of servants come to greet her. But the orderly
procession was interrupted first by the impetuosity of Canute,* the
elk-hound, who threw himself with such ardour upon his mistress
that he almost knocked her to the ground; next, by the agitation of

Mrs Grimsditch, who, making as if to curtsey, was overcome with emotion and could do no more than gasp Milord! Milady! Milady! Milord! until Orlando comforted her with a hearty kiss upon both her cheeks. After that, Mr Dupper began to read from a parchment, but the dogs barking, the huntsmen winding their horns, and the stags, who had come into the courtyard in the confusion, baying the moon, not much progress was made, and the company dispersed within after crowding about their Mistress, and testifying in every way to their great joy at her return.

No one showed an instant's suspicion that Orlando was not the Orlando they had known. If any doubt there was in the human mind the action of the deer and the dogs would have been enough to dispel it, for the dumb creatures, as is well known, are far better judges both of identity and character than we are. Moreover, said Mrs Grimsditch, over her dish of china tea, to Mr Dupper that night, if her Lord was a Lady now, she had never seen a lovelier one, nor was there a penny piece to choose between them; one was as well-favoured as the other; they were as like as two peaches on one branch; which, said Mrs Grimsditch, becoming confidential, she had always had her suspicions (here she nodded her head very mysteriously), which it was no surprise to her (here she nodded her head very knowingly), and for her part, a very great comfort; for what with the towels wanting mending and the curtains in the chaplain's parlour being moth-eaten round the fringes, it was time they had a Mistress among them.

'And some little masters and mistresses to come after her,' Mr Dupper added, being privileged by virtue of his holy office to speak his mind on such delicate matters as these.

So, while the old servants gossiped in the servants' hall, Orlando took a silver candle in her hand and roamed once more through the halls, the galleries, the courts, the bedrooms; saw loom down at her again the dark visage of this Lord Keeper, that Lord Chamberlain,* among her ancestors; sat now in this chair of state, now reclined on that canopy of delight; observed the arras, how it swayed; watched the huntsmen riding and Daphne* flying; bathed her hand, as she had loved to do as a child, in the yellow pool of light which the moonlight made falling through the heraldic Leopard in the window; slid along the polished planks of the gallery, the other side of which was rough timber; touched this silk, that satin; fancied the carved dolphins swam; brushed her hair with King James' silver brush; buried her

face in the potpourri, which was made as the Conqueror had taught
them many hundred years ago and from the same roses; looked at
the garden and imagined the sleeping crocuses, the dormant dahlias;
saw the frail nymphs gleaming white in the snow and the great yew
hedges, thick as a house, black behind them; saw the orangeries and
the giant medlars;—all this she saw, and each sight and sound, rudely
as we write it down, filled her heart with such a lust and balm of joy,
that at length, tired out, she entered the Chapel and sank into the old
red armchair in which her ancestors used to hear service. There she
lit a cheroot ('twas a habit she had brought back from the East) and
opened the Prayer Book.

It was a little book bound in velvet, stitched with gold, which had
been held by Mary Queen of Scots on the scaffold,* and the eye of
faith could detect a brownish stain, said to be made of a drop of the
Royal blood. But what pious thoughts it roused in Orlando, what
evil passions it soothed asleep, who dare say, seeing that of all com-
munions this with the deity is the most inscrutable? Novelist, poet,
historian all falter with their hand on that door; nor does the believer
himself enlighten us, for is he more ready to die than other people,
or more eager to share his goods? Does he not keep as many maids
and carriage horses as the rest? and yet with it all, holds a faith he
says which should make goods a vanity and death desirable. In the
Queen's prayer-book, along with the blood-stain, was also a lock of
hair and a crumb of pastry; Orlando now added to these keepsakes
a flake of tobacco, and so, reading and smoking, was moved by the
humane jumble of them all—the hair, the pastry, the blood-stain, the
tobacco—to such a mood of contemplation as gave her a reverent
air suitable in the circumstances, though she had, it is said, no traffic
with the usual God. Nothing, however, can be more arrogant, though
nothing is commoner than to assume that of Gods there is only one,
and of religions none but the speaker's. Orlando, it seemed, had
a faith of her own. With all the religious ardour in the world, she now
reflected upon her sins and the imperfections that had crept into her
spiritual state. The letter S, she reflected, is the serpent in the poet's
Eden. Do what she would there were still too many of these sinful
reptiles in the first stanzas of 'The Oak Tree'. But 'S' was nothing, in
her opinion, compared with the termination 'ing'. The present par-
ticiple is the Devil himself, she thought (now that we are in the place
for believing in Devils). To evade such temptations is the first duty

of the poet, she concluded, for as the ear is the antechamber to the soul, poetry can adulterate and destroy more surely than lust or gunpowder. The poet's, then, is the highest office of all, she continued. His words reach where others fall short. A silly song of Shakespeare's has done more for the poor and the wicked than all the preachers and philanthropists in the world. No time, no devotion, can be too great, therefore, which makes the vehicle of our message less distorting. We must shape our words till they are the thinnest integument for our thoughts. Thoughts are divine, etc.* Thus it is obvious that she was back in the confines of her own religion which time had only strengthened in her absence, and was rapidly acquiring the intolerance of belief.

'I am growing up,' she thought, taking her taper at last. 'I am losing some illusions,' she said, shutting Queen Mary's book, 'perhaps to acquire others,' and she descended among the tombs where the bones of her ancestors lay.

But even the bones of her ancestors, Sir Miles, Sir Gervase, and the rest, had lost something of their sanctity since Rustum el Sadi had waved his hand that night in the Asian mountains. Somehow the fact that only three or four hundred years ago these skeletons had been men with their way to make in the world like any modern upstart, and that they had made it by acquiring houses and offices, garters and ribbands, as any other upstart does, while poets, perhaps, and men of great mind and breeding had preferred the quietude of the country, for which choice they paid the penalty by extreme poverty, and now hawked broadsheets in the Strand, or herded sheep in the fields, filled her with remorse. She thought of the Egyptian pyramids and what bones lie beneath them as she stood in the crypt; and the vast, empty hills which lie above the Sea of Marmara seemed, for the moment, a finer dwelling-place than this many-roomed mansion in which no bed lacked its quilt and no silver dish its silver cover.

'I am growing up,' she thought, taking her taper. 'I am losing my illusions, perhaps to acquire new ones,' and she paced down the long gallery to her bedroom. It was a disagreeable process, and a troublesome. But it was interesting, amazingly, she thought, stretching her legs out to her log fire (for no sailor was present), and she reviewed, as if it were an avenue of great edifices, the progress of her own self along her own past.

How she had loved sound when she was a boy, and thought the

volley of tumultuous syllables from the lips the finest of all poetry. Then—it was the effect of Sasha and her disillusionment perhaps— into this high frenzy was let fall some black drop, which turned her rhapsody into sluggishness. Slowly there had opened within her something intricate and many-chambered, which one must take a torch to explore, in prose not verse; and she remembered how passionately she had studied that doctor at Norwich, Browne, whose book was at her hand there. She had formed here in solitude after her affair with Greene, or tried to form, for Heaven knows these growths are agelong in coming, a spirit capable of resistance. 'I will write', she had said, 'what I enjoy writing'; and so had scratched out twenty-six volumes. Yet still, for all her travels and adventures and profound thinkings and turnings this way and that, she was only in process of fabrication. What the future might bring, Heaven only knew. Change was incessant, and change perhaps would never cease. High battlements of thought, habits that had seemed durable as stone, went down like shadows at the touch of another mind and left a naked sky and fresh stars twinkling in it. Here she went to the window, and in spite of the cold could not help unlatching it. She leant out into the damp night air. She heard a fox bark in the woods, and the clutter of a pheasant trailing through the branches. She heard the snow slither and flop from the roof to the ground. 'By my life,' she exclaimed, 'this is a thousand times better than Turkey. Rustum,' she cried, as if she were arguing with the gipsy (and in this new power of bearing an argument in mind and continuing it with someone who was not there to contradict she showed again the development of her soul), 'you were wrong. This is better than Turkey. Hair, pastry, tobacco— of what odds and ends are we compounded,' she said (thinking of Queen Mary's prayer-book). 'What a phantasmagoria the mind is and meeting-place of dissemblables! At one moment we deplore our birth and state and aspire to an ascetic exaltation; the next we are overcome by the smell of some old garden path and weep to hear the thrushes sing.' And so bewildered as usual by the multitude of things which call for explanation and imprint their message without leaving any hint as to their meaning, she threw her cheroot out of the window and went to bed.

Next morning, in pursuance of these thoughts, she had out her pen and paper, and started afresh upon 'The Oak Tree', for to have ink and paper in plenty when one has made do with berries and margins is a delight not to be conceived. Thus she was now striking out a phrase in the depths of despair, now in the heights of ecstasy writing one in, when a shadow darkened the page. She hastily hid her manuscript.*

As her window gave on to the most central of the courts, as she had given orders that she would see no one, as she knew no one and was herself legally unknown, she was first surprised at the shadow, then indignant at it, then (when she looked up and saw what caused it) overcome with merriment. For it was a familiar shadow, a grotesque shadow, the shadow of no less a personage than the Archduchess Harriet Griselda of Finster-Aarhorn and Scand-op-Boom in the Roumanian territory. She was loping across the court in her old black riding-habit and mantle as before. Not a hair of her head was changed. This then was the woman who had chased her from England! This was the eyrie of that obscene vulture—this the fatal fowl herself! At the thought that she had fled all the way to Turkey to avoid her seductions (now become excessively flat), Orlando laughed aloud. There was something inexpressibly comic in the sight. She resembled, as Orlando had thought before, nothing so much as a monstrous hare. She had the staring eyes, the lank cheeks, the high headdress of that animal. She stopped now, much as a hare sits erect in the corn when thinking itself unobserved, and stared at Orlando, who stared back at her from the window. After they had stared like this for a certain time, there was nothing for it but to ask her in, and soon the two ladies were exchanging compliments while the Archduchess struck the snow from her mantle.

'A plague on women,' said Orlando to herself, going to the cupboard to fetch a glass of wine, 'they never leave one a moment's peace. A more ferreting, inquisiting, busybodying set of people don't exist. It was to escape this Maypole that I left England, and now'—here she turned to present the Archduchess with the salver, and behold—in her place stood a tall gentleman in black. A heap of clothes lay in the fender. She was alone with a man.

Recalled thus suddenly to a consciousness of her sex, which she had completely forgotten, and of his, which was now remote enough to be equally upsetting, Orlando felt seized with faintness.

'La!' she cried, putting her hand to her side, 'how you frighten me!'

'Gentle creature,' cried the Archduchess, falling on one knee and at the same time pressing a cordial to Orlando's lips, 'forgive me for the deceit I have practised on you!'

Orlando sipped the wine and the Archduke knelt and kissed her hand.

In short, they acted the parts of man and woman for ten minutes with great vigour and then fell into natural discourse. The Archduchess (but she must in future be known as the Archduke) told his story—that he was a man and always had been one; that he had seen a portrait of Orlando and fallen hopelessly in love with him; that to compass his ends, he had dressed as a woman and lodged at the Baker's shop; that he was desolated when he fled to Turkey; that he had heard of her change and hastened to offer his services (here he teed and heed intolerably). For to him, said the Archduke Harry, she was and would ever be the Pink, the Pearl, the Perfection of her sex. The three p's would have been more persuasive if they had not been interspersed with tee-hees and haw-haws of the strangest kind. 'If this is love,' said Orlando to herself, looking at the Archduke on the other side of the fender, and now from the woman's point of view, 'there is something highly ridiculous about it.'

Falling on his knees, the Archduke Harry made the most passionate declaration of his suit. He told her that he had something like twenty million ducats in a strong box at his castle. He had more acres than any nobleman in England. The shooting was excellent: he could promise her a mixed bag of ptarmigan and grouse such as no English moor, or Scotch either, could rival. True, the pheasants had suffered from the gape* in his absence, and the does had slipped their young, but that could be put right, and would be with her help when they lived in Roumania together.

As he spoke, enormous tears formed in his rather prominent eyes and ran down the sandy tracts of his long and lanky cheeks.

That men cry as frequently and as unreasonably as women, Orlando knew from her own experience as a man; but she was beginning to be aware that women should be shocked when men display emotion in their presence, and so, shocked she was.

The Archduke apologized. He commanded himself sufficiently to say that he would leave her now, but would return on the following day for his answer.

That was a Tuesday. He came on Wednesday; he came on Thursday; he came on Friday; and he came on Saturday. It is true that each visit began, continued, or concluded with a declaration of love, but in between there was much room for silence. They sat on either side of the fireplace and sometimes the Archduke knocked over the fire-irons and Orlando picked them up again. Then the Archduke would bethink him how he had shot an elk in Sweden, and Orlando would ask, was it a very big elk, and the Archduke would say that it was not as big as the reindeer which he had shot in Norway; and Orlando would ask, had he ever shot a tiger, and the Archduke would say he had shot an albatross, and Orlando would say (half hiding her yawn) was an albatross as big as an elephant, and the Archduke would say—something very sensible, no doubt, but Orlando heard it not, for she was looking at her writing-table, out of the window, at the door. Upon which the Archduke would say, 'I adore you', at the very same moment that Orlando said 'Look, it's beginning to rain', at which they were both much embarrassed, and blushed scarlet, and could neither of them think what to say next. Indeed, Orlando was at her wits' end what to talk about and had she not bethought her of a game called Fly Loo,* at which great sums of money can be lost with very little expense of spirit,* she would have had to marry him, she supposed; for how else to get rid of him she knew not. By this device, however, and it was a simple one, needing only three lumps of sugar and a sufficiency of flies, the embarrassment of conversation was overcome and the necessity of marriage avoided. For now, the Archduke would bet her five hundred pounds to a tester that a fly would settle on this lump and not on that. Thus, they would have occupation for a whole morning watching the flies (who were naturally sluggish at this season and often spent an hour or so circling round the ceiling) until at length some fine blue-bottle made his choice and the match was won. Many hundreds of pounds changed hands between them at this game, which the Archduke, who was a born gambler, swore was every bit as good as horse racing, and vowed he could play at for ever. But Orlando soon began to weary.

'What's the good of being a fine young woman in the prime of life', she asked, 'if I have to pass all my mornings watching blue-bottles with an Archduke?'

She began to detest the sight of sugar; flies made her dizzy. Some way out of the difficulty there must be, she supposed, but she was still awkward in the arts of her sex, and as she could no longer knock a man over the head or run him through the body with a rapier, she could think of no better method than this. She caught a blue-bottle, gently pressed the life out of it (it was half dead already, or her kindness for

the dumb creatures would not have permitted it) and secured it by
a drop of gum arabic to a lump of sugar. While the Archduke was gazing at the ceiling, she deftly substituted this lump for the one she had
laid her money on, and crying 'Loo Loo!' declared that she had won
her bet. Her reckoning was that the Archduke, with all his knowledge
of sport and horse-racing, would detect the fraud and, as to cheat at
Loo is the most heinous of crimes, and men have been banished from
the society of mankind to that of apes in the tropics for ever because
of it, she calculated that he would be manly enough to refuse to have
anything further to do with her. But she misjudged the simplicity
of the amiable nobleman. He was no nice judge of flies. A dead fly
looked to him much the same as a living one. She played the trick
twenty times on him and he paid her over £17,250 (which is about
£40,885:6:8* of our own money) before Orlando cheated so grossly
that even he could be deceived no longer. When she realized the truth
at last, a painful scene ensued. The Archduke rose to his full height.
He coloured scarlet. Tears rolled down his cheeks one by one. That
she had won a fortune from him was nothing—she was welcome to it;
that she had deceived him was something—it hurt him to think her
capable of it; but that she had cheated at Loo was everything. To love
a woman who cheated at play was, he said, impossible. Here he broke
down completely. Happily, he said, recovering slightly, there were no
witnesses. She was, after all, only a woman, he said. In short, he was
preparing in the chivalry of his heart to forgive her and had bent
to ask her pardon for the violence of his language, when she cut the
matter short, as he stooped his proud head, by dropping a small toad
between his skin and his shirt.

In justice to her, it must be said that she would infinitely have
preferred a rapier. Toads are clammy things to conceal about one's
person a whole morning. But if rapiers are forbidden, one must have
recourse to toads. Moreover toads and laughter between them sometimes do what cold steel cannot. She laughed. The Archduke blushed.
She laughed. The Archduke cursed. She laughed. The Archduke
slammed the door.

'Heaven be praised!' cried Orlando still laughing. She heard the
sound of chariot wheels driven at a furious pace down the courtyard.
She heard them rattle along the road. Fainter and fainter the sound
became. Now it faded away altogether.

'I am alone,' said Orlando, aloud since there was no one to hear.

That silence is more profound after noise still wants the confirm-ation of science. But that loneliness is more apparent directly after one has been made love to, many women would take their oath. As the sound of the Archduke's chariot wheels died away, Orlando felt drawing further from her and further from her an Archduke (she did not mind that), a fortune (she did not mind that), a title (she did not mind that), the safety and circumstance of married life (she did not mind that), but life she heard going from her, and a lover. 'Life and a lover,' she murmured; and going to her writing-table she dipped her pen in the ink and wrote:

'Life and a lover'—a line which did not scan and made no sense with what went before—something about the proper way of dipping sheep* to avoid the scab. Reading it over she blushed and repeated,

'Life and a lover.' Then laying her pen aside she went into her bed-room, stood in front of her mirror, and arranged her pearls about her neck. Then since pearls do not show to advantage against a morning gown of sprigged cotton, she changed to a dove grey taffeta; thence to one of peach bloom; thence to a wine-coloured brocade. Perhaps a dash of powder was needed, and if her hair were disposed—so—about her brow, it might become her. Then she slipped her feet into pointed slippers, and drew an emerald ring upon her finger. 'Now,' she said when all was ready and lit the silver sconces on either side of the mirror. What woman would not have kindled to see what Orlando saw then burning in the snow—for all about the looking-glass were snowy lawns, and she was like a fire, a burning bush, and the candle flames about her head were silver leaves; or again, the glass was green water, and she a mermaid, slung with pearls, a siren in a cave,* sing-ing so that oarsmen leant from their boats and fell down, down to embrace her; so dark, so bright, so hard, so soft, was she,* so aston-ishingly seductive that it was a thousand pities that there was no one there to put it in plain English, and say outright, 'Damn it, Madam, you are loveliness incarnate,' which was the truth. Even Orlando (who had no conceit of her person) knew it, for she smiled the involuntary smile which women smile when their own beauty, which seems not their own, forms like a drop falling or a fountain rising and confronts them all of a sudden in the glass—this smile she smiled and then she listened for a moment and heard only the leaves blowing and the sparrows twittering, and then she sighed, 'Life, a lover,' and then she turned on her heel with extraordinary rapidity; whipped her pearls from her neck, stripped the satins from her back, stood erect in the neat black silk knickerbockers of an ordinary nobleman, and rang the bell. When the servant came, she told him to order a coach and six to be in readiness instantly. She was summoned by urgent affairs to London. Within an hour of the Archduke's departure, off she drove.

And as she drove, we may seize the opportunity, since the landscape was of a simple English kind which needs no description, to draw the reader's attention more particularly than we could at the moment to one or two remarks which have slipped in here and there in the course of the narrative. For example, it may have been observed that Orlando hid her manuscripts when interrupted. Next, that she looked long and intently in the glass; and now, as she drove to London, one might notice her starting and suppressing a cry when the horses galloped faster than she liked. Her modesty as to her writing, her vanity as to her person, her fears for her safety all seems to hint that what was said a short time ago about there being no change in Orlando the man and Orlando the woman, was ceasing to be altogether true. She was becoming a little more modest, as women are, of her brains, and a little more vain, as women are, of her person. Certain susceptibilities were asserting themselves, and others were diminishing. The change of clothes had, some philosophers will say, much to do with it. Vain trifles as they seem, clothes have, they say, more important offices than merely to keep us warm. They change our view of the world and the world's view of us. For example, when Captain Bartolus saw Orlando's skirt, he had an awning stretched for her immediately, pressed her to take another slice of beef, and invited her to go ashore with him in the long-boat. These compliments would certainly not have been paid her had her skirts, instead of flowing, been cut tight to her legs in the fashion of breeches. And when we are paid compliments, it behoves us to make some return. Orlando curtseyed; she complied; she flattered the good man's humours as she would not have done had his neat breeches been a woman's skirts, and his braided coat a woman's satin bodice. Thus, there is much to support the view that it is clothes that wear us and not we them; we may make them take the mould of arm or breast, but they mould our hearts, our brains, our tongues to their liking. So, having now worn skirts for a considerable time, a certain change was visible in Orlando, which is to be found if the reader will look at page 94, even in her face. If we compare the picture of Orlando as a man with that of Orlando as a woman we shall see that though both are undoubtedly one and the same person, there are certain changes. The man has his hand free to seize his sword, the woman must use hers to keep the satins from slipping from her shoulders. The man looks the world full in the face, as if it were made for his uses and fashioned to his liking. The woman takes a sidelong glance at it, full of subtlety, even of suspicion. Had they both worn the same clothes, it is possible that their outlook might have been the same.

That is the view of some philosophers and wise ones, but on the whole, we incline to another. The difference between the sexes is, happily, one of great profundity. Clothes are but a symbol of something hid deep beneath. It was a change in Orlando herself that dictated her choice of a woman's dress and of a woman's sex. And perhaps in this she was only expressing rather more openly than usual—openness indeed was the soul of her nature—something that happens to most people without being thus plainly expressed. For here again, we come to a dilemma. Different though the sexes are, they intermix. In every human being a vacillation from one sex to the other takes place, and often it is only the clothes that keep the male or female likeness, while underneath the sex is the very opposite of what it is above. Of the complications and confusions which thus result everyone has had experience; but here we leave the general question and note only the odd effect it had in the particular case of Orlando herself.

For it was this mixture in her of man and woman, one being uppermost and then the other, that often gave her conduct an unexpected turn. The curious of her own sex would argue, for example, if Orlando was a woman, how did she never take more than ten minutes to dress? And were not her clothes chosen rather at random, and sometimes worn rather shabby? And then they would say, still, she has none of the formality of a man, or a man's love of power. She is excessively tender-hearted. She could not endure to see a donkey beaten or a kitten drowned. Yet again, they noted, she detested household matters, was up at dawn and out among the fields in summer before the sun had risen. No farmer knew more about the crops than she did. She could drink with the best and liked games of hazard. She rode well and drove six horses at a gallop over London Bridge. Yet again, though bold and active as a man, it was remarked that the sight of another in danger brought on the most womanly palpitations. She would burst into tears on slight provocation. She was unversed in geography, found mathematics intolerable, and held some caprices which are more common among women than men, as for instance that to travel south is to travel downhill. Whether, then, Orlando was most man or woman, it is difficult to say and cannot now be decided. For her coach was now rattling on the cobbles. She had reached her home in the city. The steps were being let down; the iron gates were being opened. She was entering her father's house at Blackfriars, which though fashion was fast deserting that end of the town, was still a pleasant, roomy mansion, with gardens running down to the river, and a pleasant grove of nut trees to walk in.

Here she took up her lodging and began instantly to look about her for what she had come in search of—that is to say, life and a lover. About the first there might be some doubt; the second she found without the least difficulty two days after her arrival. It was a Tuesday that she came to town. On Thursday she went for a walk in the Mall,* as was then the habit of persons of quality. She had not made more than a turn or two of the avenue before she was observed by a lit- tle knot of vulgar people who go there to spy upon their betters. As she came past them, a common woman carrying a child at her breast stepped forward, peered familiarly into Orlando's face, and cried out, 'Lawk upon us, if it ain't the Lady Orlando!' Her companions came crowding round, and Orlando found herself in a moment the centre of a mob of staring citizens and tradesmen's wives, all eager to gaze upon the heroine of the celebrated lawsuit.* Such was the interest that the case excited in the minds of the common people. She might, indeed, have found herself gravely discommoded by the pressure of the crowd—she had forgotten that ladies are not supposed to walk in public places alone—had not a tall gentleman at once stepped for- ward and offered her the protection of his arm. It was the Archduke. She was overcome with distress and yet with some amusement at the sight. Not only had this magnanimous nobleman forgiven her, but in order to show that he took her levity with the toad in good part, he had procured a jewel made in the shape of that reptile which he pressed upon her with a repetition of his suit as he handed her to her coach.

What with the crowd, what with the Duke, what with the jewel, she drove home in the vilest temper imaginable. Was it impossible

then to go for a walk without being half-suffocated, presented with
a toad set in emeralds, and asked in marriage by an Archduke?
She took a kinder view of the case next day when she found on her
breakfast table half a dozen billets from some of the greatest ladies
in the land—Lady Suffolk, Lady Salisbury, Lady Chesterfield, Lady
Tavistock,* and others who reminded her in the politest manner of
old alliances between their families and her own, and desired the
honour of her acquaintance. Next day, which was a Saturday, many of
these great ladies waited on her in person. On Tuesday, about noon,
their footmen brought cards of invitation to various routs,* dinners,
and assemblies in the near future; so that Orlando was launched without delay, and with some splash and foam at that, upon the waters of
London society.

To give a truthful account of London society at that or indeed at
any other time, is beyond the powers of the biographer or the historian. Only those who have little need of the truth, and no respect for
it—the poets and the novelists—can be trusted to do it, for this is one
of the cases where the truth does not exist. Nothing exists. The whole
thing is a miasma—a mirage. To make our meaning plain—Orlando
would come home from one of these routs at three or four in the
morning with cheeks like a Christmas tree and eyes like stars. She
would untie a lace, pace the room a score of times, untie another lace,
stop, and pace the room again. Often the sun would be blazing over
Southwark* chimneys before she could persuade herself to get into
bed, and there she would lie, pitching and tossing, laughing and sigh-
ing for an hour or longer, before she slept at last. And what was all
this stir about? Society. And what had society said or done to throw
a reasonable lady into such an excitement? In plain language, nothing. Rack her memory as she would, next day Orlando could never
remember a single word to magnify into the name something. Lord
O. had been gallant. Lord A. polite. The Marquis of C. charming.
Mr M. amusing. But when she tried to recollect in what their gallantry, politeness, charm, or wit had consisted, she was bound to suppose her memory at fault, for she could not name a thing. It was the
same always. Nothing remained over the next day, yet the excitement
of the moment was intense. Thus we are forced to conclude that society is one of those brews such as skilled housekeepers serve hot about
Christmas time, whose flavour depends upon the proper mixing and
stirring of a dozen different ingredients. Take one out, and it is in

itself insipid. Take away Lord O., Lord A., Lord C., or Mr M., and separately each is nothing. Stir them all together and they combine to give off the most intoxicating of flavours, the most seductive of scents. Yet this intoxication, this seductiveness, entirely evade our analysis. At one and the same time, therefore, society is everything and society is nothing. Society is the most powerful concoction in the world and society has no existence whatsoever. Such monsters the poets and the novelists alone can deal with; with such something-nothings their works are stuffed out to prodigious size; and to them with the best will in the world we are content to leave it.

Following the example of our predecessors, therefore, we will only say that society in the reign of Queen Anne* was of unparalleled brilliance. To have the entry there was the aim of every well-bred person. The graces were supreme. Fathers instructed their sons, mothers their daughters. No education was complete for either sex which did not include the science of deportment, the art of bowing and curtseying, the management of the sword and the fan, the care of the teeth, the conduct of the leg, the flexibility of the knee, the proper methods of entering and leaving the room, with a thousand etceteras, such as will immediately suggest themselves to anybody who has himself been in society. Since Orlando had won the praise of Queen Elizabeth for the way she handed a bowl of rose water as a boy, it must be supposed that she was sufficiently expert to pass muster. Yet it is true that there was an absent-mindedness about her which sometimes made her clumsy; she was apt to think of poetry when she should have been thinking of taffeta; her walk was a little too much of a stride for a woman, perhaps, and her gestures, being abrupt, might endanger a cup of tea on occasion.

Whether this slight disability was enough to counterbalance the splendour of her bearing, or whether she inherited a drop too much of that black humour which ran in the veins of all her race,* certain it is that she had not been in the world more than a score of times before she might have been heard to ask herself, had there been anybody but her spaniel Pippin* to hear her, 'What the devil is the matter with me?' The occasion was Tuesday, the 16th of June 1712; she had just returned from a great ball at Arlington House;* the dawn was in the sky, and she was pulling off her stockings. 'I don't care if I never meet another soul as long as I live,' cried Orlando, bursting into tears. Lovers she had in plenty, but life, which is, after all, of some importance in its way, escaped her. 'Is this', she asked—but there was none to answer, 'is this', she finished her sentence all the same, 'what people call life?' The spaniel raised her forepaw in token of sympathy. The spaniel licked Orlando with her tongue. Orlando stroked the spaniel with her hand. Orlando kissed the spaniel with her lips. In short, there was the truest sympathy between them that can be between a dog and its mistress, and yet it cannot be denied that the dumbness of animals is a great impediment to the refinements of intercourse. They wag their tails; they bow the front part of the body and elevate the hind; they roll, they jump, they paw, they whine, they bark, they slobber, they have all sorts of ceremonies and artifices of their own, but the whole thing is of no avail, since speak they cannot. Such was her quarrel, she thought, setting the dog gently on to the floor, with the great people at Arlington House. They, too, wag their tails, bow, roll, jump, paw, and slobber, but talk they cannot. 'All these months that I've been out in the world', said Orlando, pitching one stocking across the room, 'I've heard nothing but what Pippin might have said. I'm cold. I'm happy. I'm hungry. I've caught a mouse. I've buried a bone. Please kiss my nose.' And it was not enough.

How, in so short a time, she had passed from intoxication to disgust we will only seek to explain by supposing that this mysterious composition which we call society, is nothing absolutely good or bad in itself, but has a spirit in it, volatile but potent, which either makes you drunk when you think it, as Orlando thought it, delightful, or gives you a headache when you think it, as Orlando thought it, repulsive. That the faculty of speech has much to do with it either way, we take leave to doubt. Often a dumb hour is the most ravishing of all; brilliant wit can be tedious beyond description. But to the poets we leave it, and so on with our story.

Orlando threw the second stocking after the first and went to bed dismally enough, determined that she would forswear society for ever. But again as it turned out, she was too hasty in coming to her conclusions. For the very next morning she woke to find, among the usual cards of invitation upon her table, one from a certain great Lady, the Countess of R. Having determined overnight that she would never go into society again, we can only explain Orlando's behaviour—she sent a messenger hot-foot to R—— House to say that she would attend her Ladyship with all the pleasure in the world—by the fact that she was still suffering from the effect of three honeyed

words dropped into her ear on the deck of the *Enamoured Lady* by
Captain Nicholas Benedict Bartolus as they sailed down the Thames.
Addison, Dryden, Pope, he had said, pointing to the Cocoa Tree, and
Addison, Dryden, Pope had chimed in her head like an incantation
ever since. Who can credit such folly? but so it was. All her experience
with Nick Greene had taught her nothing. Such names still exercised
over her the most powerful fascination. Something, perhaps, we must
believe in, and as Orlando, we have said, had no belief in the usual
divinities she bestowed her credulity upon great men—yet with a distinction. Admirals, soldiers, statesmen, moved her not at all. But the
very thought of a great writer stirred her to such a pitch of belief that
she almost believed him to be invisible. Her instinct was a sound one.
One can only believe entirely, perhaps, in what one cannot see. The
little glimpse she had of these great men from the deck of the ship was
of the nature of a vision. That the cup was china, or the gazette paper,
she doubted. When Lord O. said one day that he had dined with
Dryden the night before, she flatly disbelieved him. Now, the Lady
R.'s reception room had the reputation of being the antechamber to
the presence room of genius; it was the place where men and women
met to swing censers and chant hymns to the bust of genius in a niche
in the wall. Sometimes the God himself vouchsafed his presence for
a moment. Intellect alone admitted the suppliant, and nothing (so the
report ran) was said inside that was not witty.

It was thus with great trepidation that Orlando entered the room.
She found a company already assembled in a semicircle round the fire.
Lady R., an oldish lady, of dark complexion, with a black lace mantilla
on her head, was seated in a great armchair in the centre. Thus being
somewhat deaf, she could control the conversation on both sides of
her. On both sides of her sat men and women of the highest distinction. Every man, it was said, had been a Prime Minister and every
woman, it was whispered, had been the mistress of a king. Certain it
is that all were brilliant, and all were famous. Orlando took her seat
with a deep reverence in silence. . . . After three hours, she curtseyed
profoundly and left.

But what, the reader may ask with some exasperation, happened
in between? In three hours, such a company must have said the wittiest, the profoundest, the most interesting things in the world. So it
would seem indeed. But the fact appears to be that they said nothing. It is a curious characteristic which they share with all the most

brilliant societies that the world has seen. Old Madame du Deffand*
and her friends talked for fifty years without stopping. And of it all,
what remains? Perhaps three witty sayings. So that we are at liberty to
suppose either that nothing was said, or that nothing witty was said,
or that the fraction of three witty sayings lasted eighteen thousand
two hundred and fifty nights, which does not leave a liberal allowance
of wit for any one of them.

The truth would seem to be—if we dare use such a word in such
a connection—that all these groups of people lie under an enchant-
ment. The hostess is our modern Sibyl.* She is a witch who lays her
guests under a spell. In this house they think themselves happy; in
that witty; in a third profound. It is all an illusion (which is nothing against it, for illusions are the most valuable and necessary of
all things, and she who can create one is among the world's greatest benefactors), but as it is notorious that illusions are shattered by
conflict with reality, so no real happiness, no real wit, no real profundity are tolerated where the illusion prevails. This serves to explain
why Madame du Deffand said no more than three witty things in
the course of fifty years. Had she said more, her circle would have
been destroyed. The witticism, as it left her lips, bowled over the current conversation as a cannon ball lays low the violets and the daisies.
When she made her famous 'mot de Saint Denis'* the very grass was
singed. Disillusionment and desolation followed. Not a word was
uttered. 'Spare us another such, for Heaven's sake, Madame!' her
friends cried with one accord. And she obeyed. For almost seventeen
years she said nothing memorable and all went well. The beautiful
counterpane of illusion lay unbroken on her circle as it lay unbroken
on the circle of Lady R. The guests thought that they were happy,
thought that they were witty, thought that they were profound, and,
as they thought this, other people thought it still more strongly; and
so it got about that nothing was more delightful than one of Lady
R.'s assemblies; everyone envied those who were admitted; those who
were admitted envied themselves because other people envied them;
and so there seemed no end to it—except that which we have now to
relate.

For about the third time Orlando went there a certain incident
occurred. She was still under the illusion that she was listening to
the most brilliant epigrams in the world, though, as a matter of fact,
old General C. was only saying, at some length, how the gout had

left his left leg and gone to his right, while Mr L. interrupted when
any proper name was mentioned, 'R.? Oh! I know Billy R. as well as
I know myself. S.? My dearest friend. T.? Stayed with him a fortnight
in Yorkshire'—which, such is the force of illusion, sounded like the
wittiest repartee, the most searching comment upon human life, and
kept the company in a roar; when the door opened and a little gentleman entered whose name Orlando did not catch. Soon a curiously
disagreeable sensation came over her. To judge from their faces, the
rest began to feel it as well. One gentleman said there was a draught.
The Marchioness of C. feared a cat must be under the sofa. It was
as if their eyes were being slowly opened after a pleasant dream and
nothing met them but a cheap wash-stand and a dirty counterpane. It
was as if the fumes of some delicious wine were slowly leaving them.
Still the General talked and still Mr L. remembered. But it became
more and more apparent how red the General's neck was, how bald
Mr L.'s head was. As for what they said—nothing more tedious and
trivial could be imagined. Everybody fidgeted and those who had fans
yawned behind them. At last Lady R. rapped with hers upon the arm
of her great chair. Both gentlemen stopped talking.

Then the little gentleman said,

He said next,

He said finally,[1]

Here, it cannot be denied, was true wit, true wisdom, true profundity. The company was thrown into complete dismay. One such
saying was bad enough; but three, one after another, on the same
evening! No society could survive it.

'Mr Pope,' said old Lady R. in a voice trembling with sarcastic
fury, 'you are pleased to be witty.' Mr Pope flushed red. Nobody
spoke a word. They sat in dead silence some twenty minutes. Then,
one by one, they rose and slunk from the room. That they would ever
come back after such an experience was doubtful. Link-boys* could
be heard calling their coaches all down South Audley Street.* Doors
were slammed and carriages drove off. Orlando found herself near
Mr Pope on the staircase. His lean and misshapen frame was shaken
by a variety of emotions. Darts of malice, rage, triumph, wit, and terror (he was shaking like a leaf) shot from his eyes. He looked like some
squat reptile set with a burning topaz in its forehead.* At the same

---

[1] These sayings are too well known to require repetition, and besides, they are all to be
found in his published works.

time, the strangest tempest of emotion seized now upon the luckless
Orlando. A disillusionment so complete as that inflicted not an hour
ago leaves the mind rocking from side to side. Everything appears ten
times more bare and stark than before. It is a moment fraught with
the highest danger for the human spirit. Women turn nuns and men
priests in such moments. In such moments, rich men sign away their
wealth; and happy men cut their throats with carving knives. Orlando
would have done all willingly, but there was a rasher thing still for her
to do, and this she did. She invited Mr Pope to come home with her.

For if it is rash to walk into a lion's den unarmed, rash to navigate
the Atlantic in a rowing boat, rash to stand on one foot on the top of
St Paul's,* it is still more rash to go home alone with a poet. A poet
is Atlantic and lion in one. While one drowns us the other gnaws us.
If we survive the teeth, we succumb to the waves. A man who can
destroy illusions is both beast and flood. Illusions are to the soul
what atmosphere is to the earth. Roll up that tender air and the plant
dies, the colour fades. The earth we walk on is a parched cinder. It is
marl we tread and fiery cobbles scorch our feet. By the truth we are
undone. Life is a dream. 'Tis waking that kills us.* He who robs us of
our dreams robs us of our life—(and so on for six pages if you will,
but the style is tedious and may well be dropped).

On this showing, however, Orlando should have been a heap of cinders by the time the chariot drew up at her house in Blackfriars. That
she was still flesh and blood, though certainly exhausted, is entirely
due to a fact to which we drew attention earlier in the narrative. The
less we see the more we believe. Now the streets that lie between
Mayfair and Blackfriars were at that time very imperfectly lit. True,
the lighting was a great improvement upon that of the Elizabethan
age. Then the benighted traveller had to trust to the stars or the red
flame of some night watchman to save him from the gravel pits at
Park Lane or the oak woods where swine rootled in the Tottenham
Court Road.* But even so it wanted much of our modern efficiency.
Lamp-posts lit with oil-lamps occurred every two hundred yards or
so, but between lay a considerable stretch of pitch darkness. Thus
for ten minutes Orlando and Mr Pope would be in blackness; and
then for about half a minute again in the light. A very strange state of
mind was thus bred in Orlando. As the light faded, she began to feel
steal over her the most delicious balm. 'This is indeed a very great
honour for a young woman, to be driving with Mr Pope,' she began

to think, looking at the outline of his nose. 'I am the most blessed of my sex. Half an inch from me—indeed, I feel the knot of his knee ribbons pressing against my thigh—is the greatest wit in Her Majesty's dominions. Future ages will think of us with curiosity and envy me with fury.' Here came the lamp-post again. 'What a foolish wretch I am!' she thought. 'There is no such thing as fame and glory. Ages to come will never cast a thought on me or on Mr Pope either. What's an "age", indeed? What are "we"?' and their progress through Berkeley Square* seemed the groping of two blind ants, momentarily thrown together without interest or concern in common, across a blackened desert. She shivered. But here again was darkness. Her illusion revived. 'How noble his brow is,' she thought (mistaking a hump on a cushion for Mr Pope's forehead in the darkness). 'What a weight of genius lives in it! What wit, wisdom, and truth—what a wealth of all those jewels, indeed, for which people are ready to barter their lives! Yours is the only light that burns for ever. But for you the human pilgrimage would be performed in utter darkness'; (here the coach gave a great lurch as it fell into a rut in Park Lane) 'without genius we should be upset and undone. Most august, most lucid of beams,'—thus she was apostrophizing the hump on the cushion when they drove beneath one of the street lamps in Berkeley Square and she realized her mistake. Mr Pope had a forehead no bigger than another man's. 'Wretched man,' she thought, 'how you have deceived me! I took that hump for your forehead. When one sees you plain, how ignoble, how despicable you are! Deformed and weakly, there is nothing to venerate in you, much to pity, most to despise.'

Again they were in darkness and her anger became modified directly she could see nothing but the poet's knees.

'But it is I that am a wretch,' she reflected, once they were in complete obscurity again, 'for base as you may be, am I not still baser? It is you who nourish and protect me, you who scare the wild beast, frighten the savage, make me clothes of the silkworm's wool, and carpets of the sheep's. If I want to worship, have you not provided me with an image of yourself and set it in the sky? Are not evidences of your care everywhere? How humble, how grateful, how docile, should I not be, therefore? Let it be all my joy to serve, honour, and obey you.'

Here they reached the big lamp-post at the corner of what is now Piccadilly Circus. The light blazed in her eyes, and she saw, besides some degraded creatures* of her own sex, two wretched pigmies on a stark desert land. Both were naked, solitary, and defenceless. The one was powerless to help the other. Each had enough to do to look after itself. Looking Mr Pope full in the face, 'It is equally vain', she thought, 'for you to think you can protect me, or for me to think I can worship you. The light of truth beats upon us without shadow, and the light of truth is damnably unbecoming to us both.'

All this time, of course, they went on talking agreeably, as people of birth and education use, about the Queen's temper and the Prime Minister's gout, while the coach went from light to darkness down the Haymarket, along the Strand, up Fleet Street, and reached, at length, her house in Blackfriars. For some time the dark spaces between the lamps had been becoming brighter and the lamps themselves less bright—that is to say, the sun was rising, and it was in the equable but confused light of a summer's morning in which everything is seen but nothing is seen distinctly that they alighted, Mr Pope handing Orlando from her carriage and Orlando curtseying Mr Pope to precede her into her mansion with the most scrupulous attention to the rites of the Graces.

From the foregoing passage, however, it must not be supposed that genius (but the disease is now stamped out in the British Isles, the late Lord Tennyson,* it is said, being the last person to suffer from it) is constantly alight, for then we should see everything plain and perhaps should be scorched to death in the process. Rather it resembles the lighthouse in its working, which sends one ray and then no more for a time; save that genius is much more capricious in its manifestations and may flash six or seven beams in quick succession (as Mr Pope did that night) and then lapse into darkness for a year or for ever. To steer by its beams is therefore impossible, and when the dark spell is on them men of genius are, it is said, much like other people.

It was happy for Orlando, though at first disappointing, that this should be so, for she now began to live much in the company of men of genius. Nor were they so different from the rest of us as one might have supposed. Addison, Pope, Swift, proved, she found, to be fond of tea. They liked arbours. They collected little bits of coloured glass. They adored grottos. Rank was not distasteful to them. Praise was delightful. They wore plum-coloured suits one day and grey another. Mr Swift had a fine malacca cane. Mr Addison scented his handkerchiefs. Mr Pope suffered with his head. A piece of gossip did not come amiss. Nor were they without their jealousies. (We are jotting down a few reflections that came to Orlando higgledy-piggledy.) At first, she was annoyed with herself for noticing such trifles, and kept a book in which to write down their memorable sayings, but the page remained empty. All the same, her spirits revived, and she took to tearing up her cards of invitation to great parties; kept her evenings free; began to look forward to Mr Pope's visit, to Mr Addison's, to Mr Swift's—and so on and so on. If the reader will here refer to the *Rape of the Lock*, to the *Spectator*, to *Gulliver's Travels*,* he will understand precisely what these mysterious words may mean. Indeed, biographers and critics might save themselves all their labours if readers would only take this advice. For when we read:

> Whether the Nymph shall break Diana's Law,
> Or some frail China Jar receive a Flaw,
> Or stain her Honour, or her new Brocade,
> Forget her Pray'rs or miss a Masquerade,
> Or lose her Heart, or Necklace, at a Ball.*

—we know as if we heard him how Mr Pope's tongue flickered like a lizard's, how his eyes flashed, how his hand trembled, how he loved, how he lied, how he suffered. In short, every secret of a writer's soul, every experience of his life, every quality of his mind is written large in his works, yet we require critics to explain the one and biographers to expound the other. That time hangs heavy on people's hands is the only explanation of the monstrous growth.

So, now that we have read a page or two of the *Rape of the Lock*, we know exactly why Orlando was so much amused and so much frightened and so very bright-cheeked and bright-eyed that afternoon.

Mrs Nelly then knocked at the door to say that Mr Addison waited on her Ladyship. At this, Mr Pope got up with a wry smile, made his congee,* and limped off. In came Mr Addison. Let us, as he takes his seat, read the following passage from the *Spectator*:*

'I consider woman as a beautiful, romantic animal, that may be adorned with furs and feathers, pearls and diamonds, ores and silks. The lynx shall cast its skin at her feet to make her a tippet, the peacock, parrot and swan shall pay contributions to her muff; the sea shall be searched for shells, and the rocks for gems, and every part of nature furnish out its share towards the embellishment of a creature that is the most consummate work of it. All this, I shall indulge them in, but as for the petticoat I have been speaking of, I neither can, nor will allow it.'

We hold that gentleman, cocked hat and all, in the hollow of our hands. Look once more into the crystal. Is he not clear to the very wrinkle in his stocking? Does not every ripple and curve of his wit lie exposed before us, and his benignity and his timidity and his urbanity and the fact that he would marry a Countess* and die very respectably in the end? All is clear. And when Mr Addison has said his say, there is a terrific rap at the door, and Mr Swift, who had these arbitrary ways with him, walks in unannounced. One moment, where is *Gulliver's Travels*? Here it is! Let us read a passage from the voyage to the Houyhnhnms:

'I enjoyed perfect Health of Body and Tranquillity of Mind; I did not find the Treachery or Inconstancy of a Friend, nor the Injuries of a secret or open Enemy. I had no occasion of bribing, flattering or pimping, to procure the Favour of any great Man or of his Minion. I wanted no Fence against Fraud or Oppression; Here was neither Physician to destroy my Body, nor Lawyer to ruin my Fortune; No Informer to watch my Words, and Actions, or forge Accusations against me for Hire: Here were no Gibers, Censurers, Backbiters, Pickpockets, Highwaymen, House-breakers, Attorneys, Bawds, Buffoons, Gamesters, Politicians, Wits, splenetick tedious Talkers. . . .'*

But stop, stop your iron pelt of words, lest you flay us all alive, and yourself too! Nothing can be plainer than that violent man. He is so coarse and yet so clean; so brutal, yet so kind; scorns the whole world, yet talks baby language to a girl, and will die, can we doubt it? in a madhouse.*

So Orlando poured out tea for them all; and sometimes, when the weather was fine, she carried them down to the country with her, and feasted them royally in the Round Parlour, which she had hung with their pictures* all in a circle, so that Mr Pope could not say that Mr Addison came before him, or the other way about. They were very witty, too (but their wit is all in their books), and taught her the most important part of style, which is the natural run of the voice in speaking—a quality which none that has not heard it can imitate, not Greene even, with all his skill; for it is born of the air, and breaks like a wave on the furniture, and rolls and fades away, and is never to be recaptured, least of all by those who prick up their ears, half a century later, and try. They taught her this, merely by the cadence of their

voices in speech; so that her style changed somewhat, and she wrote
some very pleasant, witty verses and characters in prose. And so she
lavished her wine on them and put bank-notes, which they took very
kindly, beneath their plates at dinner, and accepted their dedications,
and thought herself highly honoured by the exchange.

Thus time ran on, and Orlando could often be heard saying to
herself with an emphasis which might, perhaps, make the hearer
a little suspicious, 'Upon my soul, what a life this is!' (For she was still
in search of that commodity.) But circumstances soon forced her to
consider the matter more narrowly.

One day she was pouring out tea for Mr Pope while, as anyone can
tell from the verses quoted above, he sat very bright-eyed, observant,
and all crumpled up in a chair by her side.

'Lord,' she thought, as she raised the sugar tongs, 'how women
in ages to come will envy me! And yet——' she paused; for Mr
Pope needed her attention. And yet—let us finish her thought for
her—when anybody says 'How future ages will envy me', it is safe
to say that they are extremely uneasy at the present moment. Was
this life quite so exciting, quite so flattering, quite so glorious as it
sounds when the memoir writer has done his work upon it? For one
thing, Orlando had a positive hatred of tea; for another, the intellect, divine as it is, and all-worshipful, has a habit of lodging in the
most seedy of carcases, and often, alas, acts the cannibal among the
other faculties so that often, where the Mind is biggest, the Heart,
the Senses, Magnanimity, Charity, Tolerance, Kindliness, and the
rest of them scarcely have room to breathe. Then the high opinion
poets have of themselves; then the low one they have of others; then
the enmities, injuries, envies, and repartees in which they are constantly engaged; then the volubility with which they impart them;
then the rapacity with which they demand sympathy for them; all
this, one may whisper, lest the wits may overhear us, makes pouring
out tea a more precarious and, indeed, arduous occupation than is
generally allowed. Added to which (we whisper again lest the women
may overhear us), there is a little secret which men share among
them; Lord Chesterfield whispered it to his son* with strict injunc-
tions to secrecy, 'Women are but children of a larger growth. . . .
A man of sense only trifles with them, plays with them, humours and
flatters them',* which, since children always hear what they are not
meant to, and sometimes, even, grow up, may have somehow leaked

out, so that the whole ceremony of pouring out tea is a curious one. A woman knows very well that, though a wit sends her his poems, praises her judgement, solicits her criticism, and drinks her tea, this by no means signifies that he respects her opinions, admires her understanding, or will refuse, though the rapier is denied him, to run her through the body with his pen. All this, we say, whisper it as low as we can, may have leaked out by now; so that even with the cream jug suspended and the sugar tongs distended the ladies may fidget a little, look out of the window a little, yawn a little, and so let the sugar fall with a great plop—as Orlando did now—into Mr Pope's tea. Never was any mortal so ready to suspect an insult or so quick to avenge one as Mr Pope. He turned to Orlando and presented her instantly with the rough draught of a certain famous line in the 'Characters of Women'.* Much polish was afterwards bestowed on it, but even in the original it was striking enough. Orlando received it with a curtsey. Mr Pope left her with a bow. Orlando, to cool her cheeks, for really she felt as if the little man had struck her,* strolled in the nut grove at the bottom of the garden. Soon the cool breezes did their work. To her amazement she found that she was hugely relieved to find herself alone. She watched the merry boatloads rowing up the river. No doubt the sight put her in mind of one or two incidents in her past life. She sat herself down in profound meditation beneath a fine willow tree. There she sat till the stars were in the sky. Then she rose, turned, and went into the house, where she sought her bedroom and locked the door. Now she opened a cupboard in which hung still many of the clothes she had worn as a young man of fashion,* and from among them she chose a black velvet suit richly trimmed with Venetian lace. It was a little out of fashion, indeed, but it fitted her to perfection and dressed in it she looked the very figure of a noble Lord. She took a turn or two before the mirror to make sure that her petticoats had not lost her the freedom of her legs, and then let herself secretly out of doors.

It was a fine night early in April. A myriad stars mingling with the light of a sickle moon, which again was enforced by the street lamps, made a light infinitely becoming to the human countenance and to the architecture of Mr Wren. Everything appeared in its tenderest form, yet, just as it seemed on the point of dissolution, some drop of silver sharpened it to animation. Thus it was that talk should be, thought Orlando (indulging in foolish reverie); that society should be, that friendship should be, that love should be. For, Heaven knows why, just as we have lost faith in human intercourse some random collocation of barns and trees or a haystack and a waggon presents us with so perfect a symbol of what is unattainable that we begin the search again.

She entered Leicester Square* as she made these observations. The buildings had an airy yet formal symmetry not theirs by day. The canopy of the sky seemed most dexterously washed in to fill up the outline of roof and chimney. A young woman who sat dejectedly with one arm drooping by her side, the other reposing in her lap, on a seat beneath a plane tree in the middle of the square seemed the very figure of grace, simplicity, and desolation. Orlando swept her hat off to her in the manner of a gallant paying his addresses to a lady of fashion in a public place. The young woman raised her head. It was of the most exquisite shapeliness. The young woman raised her eyes. Orlando saw them to be of a lustre such as is sometimes seen on tea-pots but rarely in a human face. Through this silver glaze the young woman looked up at him (for a man he was to her) appealing, hop-ing, trembling, fearing. She rose; she accepted his arm. For—need we stress the point?—she was of the tribe which nightly burnishes their wares, and sets them in order on the common counter to wait the highest bidder. She led Orlando to the room in Gerrard Street* which was her lodging. To feel her hanging lightly yet like a suppliant on her arm, roused in Orlando all the feelings which become a man. She looked, she felt, she talked like one. Yet, having been so lately a woman herself, she suspected that the girl's timidity and her hesi-tating answers and the very fumbling with the key in the latch and the fold of her cloak and the droop of her wrist were all put on to gratify her masculinity. Upstairs they went, and the pains which the poor creature had been at to decorate her room and hide the fact that she had no other deceived Orlando not a moment. The deception roused her scorn; the truth roused her pity. One thing showing through the other bred the oddest assortment of feeling, so that she did not know whether to laugh or to cry. Meanwhile Nell, as the girl called her-self, unbuttoned her gloves; carefully concealed the left-hand thumb, which wanted mending; then drew behind a screen, where, perhaps, she rouged her cheeks, arranged her clothes, fixed a new kerchief round her neck—all the time prattling as women do, to amuse her lover, though Orlando could have sworn, from the tone of her voice, that her thoughts were elsewhere. When all was ready, out she came, prepared—but here Orlando could stand it no longer. In the strangest torment of anger, merriment, and pity she flung off all disguise and admitted herself a woman.

At this, Nell burst into such a roar of laughter as might have been heard across the way.

'Well, my dear,' she said, when she had somewhat recovered, 'I'm by no means sorry to hear it. For the plain Dunstable of the matter* is' (and it was remarkable how soon, on discovering that they were of the same sex, her manner changed and she dropped her plaintive, appealing ways), 'the plain Dunstable of the matter is, that I'm not in the mood for the society of the other sex tonight. Indeed, I'm in the devil of a fix.' Whereupon, drawing up the fire and stirring a bowl of punch, she told Orlando the whole story of her life. Since it is Orlando's life that engages us at present, we need not relate the adventures of the other lady, but it is certain that Orlando had never known the hours speed faster or more merrily, though Mistress Nell had not a particle of wit about her, and when the name of Mr Pope came up in talk asked innocently if he were connected with the perruque maker of that name in Jermyn Street.* Yet, to Orlando, such is the charm of ease and the seduction of beauty, this poor girl's talk, larded though it was with the commonest expressions of the street corners, tasted like wine after the fine phrases she had been used to, and she was forced to the conclusion that there was something in the sneer of Mr Pope, in the condescension of Mr Addison, and in the secret of Lord Chesterfield which took away her relish for the society of wits, deeply though she must continue to respect their works.

These poor creatures, she ascertained, for Nell brought Prue, and Prue Kitty, and Kitty Rose, had a society of their own of which they now elected her a member. Each would tell the story of the adventures which had landed her in her present way of life. Several were the natural daughters of earls* and one was a good deal nearer than she should have been to the King's person. None was too wretched or too poor but to have some ring or handkerchief in her pocket which stood her in lieu of pedigree. So they would draw round the punch-bowl which Orlando made it her business to furnish generously, and many were the fine tales they told and many the amusing observations they made, for it cannot be denied that when women get together—but hist—they are always careful to see that the doors are shut and that

not a word of it gets into print. All they desire is—but hist again—is
that not a man's step on the stair? All they desire, we were about to say
when the gentleman took the very words out of our mouths. Women
have no desires, says this gentleman, coming into Nell's parlour; only
affectations. Without desires (she has served him and he is gone)
their conversation cannot be of the slightest interest to anyone. 'It is
well known', says Mr S. W.,* 'that when they lack the stimulus of the
other sex, women can find nothing to say to each other. When they
are alone, they do not talk, they scratch.' And since they cannot talk
together and scratching cannot continue without interruption and it
is well known (Mr T. R. has proved it) 'that women are incapable of
any feeling of affection for their own sex and hold each other in the
greatest aversion', what can we suppose that women do when they
seek out each other's society?

As that is not a question that can engage the attention of a sensible
man, let us, who enjoy the immunity of all biographers and historians
from any sex whatever, pass it over, and merely state that Orlando
professed great enjoyment in the society of her own sex, and leave it
to the gentlemen to prove, as they are very fond of doing, that this is
impossible.

But to give an exact and particular account of Orlando's life at this
time becomes more and more out of the question. As we peer and
grope in the ill-lit, ill-paved, ill-ventilated courtyards that lay about
Gerrard Street and Drury Lane* at that time, we seem now to catch
sight of her and then again to lose it. The task is made still more difficult by the fact that she found it convenient at this time to change
frequently from one set of clothes to another. Thus she often occurs
in contemporary memoirs as 'Lord' So-and-so, who was in fact her
cousin; her bounty is ascribed to him, and it is he who is said to have
written the poems that were really hers. She had, it seems, no difficulty in sustaining the different parts, for her sex changed far more
frequently than those who have worn only one set of clothing can
conceive; nor can there be any doubt that she reaped a twofold harvest
by this device; the pleasures of life were increased and its experiences
multiplied. For the probity of breeches she exchanged the seductiveness of petticoats and enjoyed the love of both sexes equally.

So then one may sketch her spending her morning in a China robe
of ambiguous gender among her books; then receiving a client or
two (for she had many scores of suppliants) in the same garment;

then she would take a turn in the garden and clip the nut trees—for which knee-breeches were convenient; then she would change into a flowered taffeta which best suited a drive to Richmond and a proposal of marriage from some great nobleman; and so back again to town, where she would don a snuff-coloured gown like a lawyer's and visit the courts to hear how her cases were doing,—for her fortune was wasting hourly and the suits seemed no nearer consummation than they had been a hundred years ago; and so, finally, when night came, she would more often than not become a nobleman complete from head to toe and walk the streets in search of adventure.

Returning from some of these junketings—of which there were many stories told at the time, as, that she fought a duel, served on one of the King's ships as a captain, was seen to dance naked on a balcony, and fled with a certain lady to the Low Countries where the lady's husband followed them*—but of the truth or otherwise of these stories, we express no opinion—returning from whatever her occupation may have been, she made a point sometimes of passing beneath the windows of a coffee house, where she could see the wits without being seen, and thus could fancy from their gestures what wise, witty, or spiteful things they were saying without hearing a word of them; which was perhaps an advantage; and once she stood half an hour watching three shadows on the blind drinking tea together in a house in Bolt Court.*

Never was any play so absorbing. She wanted to cry out, Bravo! Bravo! For, to be sure, what a fine drama it was—what a page torn from the thickest volume of human life! There was the little shadow with the pouting lips, fidgeting this way and that on his chair, uneasy, petulant, officious; there was the bent female shadow, crooking a finger in the cup to feel how deep the tea was, for she was blind; and there was the Roman-looking rolling shadow in the big armchair— he who twisted his fingers so oddly and jerked his head from side to side and swallowed down the tea in such vast gulps. Dr Johnson, Mr Boswell, and Mrs Williams,*—those were the shadows' names. So absorbed was she in the sight, that she forgot to think how other ages would have envied her, though it seems probable that on this occasion they would. She was content to gaze and gaze. At length Mr Boswell rose. He saluted the old woman with tart asperity. But with what humility did he not abase himself before the great Roman shadow, who now rose to its full height and rocking somewhat as he

stood there rolled out the most magnificent phrases that ever left
human lips; so Orlando thought them, though she never heard a word
that any of the three shadows said as they sat there drinking tea.

At length she came home one night after one of these saunter-
ings and mounted to her bedroom. She took off her laced coat and
stood there in shirt and breeches looking out of the window. There
was something stirring in the air which forbade her to go to bed.
A white haze lay over the town, for it was a frosty night in midwinter
and a magnificent vista lay all round her. She could see St Paul's,
the Tower, Westminster Abbey, with all the spires and domes of the
city churches, the smooth bulk of its banks, the opulent and ample
curves of its halls and meeting-places. On the north rose the smooth,
shorn heights of Hampstead,* and in the west the streets and squares
of Mayfair shone out in one clear radiance. Upon this serene and
orderly prospect the stars looked down, glittering, positive, hard,
from a cloudless sky. In the extreme clearness of the atmosphere
the line of every roof, the cowl of every chimney, was perceptible;
even the cobbles in the streets showed distinct one from another,
and Orlando could not help comparing this orderly scene with the
irregular and huddled purlieus which had been the city of London
in the reign of Queen Elizabeth. Then, she remembered, the city, if
such one could call it, lay crowded, a mere huddle and conglomeration of houses, under her windows at Blackfriars. The stars reflected
themselves in deep pits of stagnant water which lay in the middle of
the streets. A black shadow at the corner where the wine shop used to
stand was, as likely as not, the corpse of a murdered man. She could
remember the cries of many a one wounded in such night brawlings,
when she was a little boy, held to the diamond-paned window in her
nurse's arms. Troops of ruffians, men and women, unspeakably inter-
laced, lurched down the streets, trolling out wild songs with jewels
flashing in their ears, and knives gleaming in their fists. On such
a night as this the impermeable tangle of the forests on Highgate*
and Hampstead would be outlined, writhing in contorted intricacy
against the sky. Here and there, on one of the hills which rose above
London, was a stark gallows tree, with a corpse nailed to rot or parch
on its cross; for danger and insecurity, lust and violence, poetry and
filth swarmed over the tortuous Elizabethan highways and buzzed
and stank—Orlando could remember even now the smell of them
on a hot night—in the little rooms and narrow pathways of the city.

Now—she leant out of her window—all was light, order, and serenity. There was the faint rattle of a coach on the cobbles. She heard
the far-away cry of the night watchman—'Just twelve o'clock on
a frosty morning'. No sooner had the words left his lips than the first
stroke of midnight sounded. Orlando then for the first time noticed
a small cloud gathered behind the dome of St Paul's. As the strokes
sounded, the cloud increased, and she saw it darken and spread with
extraordinary speed. At the same time a light breeze rose and by the
time the sixth stroke of midnight had struck the whole of the eastern
sky was covered with an irregular moving darkness, though the sky to
the west and north stayed clear as ever. Then the cloud spread north.
Height upon height above the city was engulfed by it. Only Mayfair,
with all its lights shining, burnt more brilliantly than ever by contrast. With the eighth stroke, some hurrying tatters of cloud sprawled
over Piccadilly. They seemed to mass themselves and to advance with
extraordinary rapidity towards the west end. As the ninth, tenth, and
eleventh strokes struck, a huge blackness sprawled over the whole of
London. With the twelfth stroke of midnight, the darkness was complete. A turbulent welter of cloud covered the city. All was darkness;
all was doubt; all was confusion. The Eighteenth century was over;
the Nineteenth century had begun.

CHAPTER V

THE great cloud which hung, not only over London, but over the whole of the British Isles on the first day of the nineteenth century stayed, or rather, did not stay, for it was buffeted about constantly by blustering gales, long enough to have extraordinary consequences upon those who lived beneath its shadow. A change seemed to have come over the climate of England. Rain fell frequently, but only in fitful gusts,* which were no sooner over than they began again. The sun shone, of course, but it was so girt about with clouds and the air was so saturated with water, that its beams were discoloured and purples, oranges, and reds of a dull sort took the place of the more positive landscapes of the eighteenth century. Under this bruised and sullen canopy the green of the cabbages was less intense, and the white of the snow was muddied. But what was worse, damp now began to make its way into every house—damp, which is the most insidious of all enemies, for while the sun can be shut out by blinds, and the frost roasted by a hot fire, damp steals in while we sleep; damp is silent, imperceptible, ubiquitous. Damp swells the wood, furs the kettle, rusts the iron, rots the stone. So gradual is the process, that it is not until we pick up some chest of drawers, or coal scuttle, and the whole thing drops to pieces in our hands, that we suspect even that the disease is at work.

Thus, stealthily and imperceptibly, none marking the exact day or hour of the change, the constitution of England was altered and nobody knew it. Everywhere the effects were felt. The hardy country gentleman, who had sat down gladly to a meal of ale and beef in a room designed, perhaps by the brothers Adam,* with classic dignity, now felt chilly. Rugs appeared; beards were grown; trousers were fastened tight under the instep. The chill which he felt in his legs the country gentleman soon transferred to his house; furniture was muffled; walls and tables were covered; nothing was left bare. Then a change of diet became essential. The muffin was invented and the crumpet. Coffee supplanted the after-dinner port, and, as coffee led to a drawing-room in which to drink it, and a drawing-room to glass cases, and glass cases to artificial flowers, and artificial flowers to mantelpieces, and mantelpieces to pianofortes, and pianofortes to drawing-room ballads, and drawing-room ballads (skipping a stage or two) to innumerable little dogs, mats, and china ornaments, the home—which had become extremely important—was completely altered.

Outside the house—it was another effect of the damp—ivy grew in unparalleled profusion. Houses that had been of bare stone were smothered in greenery. No garden, however formal its original design, lacked a shrubbery, a wilderness, a maze. What light penetrated to the bedrooms where children were born was naturally of an obfusc* green, and what light penetrated to the drawing-rooms where grown men and women lived came through curtains of brown and purple plush. But the change did not stop at outward things. The damp struck within. Men felt the chill in their hearts; the damp in their minds. In a desperate effort to snuggle their feelings into some sort of warmth one subterfuge was tried after another. Love, birth, and death were all swaddled in a variety of fine phrases. The sexes drew further and further apart. No open conversation was tolerated. Evasions and concealments were sedulously practised on both sides. And just as the ivy and the evergreen rioted in the damp earth outside, so did the same fertility show itself within. The life of the average woman was a succession of childbirths. She married at nineteen and had fifteen or eighteen children by the time she was thirty; for twins abounded. Thus the British Empire came into existence; and thus—for there is no stopping damp; it gets into the inkpot as it gets into the woodwork—sentences swelled, adjectives multiplied, lyrics became epics, and little trifles that had been essays a column long were now encyclopaedias in ten or twenty volumes. But Eusebius Chubb* shall be our witness to the effect this all had upon the mind of a sensitive man who could do nothing to stop it. There is a passage towards the end of his memoirs where he describes how, after writing thirty-five folio pages one morning 'all about nothing' he screwed the lid on his inkpot and went for a turn in his garden. Soon he found himself involved in the shrubbery. Innumerable leaves creaked and glistened above his head. He seemed to himself 'to crush the mould of a million more under his feet'. Thick smoke exuded from a damp bonfire at the end of the garden. He reflected that no fire on earth could ever hope to consume that vast vegetable encumbrance. Wherever he looked, vegetation was rampant. Cucumbers 'came scrolloping* across the grass to his feet'. Giant cauliflowers towered deck above deck till they rivalled, to his disordered imagination, the elm trees themselves.

Hens laid incessantly eggs of no special tint. Then, remembering with a sigh his own fecundity and his poor wife Jane, now in the throes of her fifteenth confinement indoors, how, he asked himself, could he blame the fowls? He looked upwards into the sky. Did not heaven itself, or that great frontispiece of heaven, which is the sky, indicate the assent, indeed, the instigation of the heavenly hierarchy? For there, winter or summer, year in year out, the clouds turned and tumbled, like whales,* he pondered, or elephants rather; but no, there was no escaping the simile which was pressed upon him from a thousand airy acres; the whole sky itself as it spread wide above the British Isles was nothing but a vast feather bed; and the undistinguished fecundity of the garden, the bedroom and the henroost was copied there. He went indoors, wrote the passage quoted above, laid his head in a gas oven, and when they found him later he was past revival.

While this went on in every part of England, it was all very well for Orlando to mew herself in her house at Blackfriars and pretend that the climate was the same; that one could still say what one liked and wear knee-breeches or skirts as the fancy took one. Even she, at length, was forced to acknowledge that times were changed. One afternoon in the early part of the century she was driving through St James's Park* in her old panelled coach when one of those sunbeams, which occasionally, though not often, managed to come to earth, struggled through, marbling the clouds with strange prismatic colours as it passed. Such a sight was sufficiently strange after the clear and uniform skies of the eighteenth century to cause her to pull the window down and look at it. The puce and flamingo clouds made her think with a pleasurable anguish, which proves that she was insensibly afflicted with the damp already, of dolphins dying in Ionian seas. But what was her surprise when, as it struck the earth, the sunbeam seemed to call forth, or to light up, a pyramid, hecatomb, or trophy (for it had something of a banquet-table air)—a conglomeration at any rate of the most heterogeneous and ill-assorted objects, piled higgledy-piggledy in a vast mound where the statue of Queen Victoria now stands!* Draped about a vast cross of fretted and floriated gold were widow's weeds and bridal veils; hooked on to other excrescences were crystal palaces,* bassinettes,* military helmets, memorial wreaths, trousers, whiskers, wedding cakes, cannon, Christmas trees, telescopes, extinct monsters, globes, maps, elephants, and mathematical instruments—the whole supported like a gigantic coat of arms on the right side by a female figure clothed in flowing white; on the left, by a portly gentleman wearing a frock-coat and sponge-bag trousers.* The incongruity of the objects, the association of the fully clothed and the partly draped, the garishness of the different colours and their plaid-like juxtapositions afflicted Orlando with the most profound dismay. She had never, in all her life, seen anything at once so indecent, so hideous, and so monumental. It might, and indeed it must be, the effect of the sun on the water-logged air; it would vanish with the first breeze that blew; but for all that, it looked, as she drove past, as if it were destined to endure for ever. Nothing, she felt, sinking back into the corner of her coach, no wind, rain, sun, or thunder, could ever demolish that garish erection. Only the noses would mottle and the trumpets would rust; but there they would remain, pointing east, west, south, and north, eternally. She looked back as her coach swept up Constitution Hill.* Yes, there it was, still beaming placidly in a light which—she pulled her watch out of her fob—was, of course, the light of twelve o'clock mid-day. None other could be so prosaic, so matter-of-fact, so impervious to any hint of dawn or sunset, so seemingly calculated to last for ever. She was determined not to look again. Already she felt the tides of her blood run sluggishly. But what was more peculiar, a blush, vivid and singular, overspread her cheeks as she passed Buckingham Palace and her eyes seemed forced by a superior power down upon her knees. Suddenly she saw with a start that she was wearing black breeches. She never ceased blushing till she had reached her country house, which, considering the time it takes four horses to trot thirty miles, will be taken, we hope, as a signal proof of her chastity.

Once there, she followed what had now become the most imperious need of her nature and wrapped herself as well as she could in a damask quilt which she snatched from her bed. She explained to the Widow Bartholomew (who had succeeded good old Grimsditch as housekeeper) that she felt chilly.

'So do we all, m'lady,' said the Widow, heaving a profound sigh. 'The walls is sweating,' she said, with a curious, lugubrious complacency, and sure enough, she had only to lay her hand on the oak panels for the finger-prints to be marked there. The ivy had grown so profusely that many windows were now sealed up. The kitchen was so dark that they could scarcely tell a kettle from a cullender. A poor black cat had been mistaken for coals and shovelled on the fire. Most of the maids were already wearing three or four red-flannel petticoats, though the month was August.

'But is it true, m'lady,' the good woman asked, hugging herself, while the golden crucifix heaved on her bosom, 'that the Queen, bless her, is wearing a what d'you call it, a —,' the good woman hesitated and blushed.

'A crinoline,'* Orlando helped her out with it (for the word had reached Blackfriars). Mrs Bartholomew nodded. The tears were already running down her cheeks, but as she wept she smiled. For it was pleasant to weep. Were they not all of them weak women? wearing crinolines the better to conceal the fact; the great fact; the only fact; but, nevertheless, the deplorable fact; which every modest woman did her best to deny until denial was impossible; the fact that she was about to bear a child? to bear fifteen or twenty children indeed, so that most of a modest woman's life was spent, after all, in denying what, on one day at least of every year, was made obvious.

'The muffins is keepin' 'ot,' said Mrs Bartholomew, mopping up her tears, 'in the liberry.'

And wrapped in a damask bed quilt, to a dish of muffins Orlando now sat down.

'The muffins is keepin' 'ot in the liberry'—Orlando minced out the horrid cockney phrase in Mrs Bartholomew's refined cockney accents as she drank—but no, she detested the mild fluid—her tea. It was in this very room, she remembered, that Queen Elizabeth had stood astride the fireplace with a flagon of beer in her hand, which she suddenly dashed on the table when Lord Burghley* tactlessly used the imperative instead of the subjunctive. 'Little man, little man,'— Orlando could hear her say—'is "must" a word to be addressed to princes?'* And down came the flagon on the table: there was the mark of it still.

But when Orlando leapt to her feet, as the mere thought of that great Queen commanded, the bed quilt tripped her up, and she fell back in her armchair with a curse. Tomorrow she would have to buy twenty yards or more of black bombazine,* she supposed, to make a skirt. And then (here she blushed), she would have to buy a crinoline, and then (here she blushed) a bassinette, and then another crinoline, and so on. . . . The blushes came and went with the most exquisite iteration of modesty and shame imaginable. One might see the spirit of the age blowing, now hot, now cold, upon her cheeks.

And if the spirit of the age* blew a little unequally, the crinoline being blushed for before the husband, her ambiguous position must excuse her (even her sex was still in dispute) and the irregular life she had lived before.

At length the colour on her cheeks resumed its stability and it seemed as if the spirit of the age—if such indeed it were—lay dormant for a time. Then Orlando felt in the bosom of her shirt as if for some locket or relic of lost affection, and drew out no such thing, but a roll of paper, sea-stained, blood-stained, travel-stained—the manuscript of her poem, 'The Oak Tree'. She had carried this about with her for so many years now, and in such hazardous circumstances, that many of the pages were stained, some were torn, while the straits she had been in for writing paper when with the gipsies, had forced her to overscore the margins and cross the lines till the manuscript looked like a piece of darning most conscientiously carried out. She turned back to the first page and read the date, 1586, written in her own boyish hand. She had been working at it for close on three hundred years now. It was time to make an end. Meanwhile she began turning and dipping and reading and skipping and thinking as she read, how very little she had changed all these years. She had been a gloomy boy, in love with death, as boys are; and then she had been amorous and florid; and then she had been sprightly and satirical; and sometimes she had tried prose and sometimes she had tried drama. Yet through all these changes she had remained, she reflected, fundamentally the same. She had the same brooding meditative temper, the same love of animals and nature, the same passion for the country and the seasons.

'After all,' she thought, getting up and going to the window, 'nothing has changed. The house, the garden are precisely as they were. Not a chair has been moved, not a trinket sold. There are the same walks, the same lawns, the same trees, and the same pool, which, I dare say, has the same carp in it. True, Queen Victoria is on the throne* and not Queen Elizabeth, but what difference. . . .'

No sooner had the thought taken shape, than, as if to rebuke it, the door was flung wide and in marched Basket, the butler, followed by Bartholomew, the housekeeper, to clear away tea. Orlando, who had just dipped her pen in the ink, and was about to indite some reflection upon the eternity of all things, was much annoyed to be impeded by a blot, which spread and meandered round her pen. It was some infirmity of the quill, she supposed; it was split or dirty. She dipped

it again. The blot increased. She tried to go on with what she was saying; no words came. Next she began to decorate the blot with wings
and whiskers, till it became a round-headed monster, something
between a bat and a wombat. But as for writing poetry with Basket
and Bartholomew in the room, it was impossible. No sooner had she
said 'Impossible' than, to her astonishment and alarm, the pen began
to curve and caracole* with the smoothest possible fluency. Her page
was written in the neatest sloping Italian hand with the most insipid
verse she had ever read in her life:

> I am myself but a vile link
> Amid life's weary chain,
> But I have spoken hallow'd words,
> Oh, do not say in vain!
>
> Will the young maiden, when her tears,
> Alone in moonlight shine,
> Tears for the absent and the loved,
> Murmur—*

she wrote without a stop as Bartholomew and Basket grunted and
groaned about the room, mending the fire, picking up the muffins.
    Again she dipped her pen and off it went—

> She was so changed, the soft carnation cloud
> Once mantling o'er her cheek like that which eve
> Hangs o'er the sky, glowing with roseate hue,
> Had faded into paleness, broken by
> Bright burning blushes, torches of the tomb,*

but here, by an abrupt movement she spilt the ink over the page
and blotted it from human sight she hoped for ever. She was all of
a quiver, all of a stew. Nothing more repulsive could be imagined than
to feel the ink flowing thus in cascades of involuntary inspiration.
What had happened to her? Was it the damp, was it Bartholomew,
was it Basket, what was it? she demanded. But the room was empty.
No one answered her, unless the dripping of the rain in the ivy could
be taken for an answer.
    Meanwhile, she became conscious, as she stood at the window, of
an extraordinary tingling and vibration all over her, as if she were
made of a thousand wires upon which some breeze or errant fingers
were playing scales.* Now her toes tingled; now her marrow. She had

the queerest sensations about the thigh bones. Her hairs seemed to erect themselves. Her arms sang and twanged as the telegraph wires would be singing and twanging in twenty years or so. But all this agitation seemed at length to concentrate in her hands; and then in one hand, and then in one finger of that hand, and then finally to contract itself so that it made a ring of quivering sensibility about the second finger of the left hand. And when she raised it to see what caused this agitation, she saw nothing—nothing but the vast solitary emerald which Queen Elizabeth had given her. And was that not enough? she asked. It was of the finest water. It was worth ten thousand pounds at least. The vibration seemed, in the oddest way (but remember we are dealing with some of the darkest manifestations of the human soul) to say No, that is not enough; and, further, to assume a note of interrogation, as though it were asking, what did it mean, this hiatus, this strange oversight? till poor Orlando felt positively ashamed of the second finger of her left hand without in the least knowing why. At this moment, Bartholomew came in to ask which dress she should lay out for dinner, and Orlando, whose senses were much quickened, instantly glanced at Bartholomew's left hand, and instantly perceived what she had never noticed before—a thick ring of rather jaundiced yellow circling the third finger where her own was bare.

'Let me look at your ring, Bartholomew,' she said, stretching her hand to take it.

At this, Bartholomew made as if she had been struck in the breast by a rogue. She started back a pace or two, clenched her hand and flung it away from her with a gesture that was noble in the extreme. 'No,' she said, with resolute dignity, her Ladyship might look if she pleased, but as for taking off her wedding ring, not the Archbishop nor the Pope nor Queen Victoria on her throne could force her to do that. Her Thomas had put it on her finger twenty-five years, six months, three weeks ago; she had slept in it; worked in it; washed in it; prayed in it; and proposed to be buried in it. In fact, Orlando understood her to say, but her voice was much broken with emotion, that it was by the gleam on her wedding ring that she would be assigned her station among the angels and its lustre would be tarnished for ever if she let it out of her keeping for a second.

'Heaven help us,' said Orlando, standing at the window and watching the pigeons at their pranks, 'what a world we live in! What a world to be sure!' Its complexities amazed her. It now seemed to

her that the whole world was ringed with gold. She went in to dinner.
Wedding rings abounded. She went to church. Wedding rings were
everywhere. She drove out. Gold, or pinchbeck,* thin, thick, plain,
smooth, they glowed dully on every hand. Rings filled the jewellers'
shops, not the flashing pastes and diamonds of Orlando's recollection, but simple bands without a stone in them. At the same time,
she began to notice a new habit among the town people. In the old
days, one would meet a boy trifling with a girl under a hawthorn
hedge frequently enough. Orlando had flicked many a couple with
the tip of her whip and laughed and passed on. Now, all that was
changed. Couples trudged and plodded in the middle of the road
indissolubly linked together. The woman's right hand was invariably
passed through the man's left and her fingers were firmly gripped
by his. Often it was not till the horses' noses were on them that they
budged, and then, though they moved it was all in one piece, heavily,
to the side of the road. Orlando could only suppose that some new
discovery had been made about the race; that they were somehow
stuck together, couple after couple, but who had made it, and when,
she could not guess. It did not seem to be Nature. She looked at
the doves and the rabbits and the elk-hounds and she could not see
that Nature had changed her ways or mended them, since the time
of Elizabeth at least. There was no indissoluble alliance among the
brutes that she could see. Could it be Queen Victoria then, or Lord
Melbourne? Was it from them that the great discovery of marriage
proceeded? Yet the Queen, she pondered, was said to be fond of dogs,
and Lord Melbourne,* she had heard, was said to be fond of women.
It was strange—it was distasteful; indeed, there was something in
this indissolubility of bodies which was repugnant to her sense of
decency and sanitation. Her ruminations, however, were accompanied by such a tingling and twangling of the afflicted finger that she
could scarcely keep her ideas in order. They were languishing and
ogling like a housemaid's fancies. They made her blush. There was
nothing for it but to buy one of those ugly bands and wear it like
the rest. This she did, slipping it, overcome with shame, upon her
finger in the shadow of a curtain; but without avail. The tingling
persisted more violently, more indignantly than ever. She did not
sleep a wink that night. Next morning when she took up the pen to
write, either she could think of nothing, and the pen made one large
lachrymose blot after another, or it ambled off, more alarmingly still,

into mellifluous fluencies about early death and corruption, which were worse than no thinking at all. For it would seem—her case proved it—that we write, not with the fingers, but with the whole person. The nerve which controls the pen winds itself about every fibre of our being, threads the heart, pierces the liver. Though the seat of her trouble seemed to be the left hand, she could feel herself poisoned through and through, and was forced at length to consider the most desperate of remedies, which was to yield completely and submissively to the spirit of the age, and take a husband.

That this was much against her natural temperament has been sufficiently made plain. When the sound of the Archduke's chariot wheels died away, the cry that rose to her lips was 'Life! A Lover!' not 'Life! A Husband!' and it was in pursuit of this aim that she had gone to town and run about the world as has been shown in the previous chapter. Such is the indomitable nature of the spirit of the age, however, that it batters down anyone who tries to make stand against it far more effectually than those who bend its own way. Orlando had inclined herself naturally to the Elizabethan spirit, to the Restoration spirit, to the spirit of the eighteenth century, and had in consequence scarcely been aware of the change from one age to the other. But the spirit of the nineteenth century was antipathetic to her in the extreme, and thus it took her and broke her, and she was aware of her defeat at its hands as she had never been before. For it is probable that the human spirit has its place in time assigned to it; some are born of this age, some of that; and now that Orlando was grown a woman, a year or two past thirty indeed, the lines of her character were fixed,* and to bend them the wrong way was intolerable.

So she stood mournfully at the drawing-room window (Bartholomew had so christened the library) dragged down by the weight of the crinoline which she had submissively adopted. It was heavier and more drab than any dress she had yet worn. None had ever so impeded her movements. No longer could she stride through the garden with her dogs, or run lightly to the high mound and fling herself beneath the oak tree. Her skirts collected damp leaves and straw. The plumed hat tossed on the breeze. The thin shoes were quickly soaked and mud-caked. Her muscles had lost their pliancy. She became nervous lest there should be robbers behind the wainscot and afraid, for the first time in her life, of ghosts in the corridors. All these things inclined her, step by step, to submit to the new discovery, whether Queen Victoria's

or another's, that each man and each woman has another allotted to
it for life, whom it supports, by whom it is supported, till death them
do part.* It would be a comfort, she felt, to lean; to sit down; yes, to
lie down; never, never, never to get up again. Thus did the spirit work
upon her, for all her past pride, and as she came sloping down the scale
of emotion to this lowly and unaccustomed lodging-place, those twang-
lings and tinglings which had been so captious and so interrogative
modulated into the sweetest melodies, till it seemed as if angels were
plucking harp-strings with white fingers and her whole being was per-
vaded by a seraphic harmony.

But whom could she lean upon? She asked that question of the
wild autumn winds. For it was now October, and wet as usual. Not
the Archduke; he had married a very great lady* and had hunted
hares in Roumania these many years now; nor Mr M.; he was become
a Catholic; nor the Marquis of C.; he made sacks in Botany Bay;* nor
the Lord O.; he had long been food for fishes. One way or another, all
her old cronies were gone now, and the Nells and the Kits of Drury
Lane, much though she favoured them, scarcely did to lean upon.

'Whom', she asked, casting her eyes upon the revolving clouds,
clasping her hands as she knelt on the window-sill, and looking the
very image of appealing womanhood as she did so, 'can I lean upon?'
Her words formed themselves, her hands clasped themselves, invol-
untarily, just as her pen had written of its own accord. It was not
Orlando who spoke, but the spirit of the age. But whichever it was,
nobody answered it. The rooks were tumbling pell-mell among the
violet clouds of autumn. The rain had stopped at last and there was
an iridescence in the sky which tempted her to put on her plumed hat
and her little stringed shoes and stroll out before dinner.

'Everyone is mated except myself,' she mused, as she trailed disconsolately across the courtyard. There were the rooks; Canute and
Pippin even—transitory as their alliances were, still each this evening seemed to have a partner. 'Whereas, I, who am mistress of it all,'
Orlando thought, glancing as she passed at the innumerable emblazoned windows of the hall, 'am single, am mateless, am alone.'

Such thoughts had never entered her head before. Now they bore
her down unescapably. Instead of thrusting the gate open, she tapped
with a gloved hand for the porter to unfasten it for her. One must lean
on someone, she thought, if it is only on a porter; and half wished to
stay behind and help him to grill his chop on a bucket of fiery coals,

but was too timid to ask it. So she strayed out into the park alone,
faltering at first and apprehensive lest there might be poachers or
gamekeepers or even errand-boys to marvel that a great lady should
walk alone.

At every step she glanced nervously lest some male form should
be hiding behind a furze bush or some savage cow be lowering its
horns to toss her. But there were only the rooks flaunting in the sky.
A steel-blue plume from one of them fell among the heather. She
loved wild birds' feathers. She had used to collect them as a boy. She
picked it up and stuck it in her hat. The air blew upon her spirit
somewhat and revived it. As the rooks went whirling and wheeling
above her head and feather after feather fell gleaming through the
purplish air, she followed them, her long cloak floating behind her,
over the moor, up the hill. She had not walked so far for years. Six
feathers had she picked from the grass and drawn between her fingers
and pressed to her lips to feel their smooth, glinting plumage, when
she saw, gleaming on the hillside, a silver pool, mysterious as the lake
into which Sir Bedivere flung the sword of Arthur.* A single feather
quivered in the air and fell into the middle of it. Then, some strange
ecstasy came over her. Some wild notion she had of following the
birds to the rim of the world and flinging herself on the spongy turf
and there drinking forgetfulness, while the rooks' hoarse laughter
sounded over her. She quickened her pace; she ran; she tripped; the
tough heather roots flung her to the ground. Her ankle was broken.
She could not rise. But there she lay content. The scent of the bog
myrtle and the meadow-sweet was in her nostrils. The rooks' hoarse
laughter was in her ears. 'I have found my mate,' she murmured. 'It is
the moor.* I am nature's bride,' she whispered, giving herself in rapture to the cold embraces of the grass as she lay folded in her cloak in
the hollow by the pool. 'Here will I lie. (A feather fell upon her brow.)
I have found a greener laurel than the bay. My forehead will be cool
always. These are wild birds' feathers—the owl's, the nightjar's. I shall
dream wild dreams. My hands shall wear no wedding ring,' she continued, slipping it from her finger. 'The roots shall twine about them.
Ah!' she sighed, pressing her head luxuriously on its spongy pillow,
'I have sought happiness through many ages and not found it; fame
and missed it; love and not known it; life—and behold, death is better. I have known many men and many women,' she continued; 'none
have I understood. It is better that I should lie at peace here with

ORLANDO ABOUT THE YEAR 1840

only the sky above me—as the gipsy told me years ago. That was in Turkey.' And she looked straight up into the marvellous golden foam into which the clouds had churned themselves, and saw next moment a track in it, and camels passing in single file through the rocky desert among clouds of red dust; and then, when the camels had passed, there were only mountains, very high and full of clefts and with pin- nacles of rock, and she fancied she heard goat bells ringing in their passes, and in their folds were fields of irises and gentian. So the sky changed and her eyes slowly lowered themselves down and down till they came to the rain-darkened earth and saw the great hump of the South Downs, flowing in one wave along the coast; and where the land parted, there was the sea, the sea with ships passing; and she fancied she heard a gun far out at sea, and thought at first, 'That's the Armada,' and then thought 'No, it's Nelson', and then remembered how those wars were over and the ships were busy merchant ships; and the sails on the winding river were those of pleasure boats. She saw, too, cattle sprinkled on the dark fields, sheep and cows, and she saw the lights coming here and there in farm-house windows, and lanterns moving among the cattle as the shepherd went his rounds and the cowman; and then the lights went out and the stars rose and tangled themselves about the sky. Indeed, she was falling asleep with the wet feathers on her face and her ear pressed to the ground when she heard, deep within, some hammer on an anvil, or was it a heart beating? Tick-tock, tick-tock, so it hammered, so it beat, the anvil, or the heart in the middle of the earth; until, as she listened, she thought it changed to the trot of a horse's hoofs; one, two, three, four, she counted; then she heard a stumble; then, as it came nearer and nearer, she could hear the crack of a twig and the suck of the wet bog in its hoofs. The horse was almost on her. She sat upright. Towering dark against the yellow-slashed sky of dawn, with the plovers rising and falling about him, she saw a man on horseback. He started. The horse stopped.

'Madam,' the man cried, leaping to the ground, 'you're hurt!'

'I'm dead, sir!' she replied.

A few minutes later, they became engaged.

The morning after, as they sat at breakfast, he told her his name. It was Marmaduke Bonthrop Shelmerdine,* Esquire.

'I knew it!' she said, for there was something romantic and chival-
rous, passionate, melancholy, yet determined about him which went
with the wild, dark-plumed name—a name which had, in her mind,
the steel-blue gleam of rooks' wings, the hoarse laughter of their
caws, the snake-like twisting descent of their feathers in a silver pool,
and a thousand other things which will be described presently.

'Mine is Orlando,' she said. He had guessed it. For if you see
a ship in full sail* coming with the sun on it proudly sweeping across
the Mediterranean from the South Seas, one says at once, 'Orlando',
he explained.

In fact, though their acquaintance had been so short, they had
guessed, as always happens between lovers, everything of any importance about each other in two seconds at the utmost, and it now
remained only to fill in such unimportant details as what they were
called; where they lived; and whether they were beggars or people of
substance. He had a castle in the Hebrides, but it was ruined,* he told
her. Gannets feasted in the banqueting hall. He had been a soldier
and a sailor, and had explored the East. He was on his way now to join
his brig at Falmouth, but the wind had fallen and it was only when the
gale blew from the South-west that he could put out to sea. Orlando
looked hastily from the breakfast-room window at the gilt leopard on
the weather vane. Mercifully its tail pointed due east and was steady
as a rock. 'Oh! Shel, don't leave me!' she cried. 'I'm passionately in
love with you,' she said. No sooner had the words left her mouth than
an awful suspicion rushed into both their minds simultaneously.

'You're a woman, Shel!' she cried.

'You're a man, Orlando!' he cried.

Never was there such a scene of protestation and demonstration
as then took place since the world began. When it was over and they
were seated again she asked him, what was this talk of a South-west
gale? Where was he bound for?

'For the Horn,'* he said briefly, and blushed. (For a man had to
blush as a woman had, only at rather different things.) It was only
by dint of great pressure on her side and the use of much intuition
that she gathered that his life was spent in the most desperate and
splendid of adventures—which is to voyage round Cape Horn in the
teeth of a gale. Masts had been snapped off; sails torn to ribbons (she
had to drag the admission from him). Sometimes the ship had sunk,
and he had been left the only survivor on a raft with a biscuit.

'It's about all a fellow can do nowadays,' he said sheepishly, and helped himself to great spoonfuls of strawberry jam. The vision which she had thereupon of this boy (for he was little more) sucking peppermints, for which he had a passion, while the masts snapped and the stars reeled and he roared brief orders to cut this adrift, to heave that overboard, brought the tears to her eyes, tears, she noted, of a finer flavour than any she had cried before. 'I am a woman,' she thought, 'a real woman, at last.' She thanked Bonthrop from the bottom of her heart for having given her this rare and unexpected delight. Had she not been lame in the left foot, she would have sat upon his knee.

'Shel, my darling,' she began again, 'tell me . . .' and so they talked two hours or more, perhaps about Cape Horn, perhaps not, and really it would profit little to write down what they said, for they knew each other so well that they could say anything, which is tantamount to saying nothing, or saying such stupid, prosy things as how to cook an omelette, or where to buy the best boots in London, things which have no lustre taken from their setting, yet are positively of amazing beauty within it. For it has come about, by the wise economy of nature, that our modern spirit can almost dispense with language; the commonest expressions do, since no expressions do; hence the most ordinary conversation is often the most poetic, and the most poetic is precisely that which cannot be written down. For which reasons we leave a great blank here,* which must be taken to indicate that the space is filled to repletion.

After some days more of this kind of talk,

'Orlando, my dearest,' Shel was beginning, when there was a scuffling outside, and Basket the butler entered with the information that there was a couple of Peelers* downstairs with a warrant from the Queen.

'Show 'em up,' said Shelmerdine briefly, as if on his own

quarter-deck, taking up, by instinct, a stand with his hands behind him in front of the fireplace.* Two officers in bottle-green uniforms with truncheons at their hips then entered the room and stood at attention. Formalities being over, they gave into Orlando's own hands, as their commission was, a legal document of some very impressive sort, judging by the blobs of sealing wax, the ribbons, the oaths, and the signatures, which were all of the highest importance.

Orlando ran her eyes through it and then, using the first finger of her right hand as pointer, read out the following facts as being most germane to the matter.

'The lawsuits are settled,'* she read out . . . 'some in my favour, as for example . . . others not. Turkish marriage annulled (I was ambassador in Constantinople, Shel,' she explained). 'Children pronounced illegitimate (they said I had three sons by Pepita, a Spanish dancer). So they don't inherit, which is all to the good. . . . Sex? Ah! what about sex? My sex', she read out with some solemnity, 'is pronounced indisputably, and beyond the shadow of a doubt (what I was telling you a moment ago, Shel?), female. The estates which are now desequestrated in perpetuity descend and are tailed and entailed upon the heirs male of my body, or in default of marriage'—but here she grew impatient with this legal verbiage, and said, 'but there won't be any default of marriage, nor of heirs either, so the rest can be taken as read.' Whereupon she appended her own signature beneath Lord Palmerston's* and entered from that moment into the undisturbed possession of her titles, her house, and her estate—which was now so much shrunk, for the cost of the lawsuits had been prodigious, that, though she was infinitely noble again, she was also excessively poor.

When the result of the lawsuit was made known (and rumour flew much quicker than the telegraph which has supplanted it), the whole town was filled with rejoicings.

[Horses were put into carriages for the sole purpose of being taken out. Empty barouches and landaus* were trundled up and down the High Street incessantly. Addresses were read from the Bull. Replies were made from the Stag. The town was illuminated. Gold caskets were securely sealed in glass cases. Coins were well and duly laid under stones. Hospitals were founded. Rat and Sparrow clubs* were inaugurated. Turkish women by the dozen were burnt in effigy in the market-place, together with scores of peasant boys with the label 'I am a base Pretender', lolling from their mouths. The Queen's

cream-coloured ponies were soon seen trotting up the avenue with
a command to Orlando to dine and sleep at the Castle, that very same
night. Her table, as on a previous occasion, was snowed under with
invitations from the Countess of R., Lady Q., Lady Palmerston, the
Marchioness of P., Mrs W. E. Gladstone,* and others, beseeching the
pleasure of her company, reminding her of ancient alliances between
their family and her own, etc.]—all of which is properly enclosed in
square brackets, as above, for the good reason that a parenthesis it
was without any importance in Orlando's life. She skipped it, to get
on with the text. For when the bonfires were blazing in the market-
place, she was in the dark woods with Shelmerdine alone. So fine was
the weather that the trees stretched their branches motionless above
them, and if a leaf fell, it fell, spotted red and gold, so slowly that one
could watch it for half an hour fluttering and falling till it came to rest
at last, on Orlando's foot.

'Tell me, Mar,'* she would say (and here it must be explained, that
when she called him by the first syllable of his first name, she was in
a dreamy, amorous, acquiescent mood, domestic, languid a little, as
if spiced logs were burning, and it was evening, yet not time to dress,
and a thought wet perhaps outside, enough to make the leaves glisten,
but a nightingale might be singing even so among the azaleas, two or
three dogs barking at distant farms, a cock crowing—all of which the
reader should imagine in her voice)—'Tell me, Mar,' she would say,
'about Cape Horn.' Then Shelmerdine would make a little model on
the ground of the Cape with twigs and dead leaves and an empty snail
shell or two.

'Here's the north,' he would say. 'There's the south. The wind's
coming from hereabouts. Now the brig is sailing due west; we've just
lowered the top-boom mizzen; and so you see—here, where this bit of
grass is, she enters the current which you'll find marked—where's my
map and compasses, Bo'sun? Ah! thanks, that'll do, where the snail
shell is. The current catches her on the starboard side, so we must rig
the jib-boom or we shall be carried to the larboard, which is where
that beech leaf is,—for you must understand my dear—' and so he
would go on, and she would listen to every word; interpreting them
rightly, so as to see, that is to say, without his having to tell her, the
phosphorescence on the waves; the icicles clanking in the shrouds;
how he went to the top of the mast in a gale; there reflected on the
destiny of man; came down again; had a whisky and soda; went on

shore; was trapped by a black woman; repented; reasoned it out; read Pascal;* determined to write philosophy; bought a monkey; debated the true end of life; decided in favour of Cape Horn, and so on. All this and a thousand other things she understood him to say, and so when she replied, Yes, negresses are seductive, aren't they? he having told her that the supply of biscuits now gave out, he was surprised and delighted to find how well she had taken his meaning.

'Are you positive you aren't a man?' he would ask anxiously, and she would echo,

'Can it be possible you're not a woman?' and then they must put it to the proof without more ado. For each was so surprised at the quick-ness of the other's sympathy, and it was to each such a revelation that a woman could be as tolerant and free-spoken as a man, and a man as strange and subtle as a woman, that they had to put the matter to the proof at once.

And so they would go on talking or rather, understanding, which has become the main art of speech in an age when words are growing daily so scanty in comparison with ideas that 'the biscuits ran out' has to stand for kissing a negress in the dark when one has just read Bishop Berkeley's philosophy* for the tenth time. (And from this it follows that only the most profound masters of style can tell the truth, and when one meets a simple one-syllabled writer, one may conclude, without any doubt at all, that the poor man is lying.)

So they would talk; and then, when her feet were fairly covered with spotted autumn leaves, Orlando would rise and stroll away into the heart of the woods in solitude, leaving Bonthrop sitting there among the snail shells, making models of Cape Horn. 'Bonthrop,' she would say, 'I'm off,' and when she called him by his second name, 'Bonthrop', it should signify to the reader that she was in a solitary mood, felt them both as specks on a desert, was desirous only of meeting death by herself, for people die daily, die at dinner tables, or like this, out of doors in the autumn woods; and with the bonfires blazing and Lady Palmerston or Lady Derby* asking her out every night to dinner, the desire for death would overcome her, and so say-ing 'Bonthrop', she said in effect, 'I'm dead', and pushed her way as a spirit might through the spectre-pale beech trees, and so oared herself deep into solitude as if the little flicker of noise and movement were over and she were free now to take her way—all of which the reader should hear in her voice when she said 'Bonthrop'; and should also add, the better to illumine the word, that for him too the same word signified, mystically, separation and isolation and the disembodied pacing the deck of his brig in unfathomable seas.

After some hours of death, suddenly a jay shrieked 'Shelmerdine', and stooping, she picked one of those autumn crocuses which to some people signify that very word, and put it with the jay's feather that came tumbling blue through the beech woods, in her breast. Then she called 'Shelmerdine' and the word went shooting this way and that way through the woods and struck him where he sat, making models out of snail shells in the grass. He saw her, and heard her coming to him with the crocus and the jay's feather in her breast, and cried 'Orlando', which meant (and it must be remembered that when bright colours like blue and yellow mix themselves in our eyes, some of it rubs off on our thoughts) first the bowing and swaying of bracken as if something were breaking through; which proved to be a ship in full sail, heaving and tossing a little dreamily, rather as if she had a whole year of summer days to make her voyage in; and so the ship bears down, heaving this way, heaving that way, nobly, indolently, and rides over the crest of this wave and sinks into the hollow of that one, and so, suddenly stands over you (who are in a little cockle shell of a boat, looking up at her) with all her sails quivering, and then, behold, they drop all of a heap on deck—as Orlando dropped now into the grass beside him.

Eight or nine days had been spent thus, but on the tenth, which was the 26th of October, Orlando was lying in the bracken, while Shelmerdine recited Shelley* (whose entire works he had by heart), when a leaf which had started to fall slowly enough from a tree-top whipped briskly across Orlando's foot. A second leaf followed and then a third. Orlando shivered and turned pale. It was the wind. Shelmerdine—but it would be more proper now to call him Bonthrop—leapt to his feet.

'The wind!' he cried.

Together they ran through the woods, the wind plastering them with leaves as they ran, to the great court and through it and the little courts, frightened servants leaving their brooms and their saucepans to follow after till they reached the Chapel, and there a scattering of lights was lit as fast as could be, one knocking over this bench, another snuffing out that taper. Bells were rung. People were summoned. At length there was Mr Dupper catching at the ends of

his white tie and asking where was the prayer book. And they thrust
Queen Mary's prayer book in his hands and he searched hastily fluttering the pages, and said, 'Marmaduke Bonthrop Shelmerdine, and
Lady Orlando, kneel down'; and they knelt down, and now they were
bright and now they were dark as the light and shadow came flying
helter-skelter through the painted windows; and among the banging
of innumerable doors and a sound like brass pots beating, the organ
sounded, its growl coming loud and faint alternately, and Mr Dupper,
who was grown a very old man, tried now to raise his voice above the
uproar and could not be heard and then all was quiet for a moment,
and one word—it might be 'the jaws of death'—rang out clear, while
all the estate servants kept pressing in with rakes and whips still in
their hands to listen, and some sang aloud and others prayed, and
now a bird was dashed against the pane, and now there was a clap of
thunder, so that no one heard the word Obey spoken or saw, except
as a golden flash, the ring pass from hand to hand. All was movement and confusion. And up they rose with the organ booming and
the lightning playing and the rain pouring, and the Lady Orlando,
with her ring on her finger, went out into the court in her thin dress
and held the swinging stirrup, for the horse was bitted and bridled
and the foam was still on his flank, for her husband to mount, which
he did with one bound, and the horse leapt forward and Orlando,
standing there, cried out Marmaduke Bonthrop Shelmerdine! and
he answered her Orlando! and the words went dashing and circling
like wild hawks together among the belfries and higher and higher,
further and further, faster and faster they circled, till they crashed
and fell in a shower of fragments to the ground; and she went in.

CHAPTER VI

ORLANDO went indoors. It was completely still. It was very silent. There was the ink pot: there was the pen; there was the manuscript of her poem, broken off in the middle of a tribute to eternity. She had been about to say, when Basket and Bartholomew interrupted with the tea things, nothing changes. And then, in the space of three seconds and a half, everything had changed—she had broken her ankle, fallen in love, married Shelmerdine.

There was the wedding ring on her finger to prove it. It was true that she had put it there herself before she met Shelmerdine, but that had proved worse than useless. She now turned the ring round and round, with superstitious reverence, taking care lest it should slip past the joint of her finger.

'The wedding ring has to be put on the third finger of the left hand', she said, like a child cautiously repeating its lesson, 'for it to be of any use at all.'

She spoke thus, aloud and rather more pompously than was her wont, as if she wished someone whose good opinion she desired to overhear her. Indeed, she had in mind, now that she was at last able to collect her thoughts, the effect that her behaviour would have had upon the spirit of the age. She was extremely anxious to be informed whether the steps she had taken in the matter of getting engaged to Shelmerdine and marrying him met with its approval. She was certainly feeling more herself. Her finger had not tingled once, or nothing to count, since that night on the moor. Yet, she could not deny that she had her doubts. She was married, true; but if one's husband was always sailing round Cape Horn, was it marriage? If one liked him, was it marriage? If one liked other people, was it marriage? And finally, if one still wished, more than anything in the whole world, to write poetry, was it marriage? She had her doubts.

But she would put it to the test. She looked at the ring. She looked at the ink pot. Did she dare? No, she did not. But she must. No, she could not. What should she do then? Faint, if possible. But she had never felt better in her life.

'Hang it all!' she cried, with a touch of her old spirit. 'Here goes!'

And she plunged her pen neck deep in the ink. To her enormous surprise, there was no explosion. She drew the nib out. It was wet, but not dripping. She wrote. The words were a little long in coming, but come they did. Ah! but did they make sense? she wondered, a panic coming over her lest the pen might have been at some of its involuntary pranks again. She read,

> And then I came to a field where the springing grass
> Was dulled by the hanging cups of fritillaries,
> Sullen and foreign-looking, the snaky flower,
> Scarfed in dull purple, like Egyptian girls—*

As she wrote she felt some power (remember we are dealing with the most obscure manifestations of the human spirit) reading over her shoulder, and when she had written 'Egyptian girls', the power told her to stop. Grass, the power seemed to say, going back with a ruler such as governesses use to the beginning, is all right; the hanging cups of fritillaries—admirable; the snaky flower—a thought, strong from a lady's pen, perhaps, but Wordsworth, no doubt, sanctions it;* but—girls? Are girls necessary? You have a husband at the Cape, you say? Ah, well, that'll do.

And so the spirit passed on.

Orlando now performed in spirit (for all this took place in spirit) a deep obeisance to the spirit of her age, such as—to compare great things with small*—a traveller, conscious that he has a bundle of cigars in the corner of his suit case, makes to the customs officer who has obligingly made a scribble of white chalk on the lid. For she was extremely doubtful whether, if the spirit had examined the contents of her mind carefully, it would not have found something highly contraband for which she would have had to pay the full fine. She had only escaped by the skin of her teeth. She had just managed, by some dexterous deference to the spirit of the age, by putting on a ring and finding a man on a moor, by loving nature and being no satirist, cynic, or psychologist—any one of which goods would have been discovered at once—to pass its examination successfully. And she heaved a deep sigh of relief, as, indeed, well she might, for the transaction between a writer and the spirit of the age is one of infinite delicacy, and upon a nice arrangement between the two the whole fortune of his works depends. Orlando had so ordered it that she was in an extremely happy position; she need neither fight her age, nor submit to it; she was of it, yet remained herself. Now, therefore, she could write, and write she did. She wrote. She wrote. She wrote.

It was now November. After November, comes December. Then January, February, March, and April. After April comes May. June, July, August follow. Next is September. Then October, and so, behold, here we are back at November again, with a whole year accomplished.

This method of writing biography, though it has its merits, is a little bare, perhaps, and the reader, if we go on with it, may complain that he could recite the calendar for himself and so save his pocket whatever sum the Hogarth Press* may think proper to charge for this book. But what can the biographer do when his subject has put him in the predicament into which Orlando has now put us? Life, it has been agreed by everyone whose opinion is worth consulting, is the only fit subject for novelist or biographer; life, the same authorities have decided, has nothing whatever to do with sitting still in a chair and thinking. Thought and life are as the poles asunder. Therefore—since sitting in a chair and thinking is precisely what Orlando is doing now—there is nothing for it but to recite the calendar, tell one's beads, blow one's nose, stir the fire, look out of the window, until she has done. Orlando sat so still that you could have heard a pin drop. Would, indeed, that a pin had dropped! That would have been life of a kind. Or if a butterfly had fluttered through the window and settled on her chair, one could write about that. Or suppose she had got up and killed a wasp. Then, at once, we could out with our pens and write. For there would be blood shed, if only the blood of a wasp. Where there is blood there is life. And if killing a wasp is the merest trifle compared with killing a man, still it is a fitter subject for novelist or biographer than this mere wool-gathering;* this thinking; this sitting in a chair day in, day out, with a cigarette and a sheet of paper and a pen and an ink pot. If only subjects, we might complain (for our patience is wearing thin), had more consideration for their biographers! What is more irritating than to see one's subject, on whom one has lavished so much time and trouble, slipping out of one's grasp altogether and indulging—witness her sighs and gasps, her flushing, her palings, her eyes now bright as lamps, now haggard as dawns—what is more humiliating than to see all this dumb show of emotion and excitement gone through before our eyes when we know that what causes it—thought and imagination—are of no importance whatsoever?

MARMADUKE BONTHROP SHELMERDINE, ESQUIRE

But Orlando was a woman—Lord Palmerston had just proved it. And when we are writing the life of a woman, we may, it is agreed, waive our demand for action, and substitute love instead. Love, the poet has said, is woman's whole existence.* And if we look for a moment at Orlando writing at her table, we must admit that never was there a woman more fitted for that calling. Surely, since she is a woman, and a beautiful woman, and a woman in the prime of life, she will soon give over this pretence of writing and thinking and begin at least to think of a gamekeeper* (and as long as she thinks of a man, nobody objects to a woman thinking). And then she will write him a little note (and as long as she writes little notes nobody objects to a woman writing either) and make an assignation for Sunday dusk and Sunday dusk will come; and the gamekeeper will whistle under the window—all of which is, of course, the very stuff of life and the only possible subject for fiction. Surely Orlando must have done one of these things? Alas,—a thousand times, alas, Orlando did none of them. Must it then be admitted that Orlando was one of those monsters of iniquity who do not love? She was kind to dogs, faithful to friends, generosity itself to a dozen starving poets, had a passion for poetry. But love—as the male novelists define it—and who, after all, speak with greater authority?—has nothing whatever to do with kindness, fidelity, generosity, or poetry. Love is slipping off one's petticoat and—But we all know what love is. Did Orlando do that? Truth compels us to say no, she did not. If then, the subject of one's biography will neither love nor kill, but will only think and imagine, we may conclude that he or she is no better than a corpse and so leave her.

The only resource now left us is to look out of the window. There were sparrows; there were starlings; there were a number of doves, and one or two rooks, all occupied after their fashion. One finds a worm, another a snail. One flutters to a branch, another takes a little run on the turf. Then a servant crosses the courtyard, wearing a green baize apron. Presumably he is engaged on some intrigue with one of the maids in the pantry, but as no visible proof is offered us, in the courtyard, we can but hope for the best and leave it. Clouds pass, thin or thick, with some disturbance of the colour of the grass beneath. The sun-dial registers the hour in its usual cryptic way. One's mind begins tossing up a question or two, idly, vainly, about this same life. Life, it sings, or croons rather, like a kettle on a hob, Life, life, what art thou? Light or darkness, the baize apron of the under footman or the shadow of the starling on the grass?

Let us go, then, exploring, this summer morning, when all are adoring the plum blossom and the bee. And humming and hawing, let us ask of the starling (who is a more sociable bird than the lark) what he may think on the brink of the dust-bin, whence he picks among the sticks combings of scullion's hair. What's life, we ask, leaning on the farmyard gate; Life, Life, Life! cries the bird, as if he had heard, and knew precisely, what we meant by this bothering prying habit of ours of asking questions indoors and out and peeping and picking at daisies as the way is of writers when they don't know what to say next. Then they come here, says the bird, and ask me what life is; Life, Life, Life!

We trudge on then by the moor path, to the high brow of the wine-blue purple-dark hill,* and fling ourselves down there, and dream there and see there a grasshopper, carting back to his home in the hollow, a straw. And he says (if sawings like his can be given a name so sacred and tender) Life's labour, or so we interpret the whirr of his dust-choked gullet. And the ant agrees and the bees, but if we lie here long enough to ask the moths, when they come at evening, stealing among the paler heather bells, they will breathe in our ears such wild nonsense as one hears from telegraph wires in snow storms; tee hee, haw haw. Laughter, Laughter! the moths say.

Having asked then of man and of bird and the insects, for fish, men tell us, who have lived in green caves, solitary for years to hear them speak, never, never say, and so perhaps know what life is—having asked them all and grown no wiser, but only older and colder (for did we not pray once in a way to wrap up in a book something so hard, so rare, one could swear it was life's meaning?) back we must go and say straight out to the reader who waits a-tiptoe to hear what life is—alas, we don't know.

At this moment, but only just in time to save the book from extinction, Orlando pushed away her chair, stretched her arms, dropped her pen, came to the window, and exclaimed, 'Done!'

She was almost felled to the ground by the extraordinary sight which now met her eyes. There was the garden and some birds. The world was going on as usual. All the time she was writing the world had continued.

'And if I were dead, it would be just the same!' she exclaimed.

Such was the intensity of her feelings that she could even imagine that she had suffered dissolution, and perhaps some faintness actually attacked her. For a moment she stood looking at the fair, indifferent spectacle with staring eyes. At length she was revived in a singular way. The manuscript which reposed above her heart began shuffling and beating as if it were a living thing, and, what was still odder, and showed how fine a sympathy was between them, Orlando, by inclining her head, could make out what it was that it was saying. It wanted to be read. It must be read. It would die in her bosom if it were not read. For the first time in her life she turned with violence against nature. Elk-hounds and rose bushes were about her in profusion. But elk-hounds and rose bushes can none of them read. It is a lamentable oversight on the part of Providence which had never struck her before. Human beings alone are thus gifted. Human beings had become necessary. She rang the bell. She ordered the carriage to take her to London at once.

'There's just time to catch the eleven forty-five, M'Lady,' said Basket. Orlando had not yet realized the invention of the steam engine, but such was her absorption in the sufferings of a being, who, though not herself, yet entirely depended on her, that she saw a railway train for the first time, took her seat in a railway carriage, and had the rug arranged about her knees without giving a thought to 'that stupendous invention, which had (the historians say) completely changed the face of Europe in the past twenty years' (as, indeed, happens much more frequently than historians suppose). She noticed only that it was extremely smutty; rattled horribly; and the windows stuck. Lost in thought, she was whirled up to London in something less than an hour and stood on the platform at Charing Cross, not knowing where to go.

The old house at Blackfriars, where she had spent so many pleasant days in the eighteenth century, was now sold, part to the Salvation Army,* part to an umbrella factory. She had bought another in Mayfair which was sanitary, convenient, and in the heart of the fashionable world, but was it in Mayfair that her poem would be relieved of its desire? Pray God, she thought, remembering the brightness of their ladyships' eyes and the symmetry of their lordships' legs, they haven't taken to reading there. For that would be a thousand pities. Then there was Lady R.'s. The same sort of talk would be going on there still, she had no doubt. The gout might have shifted from the General's left leg to his right, perhaps. Mr L. might have stayed ten

days with R. instead of T. Then Mr Pope would come in. Oh! but
Mr Pope was dead. Who were the wits now, she wondered—but that
was not a question one could put to a porter, and so she moved on.
Her ears were now distracted by the jingling of innumerable bells on
the heads of innumerable horses. Fleets of the strangest little boxes
on wheels were drawn up by the pavement. She walked out into the
Strand. There the uproar was even worse. Vehicles of all sizes, drawn
by blood horses and by dray horses, conveying one solitary dowager
or crowded to the top by whiskered men in silk hats, were inextricably
mixed. Carriages, carts, and omnibuses seemed to her eyes, so long
used to the look of a plain sheet of foolscap, alarmingly at logger-
heads; and to her ears, attuned to a pen scratching, the uproar of the
street sounded violently and hideously cacophonous. Every inch of
the pavement was crowded. Streams of people, threading in and out
between their own bodies and the lurching and lumbering traffic with
incredible agility, poured incessantly east and west. Along the edge of
the pavement stood men, holding out trays of toys, and bawled. At
corners, women sat beside great baskets of spring flowers and bawled.
Boys running in and out of the horses' noses, holding printed sheets
to their bodies, bawled too, Disaster! Disaster! At first Orlando supposed that she had arrived at some moment of national crisis; but
whether it was happy or tragic, she could not tell. She looked anxiously at people's faces. But that confused her still more. Here would
come by a man sunk in despair, muttering to himself as if he knew
some terrible sorrow. Past him would nudge a fat, jolly-faced fellow,
shouldering his way along as if it were a festival for all the world.
Indeed, she came to the conclusion that there was neither rhyme nor
reason in any of it. Each man and each woman was bent on his own
affairs. And where was she to go?

  She walked on without thinking, up one street and down another,
by vast windows piled with handbags, and mirrors, and dressing
gowns, and flowers, and fishing rods, and luncheon baskets; while
stuff of every hue and pattern, thickness or thinness, was looped and
festooned and ballooned across and across. Sometimes she passed
down avenues of sedate mansions, soberly numbered 'one', 'two',
'three', and so on right up to two or three hundred, each the copy of
the other, with two pillars and six steps and a pair of curtains neatly
drawn and family luncheons laid on tables, and a parrot looking out
of one window and a man servant out of another, until her mind was

dizzied with the monotony. Then she came to great open squares with black shiny, tightly buttoned statues of fat men in the middle, and war horses prancing, and columns rising and fountains falling and pigeons fluttering. So she walked and walked along pavements between houses until she felt very hungry, and something fluttering above her heart rebuked her with having forgotten all about it. It was her manuscript, 'The Oak Tree'.

She was confounded at her own neglect. She stopped dead where she stood. No coach was in sight. The street, which was wide and handsome, was singularly empty. Only one elderly gentleman was approaching. There was something vaguely familiar to her in his walk. As he came nearer, she felt certain that she had met him at some time or other. But where? Could it be that this gentleman, so neat, so portly, so prosperous, with a cane in his hand and a flower in his button-hole, with a pink, plump face, and combed white moustaches, could it be, Yes, by jove, it was!—her old, her very old friend, Nick Greene!

At the same time he looked at her; remembered her; recognized her. 'The Lady Orlando!' he cried, sweeping his silk hat almost in the dust.

'Sir Nicholas!' she exclaimed. For she was made aware intuitively by something in his bearing that the scurrilous penny-a-liner,* who had lampooned her and many another in the time of Queen Elizabeth, was now risen in the world and become certainly a Knight and doubt-less a dozen other fine things into the bargain.

With another bow, he acknowledged that her conclusion was cor-rect; he was a Knight; he was a Litt.D.;* he was a Professor. He was the author of a score of volumes. He was, in short, the most influential critic of the Victorian age.

A violent tumult of emotion besieged her at meeting the man who had caused her, years ago, so much pain. Could this be the plaguy, restless fellow who had burnt holes in her carpets, and toasted cheese in the Italian fireplace and told such merry stories of Marlowe and the rest that they had seen the sun rise nine nights out of ten? He was now sprucely dressed* in a grey morning suit, had a pink flower in his button-hole, and grey suede gloves to match. But even as she marvelled, he made another profound bow, and asked her whether she would honour him by lunching with him? The bow was a thought overdone perhaps, but the imitation of fine breeding was creditable.

She followed him, wondering, into a superb restaurant, all red plush, white table-cloths, and silver cruets, as unlike as could be the old tavern or coffee house with its sanded floor, its wooden benches, its bowls of punch and chocolate, and its broadsheets and spittoons. He laid his gloves neatly on the table beside him. Still she could hardly believe that he was the same man. His nails were clean; where they used to be an inch long. His chin was shaved; where a black beard used to sprout. He wore gold sleeve-links; where his ragged linen used to dip in the broth. It was not, indeed, until he had ordered the wine, which he did with a care that reminded her of his taste in Malmsey long ago, that she was convinced he was the same man. 'Ah!' he said, heaving a little sigh, which was yet comfortable enough, 'ah! my dear lady, the great days of literature are over. Marlowe, Shakespeare, Ben Jonson—those were the giants. Dryden, Pope, Addison—those were the heroes. All, all are dead now. And whom have they left us? Tennyson, Browning, Carlyle!'*—he threw an immense amount of scorn into his voice. 'The truth of it is,' he said, pouring himself a glass of wine, 'that all our young writers are in the pay of booksellers. They turn out any trash that serves to pay their tailor's bills. It is an age', he said, helping himself to hors-d'œuvres, 'marked by precious conceits and wild experiments—none of which the Elizabethans would have tolerated for an instant.

'No, my dear lady,' he continued, passing with approval the turbot au gratin, which the waiter exhibited for his sanction, 'the great days are over. We live in degenerate times. We must cherish the past; honour those writers—there are still a few left of 'em—who take antiquity for their model and write, not for pay but——' Here Orlando almost shouted 'Glawr!' Indeed she could have sworn that she had heard him say the very same things three hundred years ago. The names were different, of course, but the spirit was the same. Nick Greene had not changed, for all his knighthood. And yet, some change there was. For while he ran on about taking Addison as one's model (it had been Cicero once, she thought) and lying in bed of a morning (which she was proud to think her pension paid quarterly enabled him to do) rolling the best works of the best authors round and round on one's tongue for an hour, at least, before setting pen to paper, so that the vulgarity of the present time and the deplorable condition of our native tongue (he had lived long in America,* she believed) might be purified—while he ran on in much the same way that Greene had run on three hundred years ago, she had time to ask herself, how was it then that he had changed? He had grown plump; but he was a man verging on seventy. He had grown sleek: literature had been a prosperous pursuit evidently; but somehow the old restless, uneasy vivacity had gone. His stories, brilliant as they were, were no longer quite so free and easy. He mentioned, it is true, 'my dear friend Pope' or 'my illustrious friend Addison' every other second, but he had an air of respectability about him which was depressing, and he preferred, it seemed, to enlighten her about the doings and sayings of her own blood relations rather than tell her, as he used to do, scandal about the poets.

Orlando was unaccountably disappointed. She had thought of literature all these years (her seclusion, her rank, her sex must be her excuse) as something wild as the wind, hot as fire, swift as lightning; something errant, incalculable, abrupt, and behold, literature was an elderly gentleman in a grey suit talking about duchesses. The violence of her disillusionment was such that some hook or button fastening the upper part of her dress burst open, and out upon the table fell 'The Oak Tree', a poem.

'A manuscript!' said Sir Nicholas, putting on his gold pince-nez. 'How interesting, how excessively interesting! Permit me to look at it.' And once more, after an interval of some three hundred years, Nicholas Greene took Orlando's poem and, laying it down among the coffee cups and the liqueur glasses, began to read it. But now his verdict was very different from what it had been then. It reminded him, he said as he turned over the pages, of Addison's *Cato*.* It compared favourably with Thomson's *Seasons*.* There was no trace in it, he was thankful to say, of the modern spirit. It was composed with a regard to truth, to nature, to the dictates of the human heart, which was rare indeed, in these days of unscrupulous eccentricity. It must, of course, be published instantly.

Really Orlando did not know what he meant. She had always carried her manuscripts about with her in the bosom of her dress. The idea tickled Sir Nicholas considerably.

'But what about royalties?' he asked.

Orlando's mind flew to Buckingham Palace and some dusky potentates who happened to be staying there.

Sir Nicholas was highly diverted. He explained that he was alluding to the fact that Messrs —— (here he mentioned a well-known

firm of publishers) would be delighted, if he wrote them a line, to put
the book on their list. He could probably arrange for a royalty of ten
per cent on all copies up to two thousand; after that it would be fifteen. As for the reviewers, he would himself write a line to Mr ——,
who was the most influential; then a compliment—say a little puff of
her own poems—addressed to the wife of the editor of the —— never
did any harm. He would call ——. So he ran on. Orlando understood
nothing of all this, and from old experience did not altogether trust
his good nature, but there was nothing for it but to submit to what
was evidently his wish and the fervent desire of the poem itself. So Sir
Nicholas made the blood-stained packet into a neat parcel; flattened
it into his breast pocket, lest it should disturb the set of his coat; and
with many compliments on both sides, they parted.

Orlando walked up the street. Now that the poem was gone,—and
she felt a bare place in her breast where she had been used to carry
it—she had nothing to do but reflect upon whatever she liked—the
extraordinary chances it might be of the human lot. Here she was in
St James's Street; a married woman; with a ring on her finger; where
there had been a coffee house once there was now a restaurant; it was
about half past three in the afternoon; the sun was shining; there were
three pigeons; a mongrel terrier dog; two hansom cabs and a barouche
landau.* What then, was Life? The thought popped into her head violently, irrelevantly (unless old Greene were somehow the cause of it).
And it may be taken as a comment, adverse or favourable, as the reader
chooses to consider it upon her relations with her husband (who was at
the Horn), that whenever anything popped violently into her head, she
went straight to the nearest telegraph office and wired to him. There
was one, as it happened, close at hand. 'My God Shel', she wired; 'life
literature Greene toady—' here she dropped into a cypher language*
which they had invented between them so that a whole spiritual state
of the utmost complexity might be conveyed in a word or two without
the telegraph clerk being any wiser, and added the words 'Rattigan
Glumphoboo', which summed it up precisely. For not only had the
events of the morning made a deep impression on her, but it cannot
have escaped the reader's attention that Orlando was growing up—
which is not necessarily growing better—and 'Rattigan Glumphoboo'
described a very complicated spiritual state—which if the reader puts
all his intelligence at our service he may discover for himself.

There could be no answer to her telegram for some hours; indeed,

it was probable, she thought, glancing at the sky, where the upper
clouds raced swiftly past, that there was a gale at Cape Horn, so
that her husband would be at the mast-head, as likely as not, or cutting away some tattered spar, or even alone in a boat with a biscuit.
And so, leaving the post office, she turned to beguile herself into the
next shop, which was a shop so common in our day that it needs no
description, yet, to her eyes, strange in the extreme; a shop where
they sold books. All her life long Orlando had known manuscripts;
she had held in her hands the rough brown sheets on which Spenser*
had written in his little crabbed hand; she had seen Shakespeare's
script and Milton's. She owned, indeed, a fair number of quartos
and folios, often with a sonnet in her praise in them and sometimes
a lock of hair. But these innumerable little volumes, bright, identical,
ephemeral, for they seemed bound in cardboard and printed on tissue paper, surprised her infinitely. The whole works of Shakespeare
cost half a crown and could be put in your pocket. One could hardly
read them, indeed, the print was so small, but it was a marvel, none
the less. 'Works'—the works of every writer she had known or heard
of and many more stretched from end to end of the long shelves. On
tables and chairs, more 'works' were piled and tumbled, and these she
saw, turning a page or two, were often works about other works by Sir
Nicholas and a score of others whom, in her ignorance, she supposed,
since they were bound and printed, to be very great writers too. So
she gave an astounding order to the bookseller to send her everything
of any importance in the shop and left.

She turned into Hyde Park, which she had known of old (beneath
that cleft tree, she remembered, the Duke of Hamilton fell run through
the body by Lord Mohun*), and her lips, which are often to blame in
the matter, began framing the words of her telegram into a sense-
less singsong; life literature Greene toady Rattigan Glumphoboo; so
that several park keepers looked at her with suspicion and were only
brought to a favourable opinion of her sanity by noticing the pearl
necklace which she wore. She had carried off a sheaf of papers and
critical journals from the book shop, and at length, flinging herself
on her elbow beneath a tree, she spread these pages round her and
did her best to fathom the noble art of prose composition as these
masters practised it. For still the old credulity was alive in her; even
the blurred type of a weekly newspaper had some sanctity in her
eyes. So she read, lying on her elbow, an article by Sir Nicholas on

the collected works of a man she had once known—John Donne.*
But she had pitched herself, without knowing it, not far from the
Serpentine.* The barking of a thousand dogs sounded in her ears.
Carriage wheels rushed ceaselessly in a circle. Leaves sighed over-
head. Now and again a braided skirt and a pair of tight scarlet trousers
crossed the grass within a few steps of her. Once a gigantic rubber ball
bounced on the newspaper. Violets, oranges, reds, and blues broke
through the interstices of the leaves and sparkled in the emerald on
her finger. She read a sentence and looked up at the sky; she looked up
at the sky and looked down at the newspaper. Life? Literature? One
to be made into the other? But how monstrously difficult! For—here
came by a pair of tight scarlet trousers—how would Addison have put
that? Here came two dogs dancing on their hind legs.* How would
Lamb* have described that? For reading Sir Nicholas and his friends
(as she did in the intervals of looking about her), she somehow got
the impression—here she rose and walked—they made one feel—
it was an extremely uncomfortable feeling—one must never, never
say what one thought. (She stood on the banks of the Serpentine.
It was a bronze colour; spider-thin boats were skimming from side
to side.) They made one feel, she continued, that one must always,
always write like somebody else. (The tears formed themselves in her
eyes.) For really, she thought, pushing a little boat off with her toe,
I don't think I could (here the whole of Sir Nicholas' article came
before her as articles do, ten minutes after they are read, with the look
of his room, his head, his cat, his writing-table, and the time of the
day thrown in), I don't think I could, she continued, considering the
article from this point of view, sit in a study, no, it's not a study, it's
a mouldy kind of drawing-room, all day long, and talk to pretty young
men, and tell them little anecdotes, which they mustn't repeat, about
what Tupper said about Smiles;* and then, she continued, weeping
bitterly, they're all so manly; and then, I do detest Duchesses; and
I don't like cake; and though I'm spiteful enough, I could never learn
to be as spiteful as all that, so how can I be a critic and write the
best English prose of my time? Damn it all! she exclaimed, launching
a penny steamer so vigorously that the poor little boat almost sank in
the bronze-coloured waves.

   Now, the truth is that when one has been in a state of mind (as
nurses call it)—and the tears still stood in Orlando's eyes—the thing
one is looking at becomes, not itself, but another thing, which is

bigger and much more important and yet remains the same thing. If one looks at the Serpentine in this state of mind, the waves soon become just as big as the waves on the Atlantic; the toy boats become indistinguishable from ocean liners. So Orlando mistook the toy boat for her husband's brig; and the wave she had made with her toe for a mountain of water off Cape Horn; and as she watched the toy boat climb the ripple, she thought she saw Bonthrop's ship climb up and up a glassy wall; up and up it went, and a white crest with a thousand deaths in it arched over it; and through the thousand deaths it went and disappeared—'It's sunk!' she cried out in an agony—and then, behold, there it was again sailing along safe and sound among the ducks on the other side of the Atlantic.

'Ecstasy!' she cried. 'Ecstasy! Where's the post office?' she wondered. 'For I must wire at once to Shel and tell him. . . .' And repeating 'A toy boat on the Serpentine', and 'Ecstasy', alternately, for the thoughts were interchangeable and meant exactly the same thing, she hurried towards Park Lane.

'A toy boat, a toy boat, a toy boat,' she repeated, thus enforcing upon herself the fact that it is not articles by Nick Greene on John Donne nor eight-hour bills nor covenants nor factory acts* that matter; it's something useless, sudden, violent; something that costs a life; red, blue, purple; a spirt; a splash; like those hyacinths (she was passing a fine bed of them); free from taint, dependence, soilure of humanity or care for one's kind; something rash, ridiculous, like my hyacinth, husband I mean, Bonthrop: that's what it is—a toy boat on the Serpentine, ecstasy—it's ecstasy that matters. Thus she spoke aloud,* waiting for the carriages to pass at Stanhope Gate,* for the consequence of not living with one's husband, except when the wind is sunk, is that one talks nonsense aloud in Park Lane. It would no doubt have been different had she lived all the year round with him as Queen Victoria recommended. As it was the thought of him would come upon her in a flash. She found it absolutely necessary to speak to him instantly. She did not care in the least what nonsense it might make, or what dislocation it might inflict on the narrative. Nick Greene's article had plunged her in the depths of despair; the toy boat had raised her to the heights of joy. So she repeated: 'Ecstasy, ecstasy', as she stood waiting to cross.

But the traffic was heavy that spring afternoon, and kept her standing there, repeating, ecstasy, ecstasy, or a toy boat on the Serpentine, while the wealth and power of England sat, as if sculptured, in hat and cloak, in four-in-hand, victoria* and barouche landau. It was as if a golden river had coagulated and massed itself in golden blocks across Park Lane. The ladies held card-cases between their fingers; the gentlemen balanced gold-mounted canes between their knees. She stood there gazing, admiring, awestruck. One thought only disturbed her, a thought familiar to all who behold great elephants, or whales of an incredible magnitude, and that is how do these leviathans to whom obviously stress, change, and activity are repugnant, propagate their kind? Perhaps, Orlando thought, looking at the stately, still faces, their time of propagation is over; this is the fruit; this is the consummation. What she now beheld was the triumph of an age. Portly and splendid there they sat. But now, the policeman let fall his hand; the stream became liquid; the massive conglomeration of splendid objects moved, dispersed, and disappeared into Piccadilly.

So she crossed Park Lane and went to her house in Curzon Street,* where, when the meadow-sweet blew there, she could remember curlew calling and one very old man with a gun.

She could remember, she thought, stepping across the threshold of her house, how Lord Chesterfield had said—but her memory was checked. Her discreet eighteenth-century hall, where she could see Lord Chesterfield putting his hat down here and his coat down there with an elegance of deportment which it was a pleasure to watch, was now completely littered with parcels. While she had been sitting in Hyde Park the bookseller had delivered her order, and the house was crammed—there were parcels slipping down the staircase—with the whole of Victorian literature done up in grey paper and neatly tied with string. She carried as many of these packets as she could to her room, ordered footmen to bring the others, and, rapidly cutting innumerable strings, was soon surrounded by innumerable volumes.

Accustomed to the little literatures of the sixteenth, seventeenth, and eighteenth centuries, Orlando was appalled by the consequences of her order. For, of course, to the Victorians themselves Victorian literature meant not merely four great names separate and distinct but four great names sunk and embedded in a mass of Alexander Smiths, Dixons, Blacks, Milmans, Buckles, Taines, Paynes, Tuppers, Jamesons*—all vocal, clamorous, prominent, and requiring as much attention as anybody else. Orlando's reverence for print had a tough job set before it, but drawing her chair to the window to get the benefit of what light might filter between the high houses of Mayfair, she tried to come to a conclusion.

And now it is clear that there are only two ways of coming to a conclusion upon Victorian literature—one is to write it out in sixty volumes octavo,* the other is to squeeze it into six lines of the length of this one. Of the two courses, economy, since time runs short, leads us to choose the second; and so we proceed. Orlando then came to the conclusion (opening half-a-dozen books) that it was very odd that there was not a single dedication to a nobleman among them; next (turning over a vast pile of memoirs) that several of these writers had family trees half as high as her own; next, that it would be impolitic in the extreme to wrap a ten-pound note round the sugar tongs when Miss Christina Rossetti* came to tea; next (here were half-a-dozen invitations to celebrate centenaries by dining) that literature since it ate all these dinners must be growing very corpulent; next (she was invited to a score of lectures on the Influence of this upon that;* the Classical revival; the Romantic survival, and other titles of the same engaging kind) that literature since it listened to all these lectures must be growing very dry; next (here she attended a reception given by a peeress) that literature since it wore all those fur tippets must be growing very respectable; next (here she visited Carlyle's sound-proof room at Chelsea*) that genius since it needed all this coddling must be growing very delicate; and so at last she reached her final conclusion, which was of the highest importance but which, as we have already much overpassed our limit of six lines, we must omit.

Orlando, having come to this conclusion, stood looking out of the window for a considerable space of time. For, when anybody comes to a conclusion it is as if they had tossed the ball over the net and must wait for the unseen antagonist to return it to them. What would be sent her next from the colourless sky above Chesterfield House,* she wondered? And with her hands clasped, she stood for a considerable space of time wondering. Suddenly she started—and here we could only wish that, as on a former occasion, Purity, Chastity, and Modesty would push the door ajar and provide, at least, a breathing space in which we could think how to wrap up what now has to be told delicately, as a biographer should. But no! Having thrown their white garment at the naked Orlando and seen it fall short by several inches, these ladies had given up all intercourse with her these many years; and were now otherwise engaged. Is nothing then, going to happen this pale March morning to mitigate, to veil, to cover, to conceal, to shroud this undeniable event whatever it may be? For after giving that sudden, violent start, Orlando—but Heaven be praised, at this very moment there struck up outside one of these frail, reedy, fluty, jerky, old-fashioned barrel-organs which are still sometimes played by Italian organ-grinders in back streets. Let us accept the intervention, humble though it is, as if it were the music of the spheres, and allow it, with all its gasps and groans, to fill this page with sound until the moment comes which it is impossible to deny is coming; which the footman has seen coming and the maid-servant; and the reader will have to see too; for Orlando herself is clearly unable to ignore it any longer—let the barrel-organ sound and transport us on thought, which is no more than a little boat, when music sounds, tossing on the waves; on thought, which is, of all carriers, the most clumsy, the most erratic, over the roof tops and the back gardens where washing is hanging to—what is this place? Do you recognize the Green and in the middle the steeple, and the gate with a lion couchant on either side? Oh yes, it is Kew!* Well, Kew will do. So here then we are at Kew, and I will show you today (the second of March) under the plum tree, a grape hyacinth, and a crocus, and a bud, too, on the almond tree; so that to walk there is to be thinking of bulbs, hairy and red, thrust into the earth in October; flowering now; and to be dreaming of more than can rightly be said, and to be taking from its case a cigarette or cigar even, and to be flinging a cloak under (as the rhyme requires) an oak, and there to sit, waiting the kingfisher, which, it is said, was seen once to cross in the evening from bank to bank.

Wait! Wait! The kingfisher comes; the kingfisher comes not.

Behold, meanwhile, the factory chimneys and their smoke; behold the city clerks flashing by in their outrigger.* Behold the old lady taking her dog for a walk and the servant girl wearing her new hat for the first time not at the right angle. Behold them all. Though Heaven has mercifully decreed that the secrets of all hearts are hidden so that we are lured on for ever to suspect something, perhaps, that does not exist; still through our cigarette smoke, we see blaze up and salute the splendid fulfilment of natural desires for a hat, for a boat, for a rat in a ditch; as once one saw blazing—such silly hops and skips the mind takes when it slops like this all over the saucer and the barrel-organ plays—saw blazing a fire in a field against minarets near Constantinople.

Hail! natural desire! Hail! happiness! divine happiness! and pleasure of all sorts, flowers and wine, though one fades and the other intoxicates; and half-crown tickets* out of London on Sundays, and singing in a dark chapel hymns about death, and anything, anything that interrupts and confounds the tapping of typewriters and filing of letters and forging of links and chains, binding the Empire together. Hail even the crude, red bows on shop girls' lips (as if Cupid, very clumsily, dipped his thumb in red ink and scrawled a token in passing). Hail, happiness! kingfisher flashing from bank to bank, and all fulfilment of natural desire, whether it is what the male novelist says it is; or prayer; or denial; hail! in whatever form it comes, and may there be more forms, and stranger. For dark flows the stream*—would it were true, as the rhyme hints 'like a dream'—but duller and worser than that is our usual lot; without dreams, but alive, smug, fluent, habitual, under trees whose shade of an olive green drowns the blue of the wing of the vanishing bird when he darts of a sudden from bank to bank.

Hail, happiness, then, and after happiness, hail not those dreams which bloat the sharp image as spotted mirrors do the face in a country-inn parlour; dreams which splinter the whole and tear us asunder and wound us and split us apart in the night when we would sleep; but sleep, sleep, so deep that all shapes are ground to dust of infinite softness, water of dimness inscrutable, and there, folded, shrouded, like a mummy, like a moth, prone let us lie on the sand at the bottom of sleep.

But wait! but wait! we are not going, this time, visiting the blind land. Blue, like a match struck right in the ball of the innermost eye, he flys, burns, bursts the seal of sleep; the kingfisher; so that now floods back refluent like a tide, the red, thick stream of life again; bubbling, dripping; and we rise, and our eyes (for how handy a rhyme is to pass us safe over the awkward transition from death to life) fall on—(here the barrel-organ stops playing abruptly).

'It's a very fine boy, M'Lady,' said Mrs Banting, the midwife, putting her first-born child into Orlando's arms. In other words Orlando was safely delivered of a son on Thursday, March the 20th, at three o'clock in the morning.

Once more Orlando stood at the window, but let the reader take courage; nothing of the same sort is going to happen today, which is not, by any means, the same day. No—for if we look out of the window, as Orlando was doing at the moment, we shall see that Park Lane itself has considerably changed. Indeed one might stand there ten minutes or more, as Orlando stood now, without seeing a single barouche landau. 'Look at that!' she exclaimed, some days later when an absurd truncated carriage without any horses began to glide about of its own accord. A carriage without any horses indeed! She was called away just as she said that, but came back again after a time and had another look out of the window. It was odd sort of weather nowadays. The sky itself, she could not help thinking, had changed. It was no longer so thick, so watery, so prismatic now that King Edward*—see, there he was, stepping out of his neat brougham* to go and visit a certain lady opposite*—had succeeded Queen Victoria. The clouds had shrunk to a thin gauze; the sky seemed made of metal, which in hot weather tarnished verdigris, copper colour or orange as metal does in a fog. It was a little alarming—this shrinkage. Everything seemed to have shrunk. Driving past Buckingham Palace last night, there was not a trace of that vast erection which she had thought everlasting; top hats, widows' weeds, trumpets, telescopes, wreaths, all had vanished and left not a stain, not a puddle even, on the pavement. But it was now—after another interval she had come back again to her favourite station in the window—now, in the evening, that the change was most remarkable. Look at the lights in the houses! At a touch, a whole room was lit; hundreds of rooms were lit; and one was precisely the same as the other. One could see everything in the little square-shaped boxes; there was no privacy; none of those lingering shadows and odd corners that there used to be; none of those women in aprons carrying wobbly lamps which they put down carefully on this table and on that. At a touch, the whole room was bright. And the sky was bright all night long; and the pavements were bright; everything was bright. She came back again at mid-day. How narrow women had grown lately! They looked like stalks of corn, straight, shining, identical. And men's faces were as bare as the palm of one's hand.* The dryness of the atmosphere brought out the colour in everything and seemed to stiffen the muscles of the cheeks. It was harder to cry now. Water was hot in two seconds. Ivy had perished or been scraped off houses. Vegetables were less fertile; families were much smaller. Curtains and covers had been frizzled up and the walls were bare so that new brilliantly coloured pictures of real things like streets, umbrellas, apples, were hung in frames, or painted upon the wood. There was something definite and distinct about the age, which reminded her of the eighteenth century, except that there was a distraction, a desperation—as she was thinking this, the immensely long tunnel in which she seemed to have been travelling for hundreds of years widened; the light poured in; her thoughts became mysteriously tightened and strung up as if a piano tuner had put his key in her back and stretched the nerves very taut; at the same time her hearing quickened; she could hear every whisper and crackle in the room so that the clock ticking on the mantelpiece beat like a hammer. And so for some seconds the light went on becoming brighter and brighter, and she saw everything more and more clearly and the clock ticked louder and louder until there was a terrific explosion right in her ear. Orlando leapt as if she had been violently struck on the head. Ten times she was struck. In fact it was ten o'clock in the morning. It was the eleventh of October. It was 1928. It was the present moment.*

No one need wonder that Orlando started, pressed her hand to her heart, and turned pale. For what more terrifying revelation can there be than that it is the present moment? That we survive the shock at all is only possible because the past shelters us on one side and the future on another. But we have no time now for reflections; Orlando was terribly late already. She ran downstairs, she jumped into her motor-car, she pressed the self-starter and was off. Vast blue blocks of building rose into the air; the red cowls of chimneys were spotted irregularly across the sky; the road shone like silver-headed nails; omnibuses bore down upon her with sculptured white-faced drivers; she noticed sponges, bird-cages, boxes of green American cloth. But she did not allow these sights to sink into her mind even the fraction of an inch as she crossed the narrow plank of the present, lest she should fall into the raging torrent beneath. 'Why don't you look where you're going to? . . . Put your hand out, can't you?' —that was all she said sharply, as if the words were jerked out of her. For the streets were immensely crowded; people crossed without looking where they were going. People buzzed and hummed round the plate-glass windows within which one could see a glow of red, a blaze of yellow, as if they were bees, Orlando thought—but her thought that they were bees was violently snipped off and she saw, regaining perspective with one flick of her eye, that they were bodies. 'Why don't you look where you're going?' she snapped out.

At last, however, she drew up at Marshall & Snelgrove's* and went into the shop. Shade and scent enveloped her. The present fell from her like drops of scalding water. Light swayed up and down like thin stuffs puffed out by a summer breeze. She took a list from her bag and began reading in a curious stiff voice at first as if she were holding the words—boy's boots, bath salts, sardines—under a tap of many-coloured water. She watched them change as the light fell on them. Bath and boots became blunt, obtuse; sardines serrated itself like a saw. So she stood in the ground-floor department of Messrs Marshall & Snelgrove; looked this way and that; snuffed this smell and that and thus wasted some seconds. Then she got into the lift, for the good reason that the door stood open; and was shot smoothly upwards. The very fabric of life now, she thought as she rose, is magic. In the eighteenth century, we knew how everything was done; but here I rise through the air; I listen to voices in America; I see men flying—but how it's done, I can't even begin to wonder. So my belief in magic returns. Now the lift gave a little jerk as it stopped at the first floor; and she had a vision of innumerable coloured stuffs flaunting in a breeze from which came distinct, strange smells; and each time the lift stopped and flung its doors open, there was another slice of the world displayed with all the smells of that world clinging to it. She was reminded of the river off Wapping in the time of Elizabeth, where the treasure ships and the merchant ships used to anchor. How richly and curiously they had smelt! How well she remembered the feel of rough rubies running through her fingers when she dabbled them in a treasure sack! And then lying with Sukey—or whatever her name was—and having Cumberland's lantern flashed on them! The Cumberlands had a house in Portland Place* now and she had lunched with them the other day and ventured a little joke with the old man about almshouses in the Sheen Road. He had winked. But here as the lift could go no higher, she must get out—Heaven knows into what 'department' as they called it. She stood still to consult her shopping list, but was blessed if she could see, as the list bade her, bath salts, or boy's boots anywhere about. And indeed, she was about to descend again, without buying anything, but was saved from that outrage by saying aloud automatically the last item on her list; which happened to be 'sheets for a double bed'.

'Sheets for a double bed,' she said to a man at a counter and, by a dispensation of Providence, it was sheets that the man at that particular counter happened to sell. For Grimsditch, no, Grimsditch was dead; Bartholomew, no, Bartholomew was dead; Louise then*— Louise had come to her in a great taking the other day, for she had found a hole in the bottom of the sheet in the royal bed. Many kings and queens had slept there—Elizabeth; James; Charles; George; Victoria; Edward; no wonder the sheet had a hole in it. But Louise was positive she knew who had done it. It was the Prince Consort.

'Sale bosch!' she said (for there had been another war;* this time against the Germans).

'Sheets for a double bed,' Orlando repeated dreamily, for a double bed with a silver counterpane in a room fitted in a taste which she now thought perhaps a little vulgar—all in silver; but she had furnished it when she had a passion for that metal. While the man went to get sheets for a double bed, she took out a little looking-glass and a powder puff. Women were not nearly as roundabout in their ways, she thought, powdering herself with the greatest unconcern, as they had been when she herself first turned woman and lay on the deck of the *Enamoured Lady*. She gave her nose the right tint deliberately. She never touched her cheeks. Honestly, though she was now thirty-six,* she scarcely looked a day older. She looked just as pouting, as sulky, as handsome, as rosy (like a million-candled Christmas tree, Sasha had said) as she had done that day on the ice, when the Thames was frozen and they had gone skating——

'The best Irish linen, Ma'am,' said the shopman, spreading the sheets on the counter,—and they had met an old woman picking up sticks. Here, as she was fingering the linen abstractedly, one of the swing-doors between the departments opened and let through, perhaps from the fancy-goods department, a whiff of scent, waxen, tinted as if from pink candles, and the scent curved like a shell round a figure—was it a boy's or was it a girl's?—young, slender, seductive—a girl, by God! furred, pearled, in Russian trousers; but faithless, faithless!

'Faithless!' cried Orlando (the man had gone) and all the shop seemed to pitch and toss with yellow water and far off she saw the masts of the Russian ship standing out to sea, and then, miraculously (perhaps the door opened again) the conch which the scent had made became a platform, a dais, off which stepped a fat, furred woman, marvellously well preserved, seductive, diademed, a Grand Duke's mistress; she who, leaning over the banks of the Volga, eating sandwiches, had watched men drown; and began walking down the shop towards her.

'Oh Sasha!' Orlando cried. Really, she was shocked that she should have come to this; she had grown so fat; so lethargic; and she bowed her head over the linen so that this apparition of a grey woman in fur, and a girl in Russian trousers, with all these smells of wax candles, white flowers, and old ships that it brought with it might pass behind her back unseen.

'Any napkins, towels, dusters today, Ma'am?' the shopman persisted. And it is enormously to the credit of the shopping list, which Orlando now consulted, that she was able to reply with every appearance of composure, that there was only one thing in the world she wanted and that was bath salts; which was in another department.

But descending in the lift again—so insidious is the repetition of any scene—she was again sunk far beneath the present moment; and thought when the lift bumped on the ground, that she heard a pot broken against a river bank. As for finding the right department, whatever it might be, she stood engrossed among the handbags, deaf to the suggestions of all the polite, black, combed, sprightly shop assistants, who descending as they did equally and some of them, perhaps, as proudly, even from such depths of the past as she did, chose to let down the impervious screen of the present so that today they appeared shop assistants in Marshall & Snelgrove's merely. Orlando stood there hesitating. Through the great glass doors she could see the traffic in Oxford Street. Omnibus seemed to pile itself upon omnibus and then to jerk itself apart. So the ice blocks had pitched and tossed that day on the Thames. An old nobleman in furred slippers had sat astride one of them. There he went—she could see him now—calling down maledictions upon the Irish rebels. He had sunk there, where her car stood.

'Time has passed over me,' she thought, trying to collect herself; 'this is the oncome of middle age. How strange it is! Nothing is any longer one thing. I take up a handbag and I think of an old bumboat woman frozen in the ice. Someone lights a pink candle and I see a girl in Russian trousers. When I step out of doors—as I do now,' here she stepped on to the pavement of Oxford Street, 'what is it that I taste? Little herbs. I hear goat bells. I see mountains. Turkey? India? Persia?' Her eyes filled with tears.

That Orlando had gone a little too far from the present moment will, perhaps, strike the reader who sees her now preparing to get into her motor-car with her eyes full of tears and visions of Persian mountains. And indeed, it cannot be denied that the most successful practitioners of the art of life, often unknown people by the way, somehow contrive to synchronize the sixty or seventy different times which beat simultaneously in every normal human system so that when eleven strikes, all the rest chime in unison, and the present is neither a violent disruption nor completely forgotten in the past. Of them we can justly say that they live precisely the sixty-eight or seventy-two years allotted them on the tombstone. Of the rest some we know to be dead though they walk among us; some are not yet born though they go through the forms of life; others are hundreds of years old though they call themselves thirty-six. The true length of a person's life, whatever the *Dictionary of National Biography** may say, is always a matter of dispute. For it is a difficult business—this time-keeping; nothing more quickly disorders it than contact with any of the arts; and it may have been her love of poetry that was to blame for making Orlando lose her shopping list and start home without the sardines, the bath salts, or the boots. Now as she stood with her hand on the door of her motor-car, the present again struck her on the head. Eleven times she was violently assaulted.

'Confound it all!' she cried, for it is a great shock to the nervous system, hearing a clock strike—so much so that for some time now there is nothing to be said of her save that she frowned slightly, changed her gears admirably, and cried out, as before, 'Look where you're going!' 'Don't you know your own mind?' 'Why didn't you say so then?' while the motor-car shot, swung, squeezed, and slid, for she was an expert driver, down Regent Street, down Haymarket, down Northumberland Avenue, over Westminster Bridge, to the left, straight on, to the right, straight on again. . . .

The Old Kent Road* was very crowded on Thursday, the eleventh of October 1928. People spilt off the pavement. There were women with shopping bags. Children ran out. There were sales at drapers' shops. Streets widened and narrowed. Long vistas steadily shrunk together. Here was a market. Here a funeral. Here a procession with banners upon which was written 'Ra—Un',* but what else? Meat was very red. Butchers stood at the door. Women almost had their heels sliced off. Amor Vin*—that was over a porch. A woman looked out of a bedroom window, profoundly contemplative, and very still.

Applejohn and Applebed, Undert——. Nothing could be seen whole
or read from start to finish. What was seen begun—like two friends
starting to meet each other across the street—was never seen ended.
After twenty minutes the body and mind were like scraps of torn
paper tumbling from a sack and, indeed, the process of motoring fast
out of London so much resembles the chopping up small of identity
which precedes unconsciousness and perhaps death itself that it is
an open question in what sense Orlando can be said to have existed
at the present moment. Indeed we should have given her over for
a person entirely disassembled were it not that here, at last, one green
screen was held out on the right, against which the little bits of paper
fell more slowly; and then another was held out on the left so that one
could see the separate scraps now turning over by themselves in the
air; and then green screens were held continuously on either side, so
that her mind regained the illusion of holding things within itself and
she saw a cottage, a farmyard and four cows, all precisely life-size.

When this happened, Orlando heaved a sigh of relief, lit a cigarette,
and puffed for a minute or two in silence. Then she called hesitatingly,
as if the person she wanted might not be there, 'Orlando?' For if there
are (at a venture) seventy-six different times all ticking in the mind at
once, how many different people are there not—Heaven help us—all
having lodgement at one time or another in the human spirit? Some
say two thousand and fifty-two. So that it is the most usual thing in
the world for a person to call, directly they are alone, Orlando? (if
that is one's name) meaning by that, Come, come! I'm sick to death
of this particular self. I want another. Hence, the astonishing changes
we see in our friends. But it is not altogether plain sailing, either,
for though one may say, as Orlando said (being out in the country
and needing another self presumably) Orlando? still the Orlando she
needs may not come; these selves of which we are built up, one on
top of another, as plates are piled on a waiter's hand, have attachments elsewhere, sympathies, little constitutions and rights of their
own, call them what you will (and for many of these things there is no
name) so that one will only come if it is raining, another in a room
with green curtains, another when Mrs Jones is not there, another
if you can promise it a glass of wine—and so on; for everybody can
multiply from his own experience the different terms which his
different selves have made with him—and some are too wildly ridiculous to be mentioned in print at all.

So Orlando, at the turn by the barn, called 'Orlando?' with a note of interrogation in her voice and waited. Orlando did not come.

'All right then,' Orlando said, with the good humour people practise on these occasions; and tried another. For she had a great variety of selves to call upon, far more than we have been able to find room for, since a biography is considered complete if it merely accounts for six or seven selves, whereas a person may well have as many thousand. Choosing then, only those selves we have found room for, Orlando may now have called on the boy who cut the nigger's head down; the boy who strung it up again; the boy who sat on the hill; the boy who saw the poet; the boy who handed the Queen the bowl of rose water; or she may have called upon the young man who fell in love with Sasha; or upon the Courtier; or upon the Ambassador; or upon the Soldier; or upon the Traveller; or she may have wanted the woman to come to her; the Gipsy; the Fine Lady; the Hermit; the girl in love with life; the Patroness of Letters; the woman who called Mar (meaning hot baths and evening fires) or Shelmerdine (meaning crocuses in autumn woods) or Bonthrop (meaning the death we die daily) or all three together—which meant more things than we have space to write out—all were different and she may have called upon any one of them.

Perhaps; but what appeared certain (for we are now in the region of 'perhaps' and 'appears') was that the one she needed most kept aloof, for she was, to hear her talk, changing her selves as quickly as she drove—there was a new one at every corner—as happens when, for some unaccountable reason, the conscious self, which is the uppermost, and has the power to desire, wishes to be nothing but one self. This is what some people call the true self, and it is, they say, compact of all the selves we have it in us to be; commanded and locked up by the Captain self, the Key self, which amalgamates and controls them all. Orlando was certainly seeking this self as the reader can judge from overhearing her talk as she drove (and if it is rambling talk, disconnected, trivial, dull, and sometimes unintelligible, it is the reader's fault for listening to a lady talking to herself; we only copy her words as she spoke them, adding in brackets which self in our opinion is speaking, but in this we may well be wrong).

'What then? Who then?' she said. 'Thirty-six; in a motor car; a woman. Yes, but a million other things as well. A snob am I? The garter in the hall? The leopards? My ancestors? Proud of them? Yes!

Greedy, luxurious, vicious? Am I? (here a new self came in). Don't
care a damn if I am. Truthful? I think so. Generous? Oh, but that
don't count* (here a new self came in). Lying in bed of a morning listening to the pigeons on fine linen; silver dishes; wine; maids;
footmen. Spoilt? Perhaps. Too many things for nothing. Hence my
books (here she mentioned fifty classical titles; which represented,
so we think, the early romantic works that she tore up). Facile, glib,
romantic. But (here another self came in) a duffer, a fumbler. More
clumsy I couldn't be. And—and—(here she hesitated for a word and
if we suggest 'Love' we may be wrong, but certainly she laughed and
blushed and then cried out—) A toad set in emeralds! Harry the
Archduke! Blue-bottles on the ceiling! (here another self came in).
But Nell, Kit, Sasha? (she was sunk in gloom: tears actually shaped
themselves and she had long given over crying). Trees, she said.
(Here another self came in.) I love trees (she was passing a clump)
growing there a thousand years. And barns (she passed a tumbledown barn at the edge of the road). And sheep dogs (here one came
trotting across the road. She carefully avoided it). And the night.
But people (here another self came in). People? (She repeated it as
a question.) I don't know. Chattering, spiteful, always telling lies.
(Here she turned into the High Street of her native town, which was
crowded, for it was market day, with farmers, and shepherds, and
old women with hens in baskets.) I like peasants. I understand crops.
But (here another self came skipping over the top of her mind like
the beam from a lighthouse). Fame! (She laughed.) Fame! Seven editions. A prize.* Photographs in the evening papers (here she alluded
to the 'Oak Tree' and 'The Burdett Coutts' Memorial Prize* which
she had won; and we must snatch space to remark how discompos-
ing it is for her biographer that this culmination to which the whole
book moved, this peroration with which the book was to end, should
be dashed from us on a laugh casually like this; but the truth is that
when we write of a woman, everything is out of place—culminations
and perorations; the accent never falls where it does with a man*).
Fame! she repeated. A poet—a charlatan; both every morning as
regularly as the post comes in. To dine, to meet; to meet, to dine;
fame—fame! (She had here to slow down to pass through the crowd
of market people. But no one noticed her. A porpoise in a fishmonger's shop* attracted far more attention than a lady who had won
a prize and might, had she chosen, have worn three coronets one on

top of another on her brow.) Driving very slowly she now hummed
as if it were part of an old song, 'With my guineas I'll buy flowering
trees, flowering trees,* flowering trees and walk among my flowering
trees and tell my sons what fame is'. So she hummed, and now all
her words began to sag here and there like a barbaric necklace of
heavy beads. 'And walk among my flowering trees,' she sang, accent-
ing the words strongly, 'and see the moon rise slow, the waggons go.
. . .' Here she stopped short and looked ahead of her intently at the
bonnet of the car in profound meditation.

'He sat at Twitchett's table', she mused, 'with a dirty ruff on. . . .
Was it old Mr Baker come to measure the timber? Or was it Sh—p—
re?' (for when we speak names we deeply reverence to ourselves we
never speak them whole). She gazed for ten minutes ahead of her,
letting the car come almost to a standstill.

'Haunted!' she cried, suddenly pressing the accelerator. 'Haunted!
ever since I was a child. There flies the wild goose. It flies past the
window out to sea. Up I jumped (she gripped the steering-wheel
tighter) and stretched after it. But the goose flies too fast. I've seen it,
here—there—there—England, Persia, Italy. Always it flies fast out
to sea and always I fling after it words like nets (here she flung her
hand out) which shrivel as I've seen nets shrivel drawn on deck with
only sea-weed in them; and sometimes there's an inch of silver—six
words—in the bottom of the net. But never the great fish who lives in
the coral groves.' Here she bent her head, pondering deeply.

And it was at this moment, when she had ceased to call 'Orlando'
and was deep in thoughts of something else, that the Orlando whom
she had called came of its own accord; as was proved by the change
that now came over her (she had passed through the lodge gates and
was entering the park).

The whole of her darkened and settled, as when some foil whose
addition makes the round and solidity of a surface is added to it, and
the shallow becomes deep and the near distant; and all is contained
as water is contained by the sides of a well. So she was now darkened,
stilled, and become, with the addition of this Orlando, what is called,
rightly or wrongly, a single self, a real self. And she fell silent. For it is
probable that when people talk aloud, the selves (of which there may
be more than two thousand) are conscious of disseverment, and are
trying to communicate, but when communication is established they
fall silent.

Masterfully, swiftly, she drove up the curving drive between the elms and oaks through the falling turf of the park whose fall was so gentle that had it been water it would have spread the beach with a smooth green tide. Planted here and in solemn groups were beech trees and oak trees. The deer stepped among them, one white as snow, another with its head on one side, for some wire netting had caught in its horns. All this, the trees, deer, and turf, she observed with the greatest satisfaction as if her mind had become a fluid that flowed round things and enclosed them completely.* Next minute she drew up in the courtyard where, for so many hundred years she had come, on horseback or in coach and six, with men riding before or coming after; where plumes had tossed, torches flashed, and the same flowering trees that let their leaves drop now had shaken their blossoms. Now she was alone. The autumn leaves were falling. The porter opened the great gates. 'Morning, James,' she said, 'there're some things in the car. Will you bring 'em in?' words of no beauty, interest, or significance themselves, it will be conceded, but now so plumped out with meaning that they fell like ripe nuts from a tree, and proved that when the shrivelled skin of the ordinary is stuffed out with meaning it satisfies the senses amazingly. This was true indeed of every movement and action now, usual though they were; so that to see Orlando change her skirt for a pair of whipcord breeches and leather jacket, which she did in less than three minutes, was to be ravished with the beauty of movement as if Madame Lopokova were using her highest art. Then she strode into the dining-room where her old friends Dryden, Pope, Swift, Addison regarded her demurely at first as who should say Here's the prize winner! but when they reflected that two hundred guineas was in question, they nodded their heads approvingly. Two hundred guineas, they seemed to say; two hundred guineas are not to be sniffed at. She cut herself a slice of bread and ham, clapped the two together and began to eat, striding up and down the room, thus shedding her company habits in a second, without thinking. After five or six such turns, she tossed off a glass of red Spanish wine,* and, filling another which she carried in her hand, strode down the long corridor and through a dozen drawing-rooms and so began a perambulation of the house, attended by such elk-hounds and spaniels as chose to follow her.

This, too, was all in the day's routine. As soon would she come home and leave her own grandmother without a kiss as come back and leave the house unvisited. She fancied that the rooms brightened as she came in; stirred, opened their eyes* as if they had been dozing in her absence. She fancied, too, that, hundreds and thousands of times as she had seen them, they never looked the same twice, as if so long a life as theirs had stored in them a myriad moods which changed with winter and summer, bright weather and dark, and her own fortunes and the people's characters who visited them. Polite, they always were to strangers, but a little weary; with her, they were entirely open and at their ease. Why not indeed? They had known each other for close on four centuries now. They had nothing to conceal. She knew their sorrows and joys. She knew what age each part of them was and its little secrets—a hidden drawer, a concealed cupboard, or some deficiency perhaps, such as a part made up, or added later. They, too, knew her in all her moods and changes. She had hidden nothing from them; had come to them as boy and woman, crying and dancing, brooding and gay. In this window-seat, she had written her first verses; in that chapel, she had been married. And she would be buried here, she reflected, kneeling on the window-sill in the long gallery and sipping her Spanish wine. Though she could hardly fancy it, the body of the heraldic leopard would be making yellow pools on the floor the day they lowered her to lie among her ancestors. She, who believed in no immortality, could not help feeling that her soul would come and go forever with the reds on the panels and the greens on the sofa. For the room—she had strolled into the Ambassador's bedroom*—shone like a shell that has lain at the bottom of the sea for centuries and has been crusted over and painted a million tints by the water; it was rose and yellow, green and sand-coloured. It was frail as a shell, as iridescent and as empty. No Ambassador would ever sleep there again. Ah, but she knew where the heart of the house still beat. Gently opening a door, she stood on the threshold so that (as she fancied) the room could not see her and watched the tapestry rising and falling on the eternal faint breeze which never failed to move it. Still the hunter rode; still Daphne flew. The heart still beat, she thought, however faintly, however far withdrawn; the frail indomitable heart of the immense building.

Now, calling her troop of dogs to her she passed down the gallery whose floor was laid with whole oak trees sawn across. Rows of chairs with all their velvets faded stood ranged against the wall holding their arms out for Elizabeth, for James, for Shakespeare it might be, for Cecil,* who never came. The sight made her gloomy. She unhooked the rope that fenced them off. She sat on the Queen's chair; she opened a manuscript book lying on Lady Betty's table;* she stirred her fingers in the aged rose leaves; she brushed her short hair with King James' silver brushes; she bounced up and down upon his bed (but no King would ever sleep there again, for all Louise's new sheets) and pressed her cheek against the worn silver counterpane that lay upon it. But everywhere were little lavender bags to keep the moth out and printed notices, 'Please do not touch', which, though she had put them there herself, seemed to rebuke her. The house was no longer hers entirely, she sighed. It belonged to time now; to history; was past the touch and control of the living. Never would beer be spilt here any more, she thought (she was in the bedroom that had been old Nick Greene's), or holes burnt in the carpet. Never two hundred servants come running and brawling down the corridors with warming pans and great branches for the great fireplaces. Never would ale be brewed and candles made and saddles fashioned and stone shaped in the workshops outside the house. Hammers and mallets were silent now. Chairs and beds were empty; tankards of silver and gold were locked in glass cases. The great wings of silence beat up and down the empty house.

So she sat at the end of the gallery with her dogs couched round her, in Queen Elizabeth's hard armchair. The gallery stretched far away to a point where the light almost failed. It was as a tunnel bored deep into the past.* As her eyes peered down it, she could see people laughing and talking; the great men she had known; Dryden, Swift, and Pope; and statesmen in colloquy; and lovers dallying in the window-seats; and people eating and drinking at the long tables; and the wood smoke curling round their heads and making them sneeze and cough. Still further down, she saw sets of splendid dancers formed for the quadrille. A fluty, frail, but nevertheless stately music began to play. An organ boomed. A coffin was borne into the chapel. A marriage procession came out of it. Armed men with helmets left for the wars. They brought banners back from Flodden and Poitiers* and stuck them on the wall. The long gallery filled itself thus, and still peering further, she thought she could make out at the very end, beyond the Elizabethans and the Tudors, some one older, further, darker, a cowled figure, monastic, severe, a monk, who went with his hands clasped, and a book in them, murmuring——

Like thunder, the stable clock struck four. Never did any earthquake so demolish a whole town. The gallery and all its occupants fell to powder. Her own face, that had been dark and sombre as she gazed, was lit as by an explosion of gunpowder. In this same light everything near her showed with extreme distinctness. She saw two flies circling round and noticed the blue sheen on their bodies; she saw a knot in the wood where her foot was, and her dog's ear twitching. At the same time, she heard a bough creaking in the garden, a sheep coughing in the park, a swift screaming past the window. Her own body quivered and tingled as if suddenly stood naked in a hard frost. Yet, she kept, as she had not done when the clock struck ten in London, complete composure (for she was now one and entire, and presented, it may be, a larger surface to the shock of time). She rose, but without precipitation, called her dogs, and went firmly but with great alertness of movement down the staircase and out into the garden. Here the shadows of the plants were miraculously distinct. She noticed the separate grains of earth in the flower beds as if she had a microscope stuck to her eye. She saw the intricacy of the twigs of every tree. Each blade of grass was distinct and the marking of veins and petals. She saw Stubbs, the gardener, coming along the path, and every button on his gaiters was visible; she saw Betty and Prince, the cart horses, and never had she marked so clearly the white star on Betty's forehead, and the three long hairs that fell down below the rest on Prince's tail. Out in the quadrangle the old grey walls of the house looked like a scraped new photograph; she heard the loud speaker condensing on the terrace a dance tune that people were listening to in the red velvet opera house at Vienna. Braced and strung up by the present moment she was also strangely afraid, as if whenever the gulf of time gaped and let a second through some unknown danger might come with it. The tension was too relentless and too rigorous to be endured long without discomfort. She walked more briskly than she liked, as if her legs were moved for her, through the garden and out into the park. Here she forced herself, by a great effort, to stop by the carpenter's shop, and to stand stock-still watching Joe Stubbs fashion a cart wheel. She was standing with her eye fixed on his hand when the quarter struck. It hurtled through her like a meteor, so hot that no fingers can hold it. She saw with disgusting vividness that the thumb on Joe's right hand was without a finger nail and there was a raised saucer of pink flesh where the nail

ORLANDO AT THE PRESENT TIME

should have been. The sight was so repulsive that she felt faint for a moment, but in that moment's darkness, when her eyelids flickered, she was relieved of the pressure of the present. There was something strange in the shadow that the flicker of her eyes cast, something which (as anyone can test for himself by looking now at the sky) is always absent from the present—whence its terror, its nondescript character—something one trembles to pin through the body with a name and call beauty, for it has no body, is as a shadow without substance or quality of its own, yet has the power to change whatever it adds itself to. This shadow now, while she flickered her eye in her faintness in the carpenter's shop, stole out, and attaching itself to the innumerable sights she had been receiving, composed them into something tolerable, comprehensible. Her mind began to toss like the sea. Yes, she thought, heaving a deep sigh of relief, as she turned from the carpenter's shop to climb the hill, I can begin to live again. I am by the Serpentine, she thought, the little boat is climbing through the white arch of a thousand deaths. I am about to understand. . . .

Those were her words, spoken quite distinctly, but we cannot conceal the fact that she was now a very indifferent witness to the truth of what was before her and might easily have mistaken a sheep for a cow, or an old man called Smith for one who was called Jones and was no relation of his whatever. For the shadow of faintness which the thumb without a nail had cast had deepened now, at the back of her brain (which is the part furthest from sight), into a pool where things dwell in darkness so deep that what they are we scarcely know. She now looked down into this pool or sea in which everything is reflected—and, indeed, some say that all our most violent passions, and art and religion, are the reflections which we see in the dark hollow at the back of the head when the visible world is obscured for the time. She looked there now, long, deeply, profoundly, and immediately the ferny path up the hill along which she was walking became not entirely a path, but partly the Serpentine; the hawthorn bushes were partly ladies and gentlemen sitting with card-cases and gold-mounted canes; the sheep were partly tall Mayfair houses; everything was partly something else, as if her mind had become a forest with glades branching here and there; things came nearer, and further, and mingled and separated and made the strangest alliances and combinations in an incessant chequer of light and shade. Except when

Canute, the elk-hound, chased a rabbit and so reminded her that it must be about half past four—it was indeed twenty-three minutes to six—she forgot the time.

The ferny path led, with many turns and windings, higher and higher to the oak tree, which stood on the top. The tree had grown bigger, sturdier, and more knotted since she had known it, somewhere about the year 1588, but it was still in the prime of life. The little sharply frilled leaves were still fluttering thickly on its branches. Flinging herself on the ground, she felt the bones of the tree running out like ribs from a spine this way and that beneath her. She liked to think that she was riding the back of the world. She liked to attach herself to something hard. As she flung herself down a little square book bound in red cloth fell from the breast of her leather jacket—her poem 'The Oak Tree'. 'I should have brought a trowel,' she reflected. The earth was so shallow over the roots that it seemed doubtful if she could do as she meant and bury the book here. Besides, the dogs would dig it up. No luck ever attends these symbolical celebrations, she thought. Perhaps it would be as well then to do without them. She had a little speech on the tip of her tongue which she meant to speak over the book as she buried it. (It was a copy of the first edition, signed by author and artist.) 'I bury this as a tribute,' she was going to have said, 'a return to the land of what the land has given me,' but Lord! once one began mouthing words aloud, how silly they sounded! She was reminded of old Greene getting upon a platform the other day comparing her with Milton (save for his blindness) and handing her a cheque for two hundred guineas.* She had thought then, of the oak tree here on its hill, and what has that got to do with this, she had wondered? What has praise and fame to do with poetry? What has seven editions (the book had already gone into no less) got to do with the value of it? Was not writing poetry a secret transaction, a voice answering a voice? So that all this chatter and praise and blame and meeting people who admired one and meeting people who did not admire one was as ill suited as could be to the thing itself—a voice answering a voice. What could have been more secret, she thought, more slow, and like the intercourse of lovers, than the stammering answer she had made all these years to the old crooning song of the woods, and the farms and the brown horses standing at the gate, neck to neck, and the smithy and the kitchen and the fields, so laboriously bearing wheat, turnips, grass, and the garden blowing irises and fritillaries?

So she let her book lie unburied and dishevelled on the ground, and watched the vast view, varied like an ocean floor this evening with the sun lightening it and the shadows darkening it. There was a village with a church tower among elm trees; a grey domed manor house in a park; a spark of light burning on some glass-house; a farmyard with yellow corn stacks. The fields were marked with black tree clumps, and beyond the fields stretched long woodlands, and there was the gleam of a river, and then hills again. In the far distance Snowdon's crags broke white among the clouds; she saw the far Scottish hills and the wild tides that swirl about the Hebrides. She listened for the sound of gun-firing out at sea. No—only the wind blew. There was no war today. Drake had gone; Nelson* had gone. 'And there', she thought, letting her eyes, which had been looking at these far distances, drop once more to the land beneath her, 'was my land once: that Castle between the downs was mine; and all that moor running almost to the sea was mine.' Here the landscape (it must have been some trick of the fading light) shook itself, heaped itself, let all this encumbrance of houses, castles, and woods slide off its tent-shaped sides. The bare mountains of Turkey were before her. It was blazing noon. She looked straight at the baked hill-side. Goats cropped the sandy tufts at her feet. An eagle soared above her. The raucous voice of old Rustum, the gipsy, croaked in her ears, 'What is your antiquity and your race, and your possessions compared with this? What do you need with four hundred bedrooms and silver lids on all your dishes, and housemaids dusting?'

At this moment some church clock chimed in the valley. The tent-like landscape collapsed and fell. The present showered down upon her head once more, but now that the light was fading, gentlier than before, calling into view nothing detailed, nothing small, but only misty fields, cottages with lamps in them, the slumbering bulk of a wood, and a fan-shaped light pushing the darkness before it along some lane. Whether it had struck nine, ten, or eleven, she could not say. Night had come—night that she loved of all times, night in which the reflections in the dark pool of the mind shine more clearly than by day. It was not necessary to faint now in order to look deep into the darkness where things shape themselves and to see in the pool of the mind now Shakespeare, now a girl in Russian trousers, now a toy boat on the Serpentine, and then the Atlantic itself, where it storms in great waves past Cape Horn. She looked into the darkness. There was her husband's brig, rising to the top of the wave! Up, it went, and up and up. The white arch of a thousand deaths rose before it. Oh rash, oh ridiculous man, always sailing, so uselessly, round Cape Horn in the teeth of a gale! But the brig was through the arch and out on the other side; it was safe at last!

'Ecstasy!' she cried, 'ecstasy!' And then the wind sank, the waters grew calm; and she saw the waves rippling peacefully in the moonlight.

'Marmaduke Bonthrop Shelmerdine!' she cried, standing by the oak tree.

The beautiful, glittering name fell out of the sky like a steel-blue feather. She watched it fall, turning and twisting like a slow-falling arrow that cleaves the deep air beautifully. He was coming, as he always came, in moments of dead calm; when the wave rippled and the spotted leaves fell slowly over her foot in the autumn woods; when the leopard was still; the moon was on the waters, and nothing moved between sky and sea. Then he came.

All was still now. It was near midnight. The moon rose slowly over the weald. Its light raised a phantom castle upon earth. There stood the great house with all its windows robed in silver. Of wall or sub-stance there was none. All was phantom. All was still. All was lit as for the coming of a dead Queen. Gazing below her, Orlando saw dark plumes tossing in the courtyard, and torches flickering and shadows kneeling. A Queen once more stepped from her chariot.

'The house is at your service, Ma'am,' she cried, curtseying deeply. 'Nothing has been changed. The dead Lord, my father, shall lead you in.'

As she spoke, the first stroke of midnight sounded. The cold breeze of the present brushed her face with its little breath of fear. She looked anxiously into the sky. It was dark with clouds now. The wind roared in her ears. But in the roar of the wind she heard the roar of an aeroplane coming nearer and nearer.

'Here! Shel, here!' she cried, baring her breast to the moon* (which now showed bright) so that her pearls glowed like the eggs of some vast moon-spider. The aeroplane rushed out of the clouds and stood over her head. It hovered above her. Her pearls burnt like a phosphorescent flare in the darkness.

And as Shelmerdine, now grown a fine sea captain, hale,

fresh-coloured, and alert, leapt to the ground, there sprang up over his head a single wild bird.

'It is the goose!' Orlando cried. 'The wild goose. . . .'

And the twelfth stroke of midnight sounded; the twelfth stroke of midnight, Thursday, the eleventh of October, Nineteen hundred and Twenty Eight.

INDEX

THE END

EXPLANATORY NOTES

I am indebted to previous editors and annotators of the novel: Rachel Bowlby, Sandra M. Gilbert, Stuart N. Clarke, J. H. Stape, and Merry Pawlowski.

ABBREVIATIONS

bap.	baptized
Bowlby	*Orlando*, ed. Rachel Bowlby (Oxford: Oxford University Press, 1992).
Diary	*The Diary of Virginia Woolf*, ed. Anne Olivier Bell assisted by Andrew McNeillie, 5 vols. (London: Hogarth Press, 1977–84).
Essays	*The Essays of Virginia Woolf*, 6 vols., ed. Andrew McNeillie (vols. i–iv) and Stuart N. Clarke (vols. v–vi) (London: Hogarth Press, 1984–2012).
Knole	Vita Sackville-West, *Knole and the Sackvilles* (London: W. Heinemann, 1922).
LE	Ben Weinreb, Christopher Hibbert, Julia Keay, and John Keay, *The London Encyclopaedia* (3rd edn., London and Basingstoke: Macmillan, 2008).
Letters	*The Letters of Virginia Woolf*, ed. Nigel Nicolson and Joanne Trautmann, 6 vols. (London: Hogarth Press, 1975–80).
Nicolson, *Portrait*	Nigel Nicolson, *Portrait of a Marriage* (London: Weidenfeld and Nicolson, 1973).
OED	*Oxford English Dictionary*
VSW	Vita Sackville-West
VW	Virginia Woolf

ILLUSTRATIONS

2 *Orlando as a Boy*: the frontispiece to the 1928 Hogarth Press edition. The painting is a detail of Edward Sackville from a double portrait at Knole by Cornelius Nuie; the full portrait, reproduced in VSW's *Knole* (facing p. 106), depicts the two sons of Edward Sackville, 4th Earl of Dorset. The arrangements for the illustrations are detailed in letters from VW to VSW in October and November 1927, and April 1928 (*Letters*, iii. 434–5, 484, 488).

33 *The Russian Princess as a Child*: a photograph of Angelica Bell, aged 9, taken by her mother Vanessa Bell.

69 *The Archduchess Harriet*: portrait of Mary, 4th Countess of Dorset (née Curzon) (1586–1645), from Lord Sackville's private collection at Knole.

75 *Orlando as Ambassador*: portrait of Lionel Sackville, 7th Earl and 1st Duke
    of Dorset (1688–1765), by Rosalba Carriera, in the collection at Knole.

94 *Orlando on her Return to England*: photograph of VSW taken by Lenare,
    Hanover Square, London, in November 1927.

144 *Orlando about the Year 1840*: photograph of VSW taken by Vanessa Bell
    and Duncan Grant, November 1927.

156 *Marmaduke Bonthrop Shelmerdine, Esquire*: portrait of an unknown man,
    artist unknown, at that time in VSW's collection.

186 *Orlando at the Present Time*: photograph of VSW probably taken by Leon-
    ard Woolf, April 1928. VW to VSW: 'It has now become essential to have
    a photograph of Orlando in country clothes in a wood, to end with' (*Let-
    ters*, iii. 488).

ORLANDO

6 *my husband*: Leonard Woolf (1880–1969). For the others named in VW's
   acknowledgements, see the List of Names, pp. 229–30.

   a gentleman in America: in matters of botany VW's *Night and Day* had drawn
   criticism for depicting roses in bloom in Lincolnshire in late December.
   In 1927 Baron Olivier (1859–1943) had criticized *To the Lighthouse*: 'my
   horticulture and natural history is in every instance wrong: there are no
   rooks, elms, or dahlias in the Hebrides; my sparrows are wrong; so are my
   carnations' (VW, letter to Vanessa Bell, 22 May 1927, *Letters*, iii. 279). The
   gentleman in America, however, is fictitious.

11 *a Moor*: a native of north-west Africa; in the Middle Ages and early mod-
    ern period, the term was also used more broadly to denote any native of
    Africa.

    fields of asphodel: asphodel, a 'genus of liliaceous plants with very hand-
    some flowers' (*OED*) common in southern Europe, was also, from classical
    Greece onwards, considered to be an immortal flower found in the place of
    the blessed dead, the Elysian fields.

    shrunk, black lips: VW's phrases borrow from Joseph Conrad's description
    of Africans' heads in *Heart of Darkness* (and see p. 32): 'I returned delib-
    erately to the first I had seen—and there it was, black, dried, sunken, with
    closed eyelids,—a head that seemed to sleep at the top of that pole, and,
    with the shrunken dry lips showing a narrow white line of the teeth, was
    smiling too, smiling continuously at some endless and jocose dream of that
    eternal slumber.'

    instantly coloured red, blue, and yellow like a butterfly's wing: the light cast by
    stained glass echoes John Keats's 'The Eve of St Agnes' (1820) in which
    glass 'diamonded with panes of quaint device, | Innumerable of stains and
    splendid dyes, | As are the tiger-moth's deep-damasked wings' (ll. 211–
    13) throws 'warm gules' on Madeline as she prays, while 'Rose-bloom fell

on her hands, together pressed, | And on her silver cross soft amethyst, | And on her hair a glory, like a saint' (ll. 220–2).

12 *'Æthelbert: A Tragedy in Five Acts'*: the title alludes to the eight novels and five plays, many on historical themes, that VSW had written between 1906 and 1910, such as 'The King's Secret', 'Edward Sackville: Tale of a Cavalier', and 'The Life of Alcibiades'. None was properly published, though she had *Chatterton: A Drama in Three Acts* privately printed in 1909 (Nicolson, *Portrait*, 62–4).

13 *the thought is too well known to be worth writing out*: though the quoted phrase 'how many suns shall I see set' appears to be an allusion, on account of its near-iambic rhythm, no source has been traced. The well-known thought may be to do with mortality, i.e., 'How many more suns shall I see set before I die.'

a trifle clumsy: VW had found VSW 'uncouth & clumsy' early in their acquaintance (*Diary*, iii. 28).

Stubbs: VW used the name of the actual gardener at Knole, VSW's ancestral home (Bowlby, 319).

one could see the English Channel: the English Channel is about 30 miles from Knole, and is not visible. In VW's very first recorded notes about *Orlando*, when she envisaged a fantasy to be called 'The Jessamy Brides', based on the Ladies of Llangollen (Lady Eleanor Butler and the Hon. Sarah Ponsonby), it was of two women 'at the top of a house': 'One can see anything (for this is all fantasy) the Tower Bridge, clouds, aeroplanes' (*Diary*, iii. 131).

15 *The Queen had come*: the house and lands at Knole were granted to Thomas Sackville, Lord Buckhurst (1536–1608), in 1566, but at that time they were under lease, and he did not gain access to Knole until 1603. If Queen Elizabeth I did visit Knole, it was not while it was occupied by the Sackville family.

Mrs Stewkley: in VSW's *Knole* (p. 78), a Mrs Stewkly [*sic*] is listed in a seventeeth-century 'catalogue' of the members of the Knole household, being one of the higher-ranking members of the staff who dined at the Parlour Table.

a rather fat, shabby man: VWs index indicates that this figure is Shakespeare. The 'globed' eyes allude to the name of his playhouse.

hodden brown: hodden is a coarse woollen cloth associated with peasants; the inversion of conventional word order derives from the phrase 'hodden grey' used by two eighteenth-century poets.

like some green stone of curious texture: it is not known what colour Shakespeare's eyes were; as the *Dictionary of National Biography* noted, those on the bust in Holy Trinity church in Stratford-upon-Avon were coloured hazel. VW's choice of green suggests the 'green-eyed monster', jealousy (*Othello*, III. iii).

16 *the waxworks at the Abbey*: Westminster Abbey preserved funeral effigies of kings, queens, and other nobility, which had been placed on top of their coffins before their funeral. Woolf had written about them in her essay 'Waxworks at the Abbey' (11 April 1928), remarking of Elizabeth I that 'It is a drawn, anguished figure, with the pursed look of someone who goes in perpetual dread of poison or of trap; [. . .]. Her eyes are wide and vigilant' (*Essays*, iv. 540–2).

the glistening poison drop and the long stiletto: means of murder in the sixteenth and seventeenth centuries; a stiletto is a short dagger, easily concealed.

she heard the guns in the Channel: in part a recollection of the First World War, when bombardments in France were audible from Kent and Sussex, and had been heard by both VSW (Bowlby, 319) and VW, who had compared the sound to 'the beating of gigantic carpets by gigantic women' ('Heard on the Downs: The Genesis of Myth' (1916), in *Essays*, ii. 40–2). However, to speak of guns *in* the channel rather than *over* or *across* it implies a naval battle.

the great monastic house: in *Knole*, VSW does not consider the medieval history of buildings on the site of the house, and though it had been owned by archbishops, there is no evidence there that it had ever been a monastery; 'monastic house' and the later reference to a monk (p. 184) may be an allusion to VW's own modest Sussex home, Monks House.

17 *Whitehall*: a royal palace, the chief London residence of the monarch in the sixteenth century.

her Treasurer and Steward: Thomas Sackville, 1st Baron Buckhurst and 1st Earl of Dorset (*c*.1536–1608), VSW's ancestor, became Lord Treasurer and Lord High Steward to Queen Elizabeth I.

the jewelled order of the Garter: Thomas Sackville was created Knight of the Garter on 24 April 1589, ten years before he became Lord Treasurer.

sent him to Scotland on a sad embassy to the unhappy Queen: in 1587 Thomas Sackville was sent to inform Mary, Queen of Scots (1542–87) that she had been sentenced to death, 'and received from her in recognition of his tact and gentleness in conveying this news the triptych and carved group of the Procession to Calvary now on the altar in the chapel at Knole' (*Knole*, 35). Mary was not in Scotland but at Fotheringay Castle in Northamptonshire. VSW had told VW this anecdote in 1924 (*Diary*, ii. 306).

the Polish wars: Stape suggests the Livonian War (1557–82), which concerned the succession to the Polish throne, though England was not directly involved (*Orlando*, ed. J. H. Stape (1998), 197).

18 *Richmond*: Richmond, in Surrey, now in the outer suburbs of south-west London, was the site of a royal palace from the fifteenth century onwards. Queen Elizabeth died there in 1603. The palace was demolished during the Commonwealth. Leonard and Virginia Woolf lived in Richmond from 1915 to 1924.

she struck violently at the mirror: the image of a mirror shattered by a woman, followed by her decline, suggests 'The Lady of Shallott' (1832) by Alfred, Lord Tennyson.

19 *Girls were roses . . . Plucked they must be before nightfall*: VW alludes to the *carpe diem* (seize the day) theme of early modern love poetry.

Doris, Chloris, Delia, or Diana: the names are typical of classically influenced poetry, particularly love poetry, of the sixteenth and seventeeth centuries. The best known is Delia, from the sonnet sequence of the same name (1591) by Samuel Daniel (1562/3–1619), and Diana features frequently in poems alluding to the classical goddess of hunting. Chloris appears in many of the songs in the third book of *Ayres and Dialogues* (1658) by Henry Lawes ((bap. 1596, d. 1662), while Doris appears in, among other places, 'To A.D. unreasonable distrustfull of her owne beauty', by Thomas Carew (1594/5–1640).

Wapping Old Stairs: stairs leading to the shoreline in Wapping, east London. The area was noted for its taverns.

Azores: islands in the North Atlantic, part of Spain in the sixteenth century. In 1586, Sir Walter Raleigh had led an expedition to the islands, as did the Earl of Cumberland in 1589; both are recounted in Richard Hakluyt's *The Principal Navigations, Voyages, Traffiques, and Discoveries of The English Nation*, vol. vii. In 1597 Robert Devereux, 2nd Earl of Essex (1565–1601), had led a failed attempt to capture the islands for England.

20 *the Indies*: a term used both for the Indian subcontinent and for what is now known as the West Indies.

Earl of Cumberland: the 3rd Earl of Cumberland, George Clifford (1558–1605), courtier and privateer.

alms houses still standing in the Sheen Road: the almshouses on the Sheen Road in Richmond (near Paradise Road, VW's home from 1913 to 1925) were built in 1834 using an endowment left in 1727 by William Hickey.

21 *the Court of King James*: James VI of Scotland and I of England (1566–1625), who became king of England in 1603.

Clorinda, Favilla, Euphrosyne: all three names might have been used in classicizing love poetry of the sixteenth and seventeenth centuries. 'Euphrosyne' had been used as the title of a collection of poems by several of Woolf's male friends (1905), and she had later used it as the name of the ship in *The Voyage Out* (1915).

address in horsemanship: 'address' in the rare sense of ability, skill, or dexterity.

drugget: a heavy cloth made of wool, or of a mixture of wool and silk or wool and linen; a wealthy woman's stockings would be made of silk.

the Irish Desmonds: VSW's *Knole* mentions a portrait of Catherine Fitzgerald, Countess of Desmond (p. 14).

22 *the Great Frost*: the Great Frost of 1608. VW took many of her details
from Thomas Dekker's pamphlet 'The Great Frost' (1608), as reprinted
in Edward Arber's anthology, *An English Garner: Ingatherings from our
History and Literature*, 7 vols. (London: E. Arber, 1877–83), i. 77–99.

23 *the north-west passage and the Spanish Armada*: the search for a northern route between the Atlantic and Pacific was a major preoccupation of
sixteenth- and seventeenth-century explorers. It is discussed briefly in
Richard Hakluyt's *Voyages* (1598–1600); in 1612 a company was formed
with the purpose of finding it. The defeat of the Spanish Armada in July
1588 by English naval forces was treated in many English histories as
a key turning point. For example, in Green: 'The defeat of the Armada,
the deliverance from Catholicism and Spain, marked the critical moment
in our political development. From that hour England's destiny was fixed.
She was to be a Protestant power' (J. R. Green, *History of the English
People*, 4 vols. (London: Macmillan, 1877–80), ii. 454).

the corantoe and lavolta: two forms of dance, both dating from the sixteenth century, the first (usually spelt *coranto*) 'characterized by a running
or gliding step' (*OED*), the second 'A lively dance for two persons, consisting a good deal in high and active bounds' (*OED*).

24 *quadrille or minuet*: two forms of dance, the first a square dance 'typically
performed by four couples' (*OED*), the second 'A stately dance for two in
triple time' (*OED*). The first term appears in English in 1605, the second
not until 1672.

He called her a melon . . . three seconds: the passage recalls and parodies both
VSW's *Challenge* (1924) and VW's *Mrs Dalloway* (1925). In the former,
VSW's hero Julian (modelled on herself) gazes at his love, Eva, who is
based on VSW's lover Violet Trefusis:

His imagination bore him away upon a flight of images that left him startled by their emphasis no less than by their fantasy. A cloak of black velvet,
he thought to himself, as he continued to gaze unseeingly at her; a dusky
voice, a gipsy among voices! the purple ripeness of a plum; the curve of
a Southern cheek; the heart of red wine. (*Challenge* (London: Virago,
2012), 102–3)

VW, on reading *Challenge*, remarked of Eva: 'She is very desirable I agree:
very' (letter to VSW [14 June 1927], *Letters*, iii. 391). In *Mrs Dalloway*, as
Clarissa Dalloway's daughter Elizabeth waits for a bus, 'People were beginning to compare her to poplar trees, early dawn, hyacinths, fawns, running
water, and garden lilies; and it made her life a burden to her' (*Mrs Dalloway*,
ed. David Bradshaw (Oxford: Oxford World's Classics, 2000), 114).

25 *Lord Francis Vere . . . the young Earl of Moray*: Sir Francis Vere (or 'de
Vere') (1560/1–1609), army officer and diplomat, and James Stuart, 3rd
Earl of Moray (1581–1638).

'Je crois . . . l'été dernier' or *'La beauté . . . la sienne'*: the first phrase trans-
lates as 'I think I met a gentleman of your family in Poland last summer';

VSW supplied VW with the French translations, and the English given
here is taken from VSW's letter of 26 April 1928 (*Letters of VSW to VW*,
ed. Louise DeSalvo and Mitchell A. Leaska (London: Hutchinson, 1984),
284). The second phrase had been given to VSW as: 'The ladies of the
English Court ravish me with their beauty. Never have I seen so graceful
a lady as your Queen or so fine a head dress.'

trulls: prostitutes; the term is used by Shakespeare in several plays.

26 *comme une grande perche mal fagotée*: 'like a tall, badly decorated pole'. If
fagotée glances at the English 'faggot', it is more likely as a term of abuse
directed at women (first recorded 1591) than as an abusive term for a male
homosexual, which was originally American (first recorded 1914) and not
widely used in England until later in the twentieth century.

which of those popinjays was George Villiers?: George Villiers, 1st Duke of
Buckingham (1592–1628), was a royal favourite; however, Villiers's association with King James did not begin until 1614, several years after the
Great Frost. 'Popinjays' are literally 'parrots', but the word is used here in
the sense of shallow, vain, or conceited persons (*OED*).

27 *The Tower, the Beefeaters, the Heads on Temple Bar*: 'The Tower' is the
Tower of London, a medieval fortress begun by William I and completed
by Edward I, while 'Beefeaters' is the popular term for its military guards,
the Yeoman Warders. Temple Bar was a gateway marking the western
limit of the City of London, its border with the City of Westminster. The
display of the heads of executed traitors dated from 1684, later than this
scene (*LE*, 909–10).

the Royal Exchange: a building in the City of London enclosing a large
piazza, intended primarily as a meeting place for merchants to conduct
their business, but which also contained small shops. It was opened in
1570 and burned down in the Great Fire of London, 1666. Its replace-
ment also burned down, and the building familiar to VW dates from 1844.

28 *of wood, of sackcloth, and of cinders*: VW asked VSW to translate this phrase
into French, but the translation raised problems, and VSW advised VW to
leave it in English.

the philosopher: the 'philosopher' is not readily identified; though Robert
Burton, author of *The Anatomy of Melancholy* (1621), might be intended,
as an Anglican he was far from believing that the Anabaptist sect was the
true church.

30 *palanquin*: a covered conveyance for one person, carried on poles by four
or six servants.

orgulous: proud; haughty.

31 *sennight*: 'a period of seven (days and) nights' (*OED*); one of several archa-
isms, e.g. Shakespeare, 'A Sennights speede' (*Othello*, II.i.77).

32 *the dome of St Paul's*: an anachronism: the medieval St Paul's Cathedral,
destroyed in 1666 by the Great Fire of London, did not have a dome.

the massy: 'massive' or 'consisting of great blocks of masonry' (*OED*). The word appears in several of Shakespeare's plays.

a knob . . . Temple Bar: in Conrad's *Heart of Darkness*, the narrator Marlow at first believes the heads on poles around Kurtz's encampment to be ornamental, 'round knobs' or 'knob[s] of wood'.

34 *they would stray into the great hall*: derives from a remark in VSW's *Knole*, though with a change of season: 'In summer the great oak doors of this second gate-house are left open, and it has sometimes happened that I have found a stag in the banqueting hall, puzzled but still dignified, strayed in from the park since no barrier checked him' (*Knole*, 4).

cressets: iron containers for fires, 'usually mounted on the top of a pole or building, or suspended from a roof' (*OED*). The phrase has antecedents in Shakespeare ('burning cressets', *Henry IV, Part 1*, III.i.15), and Milton ('blazing cressets', *Paradise Lost*, i. 728).

35 *cony catchers*: a cheat or swindler; the phrase became current following the publication of Robert Greene's *Art of Conny Catching* (1592).

ostlers: stablemen or horse grooms.

dishclout: an archaic spelling of 'dishcloth'.

A black man . . . a woman in white: as becomes clearer on the next page, Orlando is watching a performance of Shakespeare's *Othello*.

36 *Methinks . . . yawn——*: from Shakespeare's *Othello*, V.ii.102–4: Othello's speech shortly after he has murdered Desdemona.

'Jour de ma vie!': 'Day of my life!', the motto of the Sackville family, 'referring to the Battle of Crécy (1346), where one of them fought' (Nicolson in Bowlby, 322).

Drake, Hawkins, and Grenville: Sir Francis Drake (1540–96), pirate, sea captain, and explorer; Sir John Hawkins (1532–95), merchant and naval commander; and Sir Richard Grenville (1542–91), naval commander.

39 *the Irish rebels*: in April 1608, the year of the Great Frost, Sir Cahir O'Doherty [Cathaoir Ó Dochartaigh] (1587–1608), had led a rebellion against the English in the north of Ireland.

43 *Mrs Grimsditch . . . Mr Dupper*: in VSW's *Knole*, 78, Mrs Grimsditch and Mr Dupper, the Chaplain, are listed alongside Mrs Stewkly (see note to p. 15) in the 'Catalogue' as members of the staff who dine at the Parlour Table.

Mrs Field and old Nurse Carpenter: Mrs Field was another who dined at the Parlour Table; 'Nurse Carpenter' is listed among the Nursery staff (*Knole*, 78, 79).

the Judys and the Faiths: in *Knole* the 'Catalogue' lists a Judith Simpton and Faith Husband among the Laundry Maids (*Knole*, 81).

the Blackamoor whom they called Grace Robinson: listed in the 'Catalogue' among the Laundry Maids (*Knole*, 81).

44 *Sir Malise*: the most prominent nobleman by this name was Malise Graham, 3rd Earl of Strathearn and 1st Earl of Menteith (*c*.1406–90).

the Conqueror: King William I of England, also known as William the Conqueror (1027–87). The earliest recorded member of the Sackville family, Herbrand de Sackville, accompanied William to England (*Knole*, 30).

Thomas Browne . . . whose writing . . . took his fancy amazingly: Sir Thomas Browne (1605–82) was a writer and doctor. His *Urn-Burial* (full title, *Hydriotaphia, Urn-Burial, or, A Discourse of the Sepulchral Urns Lately Found in Norfolk*, 1658) may in particular be intended. VSW records that during the English Civil War, Edward Sackville recommended Browne's *Religio Medici* (1642) to his friend Sir Kenelm Digby (*Knole*, 105).

45 *foully murdered*: the phrase echoes 'murder most foul' (Shakespeare, *Hamlet*, I.v.26).

46 *Hall, the falconer, . . . Giles, the groom*: John Hall is listed as a falconer in the 'Catalogue', and Thomas Giles as Groom of the Stables (*Knole*, 80).

47 *a great inlaid cabinet*: according to Nigel Nicolson, VSW owned a cabinet like that described, and 'kept all her most intimate letters in it' (Bowlby, 322).

'The Death of Ajax' . . . 'The Return of Odysseus': a further allusion to VSW's unpublished juvenilia. As is appropriate for his era, Orlando's subjects derive from classical antiquity.

priest's holes: hiding places for Catholic priests escaping Protestant persecution.

John Ball of the Feathers and Coronet opposite St Paul's Cross, Cheapside: not an actual printer, but the form of the name is typical of seventeenth-century printers, e.g. Samuel Lee, at the Feathers in Lombard Street (active *c*.1680).

'Xenophila a Tragedy': see note on 'The Death of Ajax', p. 47.

rainbow and granite: VW had used a very similar phrase in 'The New Biography' (1927), a review of *Some People* by Harold Nicolson, VSW's husband. Woolf argued that the Victorian style of biography was obsolete. She asked her reader to consider how Victorian biographers like Lord Morley or Sidney Lee would have treated 'a few years that one has actually lived': 'how strangely all that has been most real in them would have slipped through their fingers. Nor can we name the biographer whose art is subtle and bold enough to present that queer amalgamation of dream and reality, that perpetual marriage of granite and rainbow' (*Essays*, iv. 478).

48 *even now (the first of November 1927)*: in the manuscript, this reads 'Tuesday 1st Nov. 1927', an actual date, which suggests that the first of November was the 'now' of composition. VW recorded on 20 November 1927 that she was about to begin on Chapter III.

Queen Alexandra: Queen Alexandra (1844–1925), consort of King Edward VII.

48 *as one lantern slide is half seen through the next*: the phrase alludes to 'dis-
    solving views', a very popular form of visual entertainment in Victorian
    Britain, in which one slide projection was gradually replaced by another
    (see Kate Flint, *The Victorians and the Visual Imagination* (Cambridge:
    Cambridge University Press, 2000), 147).

    old Queen Bess: a familiar name for Elizabeth I (1533–1603), queen of Eng-
    land and Ireland from 1558 to her death.

49 *thick boots such as citizens wear in Cheapside*: Cheapside is a street in the
    City of London which from medieval times to the Victorian era was
    a thriving marketplace. The 'thick boots' indicate that the marketplace was
    frequented by those of lower social orders.

    shawms: wind instruments of medieval origin, related to the oboe.

    Paynim: pagan; non-Christian.

    Sir Gawain: the name, not found in the Sackville family, is that of one of
    the legendary King Arthur's knights of the Round Table, best known from
    the anonymous fourteenth-century poem *Sir Gawain and Green Knight*.

50 *the vales of Tempe*: in Latin and later in English poetry, usually in the form
    'the vale [singular] of Tempe' or 'Tempe's vale', an ideal rural place; the
    name derives from an actual valley in Thessaly, Greece.

    Giles Isham, of Norfolk: VW knew a real Gyles Isham (1903–76), of North-
    amptonshire, son of her cousin, Millicent Vaughan, and her husband, Sir
    Vere Isham.

51 *Lady Winchilsea's fan*: a slightly anachronistic reference to the poet Anne
    Finch (née Kingsmill), Countess of Winchilsea (1661–1720). The 'fan'
    suggests the title of Oscar Wilde's play, *Lady Windermere's Fan* (1892).

    Mr Nicholas Greene: a fictitious figure, incorporating elements of several of
    Woolf's contemporaries. She very probably took the surname from Robert
    Greene (*c.*1558–92), writer and playwright. For his debts to Woolf's near-
    contemporaries Logan Pearsall Smith (1865–1946) and Edmund Gosse
    (1849–1928), see Introduction (pp. xx–xxiv) and notes to pp. 54 and 162.
    VSW was the first to make the identification of Greene with Gosse, in
    a letter to Harold Nicolson: see Victoria Glendinning, *Vita: The Life of
    Vita Sackville-West* (London: Weidenfeld and Nicolson, 1983), 202.

    at Flodden and at Agincourt: Flodden was a battle fought in north-east
    England in 1513 between forces led by James IV of Scotland and Eng-
    lish forces led by Lord Surrey. Agincourt was an earlier battle (25 Octo-
    ber 1415) fought in northern France between French forces and English
    forces led by Henry V.

52 *Malmsey*: a strong sweet wine from southern Europe; the name derives
    from Monemvasia (Napoli di Malvasia) in the Peloponnese, Greece.

53 *Marlowe, Ben Jonson, Browne, Donne*: Christopher Marlowe (bap. 1564,
    d. 1593), playwright and poet; Ben Jonson (1572–1637), poet and

playwright; for Thomas Browne, see note to p. 44; John Donne (1572–1631), poet and Church of England clergyman.

54 *La Gloire*: the French term may roughly be translated as 'glory'. The first of several references to Logan Pearsall Smith's pamphlet *The Prospects of Literature* in which he refers to posthumous fame as 'la gloire' (Hogarth Press, 1927); see Introduction, pp. xx–xxiv. Edmund Gosse had also written about 'la glore', in 'Vauvenargues and the Sentiment of "La Gloire"', *Fortnightly Review*, 103 (1918), 511–23 (at 517), and in *Some Diversions of a Man of Letters* (London: Heinemann, 1919), 279. In the latter volume, which Woolf reviewed (*Essays*, iii. 105–8), Gosse uses the term in the sense of military glory.

all young writers . . . poured out any trash that would sell: a further allusion to Logan Pearsall Smith's opinions; see Introduction, xx–xxiv. Smith had referred to 'editors' and 'publishers'; VW modifies his terminology to 'booksellers', more appropriate to the conditions of book production and distribution in Shakespeare's England.

the Cock Tavern in Fleet Street: the Cock Tavern on Fleet Street was built in 1887; it replaced an older building opposite, the sixteenth-century Cock Alehouse.

trembling on the verge of a great age in English literature: a self-reference, and another reference to Logan Pearsall Smith's *The Prospects of Literature*. VW had concluded 'Character in Fiction' (July 1924) by making 'one final and surpassingly rash prediction—we are trembling on the verge of one of the great ages of English literature' (*Essays*, iii. 436). Smith began his pamphlet by quoting this prediction, and went on to disagree. (See Introduction, xx–xxiv).

Cicero: Marcus Tullius Cicero (106–43 BC), Roman orator and statesman.

55 *printer's devils*: errand boys from printers' offices.

a teg: 'A sheep in its second year, or from the time it is weaned till its first shearing; a yearling sheep' (*OED*). VSW uses the term in her poem *The Land* (1927), where the shepherd 'shall turn little rams to little tegs' (p. 17).

ignorant of the rotation of the crops: VSW's *The Land* includes a passage on the rotation of crops.

57 *Fetter Lane*: a street in the City of London running between Fleet Street and Holborn.

Tom Fletcher: a fictitious figure, though his name recalls the playwright John Fletcher (1579–1625), who collaborated with Shakespeare on *The Two Noble Kinsmen* and other works, and the later minor poet Thomas Fletcher (1666–1713).

midden: dunghill or manure heap.

Harwich: a port in Essex, England, in VW's time used for sailings to the Netherlands, Germany, Denmark, and Sweden.

59 '*Time passed*': the phrase and some of the description preceding it is a self-mocking reference to the 'Times Passes' section of VW's *To the Lighthouse* (1927), in which the passage of time is registered in its effects on the Ramsays' neglected holiday home, and in which two old women eventually clean and prepare the house for the family's return.

diuturnity: 'Long duration or continuance; lastingness' (*OED*).

60 *deserts of vast eternity*: an allusion to 'To His Coy Mistress' by Andrew Marvell (1621–78).

> But at my back I always hear
> Time's wingèd chariot hurrying near;
> And yonder all before us lie
> Deserts of vast eternity.

62 *scrolloping*: VW's own coinage, which suggests 'scroll' and 'lollop'. VW first used it in 1923, when she compared the Hon. Vera Benedicta Birch to VSW: 'Like Vita she detests the scrolloping honours of the great, calls her family dull & stupid' (*Diary*, ii. 232).

64 *the odious Parliament days were over*: the monarchy was restored in 1660. Edward Sackville, 4th Earl of Dorset (1590–1652), was a Royalist, and early in the English Civil War, in 1642, Knole had been raided by Parliamentarian troops (*Knole*, 102).

three hundred and sixty-five bedrooms: Knole famously has as many rooms as there are days in the year, and fifty-two staircases, one for each week; VSW remarked that 'I cannot truthfully pretend I have ever verified these counts, and it may be that their accuracy is accepted solely on the strength of the legend' (*Knole*, 4).

65 '*To fifty pairs . . . for a dozen lights apiece. . . .* ': Knole frequently quotes from inventories and ledgers, and parts of Woolf's description are adapted from a 'Note of household stuff sent by SYMONDES to KNOLE the 28th of July 1624'. VSW's text includes 'a pair of Spanish blankets, 5 curtains of crimson and white taffeta, the valance to it of white satin embroidered with crimson and white silk'; 'a yellow satin chair and 3 stools, suitable with their buckram covers to them' (the 'all' in Woolf's text may come from the place name Croxall, which appears on the next line); '2 walnut tree tables'; 'A box containing 3 dozen of Venice glasses'; '6 pairs of mats to mat chambers with gt 30 yards apiece'; '9 cups of crimson damask laid with silver parchment lace'; 'In a wicker trunk, 2 brass branches for a dozen lights apiece' (*Knole*, 95–6).

to level a million molehills: Knole includes a list of expenses for Knole Park in 1628, which includes 'Paid a labourer for spreading the mole hills in the meads and for killing moles' (*Knole*, 91).

nails at 5½d. a gill . . . to repair the fence: the Knole accounts from 1628 also include the cost of 400 nails for the pales (*Knole*, 91). Nails were traditionally sold by volume; a gill is one quarter of a pint.

sawn across and laid along the gallery for flooring: the floor of the Cartoon Gallery at Knole is 'formed of black oak planks irregularly laid, the charm of which is that they are not planks at all, but solid tree-trunks, split in half, with the rounded half downwards' (*Knole*, 10).

66 *Daphne flying*: a scene from classical mythology: the nymph Daphne fled from the advances of the god Apollo, and was transformed into a laurel. There is no such arras (tapestry) at Knole, though the collection of works assembled by the 3rd Duke includes a late seventeenth-century drawing of the subject.

the silver shone . . . and dolphins swam upon the walls: the passage echoes several phrases from T. S. Eliot's *The Waste Land* (1922), an edition of which the Hogarth Press had published in 1923: in it, a chair 'Glowed on the marble'; there is no lacquer, but there is a 'laquearia', a panelled ceiling; and, by the light of a flame, 'a carvèd dolphin swam'.

67 *his private room alone*: Orlando's withdrawal echoes those of Clarissa Dalloway in *Mrs Dalloway* and Mrs Ramsay in *To the Lighthouse*.

68 *Archduchess Harriet Griselda of Finster-Aarhorn and Scand-op-Boom in the Roumanian Territory*: 'Harriet' may carry a family echo: Harriet Stephen (née Thackeray, 1840–75) was the first wife of VW's father Leslie Stephen; however, the name was relatively common in the nineteenth century. Griselda was far less common, and in literary terms echoes the patient Griselda of Chaucer's 'The Clerk's Tale' in *The Canterbury Tales*. The first part of the Archduchess's extravagant title is derived from a mountain in Switzerland, the Finsteraarhorn, the highest in the Bernese Alps, which is mentioned several times by Leslie Stephen in his mountaineering book *The Playground of Europe* (1871). The second part echoes 'Bergen-op-Zoom', in Holland, mentioned in VSW's *Knole*, 84, as the site of a duel. 'Roumania' was the usual spelling in 1928 for the country now known as Romania.

a suit of armour . . . the work of Jacobi or of Topp: *Knole* (p. 99) refers to a suit of armour 'made in 1575 by Jacob Topp or Jacobi for Sir Thomas Sackville', 'richly decorated by bands and bordering, deeply etched and partly gilt with a scroll design'. It is part of the Wallace Collection, London.

71 *King Charles*: Charles II (1630–85), who reigned after the Restoration, from 1660 until his death.

Constantinople: modern Istanbul.

Nell Gwyn: Eleanor Gwyn (1651?–1687), known as Nell Gwyn, actress and, in the mid-1660s, mistress to Charles Sackville (1643-1706); later, from around 1669, mistress to Charles II. There is a portrait of her at Knole (*Knole*, 122–6).

72 *his Bath and his Dukedom*: Edward Sackville was made a Knight of the Bath in 1616. The title of Duke came to the family with Lionel Cranfield Sackville (1688–1765), created 1st Duke of Dorset in 1720.

Santa Sofia: a domed building in Constantinople (later Istanbul) which had begun its life as a Greek Orthodox church, but which became a mosque in 1453. A few years after the publication of *Orlando* it became a museum.

Galata Bridge: the bridge crossing the channel of the Bosphorus that runs through the centre of Constantinople.

the heights of Pera: a district on Constantinople, on the European side of the city.

73 *Tunbridge Wells*: town in Kent, about 9 miles from Knole.

Circassian: 'A native or inhabitant of Circassia, a region in the northern Caucasus' (*OED*).

Janissaries: the military guard of the Turkish sultan.

74 *chanting something*: 'chanting' was not uncommon as a style of poetry recitation in the early twentieth century. W. B. Yeats was particularly well known for chanting his poetry as he wrote it and when he recited it. VW recorded that when T. S. Eliot read *The Waste Land* in 1922 'He sang it & chanted it rhythmed it' (*Diary*, ii. 178).

77 *Sir Adrian Scrope*: the name suggests that of the royalist Sir Adrian Scroope (sometimes spelled 'Scrope') (1614/15–67), who was made Knight of the Bath at the coronation of Charles II.

John Fenner Brigge: fictitious, though the naval officer's name has a teasing echo of Fenner Brockway (1888–1988), politician and pacifist campaigner.

78 *Miss Penelope Hartopp*: the surname derives from that of a British diplomat in Cairo, Charles Hartopp (1893–1930), mentioned by VSW to VW in 1926 (*Letters of VSW to VW*, 129).

negus: a drink, named after Colonel Francis Negus, made from wine (usually port or sherry) and hot water, sweetened with sugar and sometimes flavoured.

the Pantiles: a colonaded street in Tunbridge Wells.

79 *blue-jackets*: sailors.

80 *Rosina Pepita*: VSW's mother, Victoria Josefa Dolores Catalina Sackville-West (1862–1936), was the illegitimate daughter of Sir Lionel Sackville Sackville-West, 2nd Baron Sackville (1827–1908), and a Spanish dancer Josefa de la Oliva known as Pepita. VSW later wrote about her grandmother in *Pepita* (1937).

bastinado: an archaic term for a beating with a stick, especially on the soles of the feet.

82 *the still unravished heights*: an echo of the opening line of John Keats's 'Ode on a Grecian Urn' (1819), 'Thou still unravished bride of quietness'.

84 *But let other pens treat of sex and sexuality*: an echo of Jane Austen, *Mansfield Park* (1814), chapter 48: 'Let other pens dwell on guilt and misery'.

Seleuchi hound: the breed of dog more usually known as the Saluki, and referred to by VSW as a 'sloughi'. VSW wrote to VW from Baghdad (28 February 1926) that she had bought one while there, 'a marvel of elegance,—long tapering paws, and a neck no thicker than your wrist' (*Letters of VSW to VW*, 120). There is also an account in VSW's *Passenger to Teheran* (London: Hogarth Press, 1926), 59–60.

pearls of the finest orient: a pearl of the orient is one from the Indian seas, and is considered finer than a European pearl. VSW uses the phrase in *Passenger to Teheran*. Called upon to advise on the ceremonial aspects of the coronation of Reza Khan, VSW was shown the treasury of imperial Iran: 'The linen bags vomited emeralds and pearls; the green baize vanished, the table became a sea of precious stones. [. . .] Then from the inner room came the file of servants again, carrying uniforms sewn with diamonds; a cap with a tall aigrette, secured by a diamond larger than the Koh-i-Nur; two crowns like great hieratic tiaras, barbaric diadems, composed of pearls of the finest orient' (*Passenger to Teheran*, 145). She had written to VW about this moment in April 1926 (*Letters of VSW to VW*, 132–3).

Broussa: a city in Turkey, now known as Bursa. VW had been there in 1911 to help her sister return to England following a miscarriage and a breakdown.

85 *old Rustum's pipe*: the name probably derives from Matthew Arnold's poem 'Sohrab and Rustum' (1853).

the Thessalian hills: Thessaly, a region of Greece, lies west of Turkey across the Aegean Sea.

The gipsies have no word for 'beautiful': accounts of foreign languages that lack terms found in English are common in nineteenth-century linguistics. For the lack of terms for 'beauty' specifically, see S. T. Coleridge in the second of his 'Essays on the Principles of Genial Criticism' (1814), writing of Dahoma, Africa: 'a very intelligent traveller, describing the low state of the human mind in this very country, gives as an instance, that in their whole language they have no word for Beauty or the beautiful; but say either it is very nice, or it is good' (Coleridge, *Shorter Works and Fragments*, in *Collected Works*, 16 vols., ed. Kathleen Coburn (London: Routledge, 1969–2002), xi. 364. The essay had been reprinted in Joseph Cottle's *Early Recollections, Chiefly Relating to the Late Samuel Taylor Coleridge* (1837), Leslie Stephen's copy of which was among VW's books.

86 *the Sea of Marmara, the plains of Greece . . . the Acropolis*: the Sea of Marmara is an inland sea that divides the European from the Asian parts of Turkey. The Acropolis in Athens is not visible from this part of Turkey.

88 *four or five hundred years only*: the figure is close to VW's estimate of the Sackville family's age; in 1923 she recorded that 'Snob as I am, I trace her passions 500 years back' (*Diary*, ii. 235–6); and she wrote to VSW that 'Your excellence as a subject arises largely from your noble birth. (But whats 400 years of nobility, all the same?)' (*Letters*, iii. 429).

88 *Howards and Plantagenets*: the *Dictionary of National Biography* traces the Howard family back to John Howard, 1st Duke of Norfolk (1430?–1485). The Plantagenet dynasty of English kings can be traced back to Henry II (1133–89), son of Geoffrey Plantagenet, Count of Anjou, though the name was not regularly used by kings until the fifteenth century.

89 *Whigs and Tories, Liberal party and Labour party*: from 1689 to the mid-nineteenth century, the Whig and the Tory parties were the two main parliamentary political groupings. The term 'Whig' became obsolete around the mid-nineteenth century due to the rise of the Liberal party. The Labour party evolved from the Labour Representation Committee of 1900; the party first formed a government in 1924.

Mount Athos: the female Orlando's presence on Mount Athos is transgressive. The Greek peninsula on which the mountain stands is home to twenty Greek Orthodox monasteries, and women are not permitted to enter it. It had been in the news in 1927 as the Greek government sought to normalize its relation to the Greek state while preserving its distinctive status.

90 *burnous*: 'A mantle or cloak with a hood, an upper garment extensively worn by Arabs and Moors' (*OED*).

91 *paduasoy*: 'A strong, rich, silk fabric, usually slightly corded or embossed' (*OED*).

92 *Which is the greater ecstasy? The man's or the woman's?*: in Greek mythology, the gods Jupiter and Juno had posed these questions to Tiresias, who, born male, had changed sex for seven years. The story is recounted in Latin in Ovid's *Metamorphoses*, iii.

shiver: given that 'the tiniest little slice' has previously been referred to, it is possible that this is an error for 'sliver'; but it may refer to a shiver of pleasure.

plesaunce: Bowlby suggests the intended sense is that of 'a pleasure ground' or secluded part of a garden; but in another unrelated sense it refers to a fine gauzelike fabric.

Marie Rose: an echo of the name of the Tudor warship, the *Mary Rose*, which sank in 1545; the name was also used for later warships, including one launched in 1556 which fought the Spanish Armada.

93 *staying*: the act of putting stays into a laced underbodice.

D'you take sugar?: in her memoir 'Sketch of the Past', VW wrote that when she read her early literary reviews, she felt they were too suave, polite, and evasive, and laid the blame on her late Victorian 'tea-table training': rereading them, 'I see myself, not reviewing a book, but handing plates of buns to shy young men and asking them: do they take cream and sugar?' (*Moments of Being*, ed. Jeanne Schulkind (London: Pimlico, 2002), 152).

to dress up like a Guy Fawkes: on 5 November effigies of the gunpowder plotter Guy Fawkes (1570–1606) were traditionally dressed in 'grotesquely ragged and ill-assorted garments' (*OED*); here, however, VW's emphasis is on the eye-catching elaborateness of costume rather than its raggedness or ill-assortedness.

96 *mantilla*: a light veil, often of black lace, worn by women over the head and covering the shoulders.

what the poet says about truth and beauty: John Keats in the concluding lines of 'Ode on a Grecian Urn': 'Beauty is truth, truth beauty,—that is all | Ye know on earth, and all ye need to know.'

97 *samphire gatherers, hanging half-way down the cliff*: people gathering *crith-mum maritimum*, which grows on rocks by the sea, for culinary purposes. The scene and the phrasing echoes Shakespeare's *King Lear* in which Edgar deceives the blinded Gloucester into thinking that he stands on the edge of a cliff, vividly describing it:

> The crows and choughs that wing the midway air
> Show scarce so gross as beetles. Half way down
> Hangs one that gathers sampire, dreadful trade!

(*King Lear*, IV.vi.13–15)

'So good-bye and adieu to you, Ladies of Spain': a modified form of a line from a sea shanty:

> Farewell, and adieu to you grand Spanish ladies,
> Farewell, and adieu to you ladies of Spain,
> For we've received orders to sail for Old England,
> But we hope in short time for to see you again.

A variant version of the first two lines appears in Herman Melville's *Moby Dick*, chapter 40, two copies of which VW owned.

98 *St Paul's*: between 1675 and 1711 St Paul's Cathedral had been completely rebuilt to the designs of Christopher Wren (1632–1723), replacing the building destroyed by the Great Fire in 1666.

Greenwich Hospital, Queen Mary . . . his late majesty, William the Third: two of the four blocks of the Greenwich Hospital, which in 1873 became the Royal Naval College, were constructed at the instigation of Queen Mary II (1662–94) and her husband, King William III (1650–1702).

the Monument . . . a plague and a fire: the Monument, erected 1671–7, stands near the place where the Great Fire of London had begun in 1666. The 'shock of golden hair' is a sculpture in gilt bronze of flames leaping from an urn. The plague referred to was the Great Plague of 1664–5, which claimed the lives of at least 68,576 Londoners at a time when its population stood at about 400,000 (*LE*, 344–6, at 656).

99 *London Bridge*: in the eighteeenth century the bridge known by this name stood slightly downstream from the present structure; there had been a bridge there since 1209, and until 1758–62 it had many houses on it. The bridge that VW would have known, running from King William Street in

the City of London to Southwark on the south side of the Thames, was
built in 1823–31; it was itself replaced in 1967–72.

99 *the Cocoa Tree*: a coffee house in Pall Mall patronized in the eighteenth
century by Tory politicians and writers.

Mr Addison . . . Mr Dryden . . . Mr Pope: Joseph Addison (1672–1719),
writer and politician, founder of the periodicals *The Tatler* (1709–11) and
The Spectator (1711–12); John Dryden (1631–1700), poet, playwright, and
critic; Alexander Pope (1688–1744), poet. Pope suffered from a deformity
of the spine, hence the Captain's description of one man as 'humped'.

Sad dogs . . . Papists: the Captain's derogatory words are meant for Dryden
(who had converted to Catholicism in 1685) and Pope (who was born
and died a Catholic); Addison, who might seem to be included, was an
Anglican.

men of parts: men who are 'talented or accomplished in many respects'
(*OED*).

The Captain must have been mistaken . . . and so we let it stand: the Captain's
mistake is a double one: Pope had not quite reached his twelfth birthday on the date of Dryden's death, and would not have been conversing
in a coffee house with him; moreover, the Whig Addison would not have
frequented the Tory coffee shop the Cocoa Tree, preferring instead Button's Coffee House; Dryden and Pope were more closely associated with
Will's Coffee House. The Captain sees the three writers through the lens
of literary-historical categories.

100 *Blackfriars*: an area in the City of London, which from 1577 to 1655 had
been home to an important playhouse. VSW's mother lived in Dorset
House in this area.

Bow Street runners: an unofficial police force founded in the mid-
seventeenth century by magistrates in Bow Street, central London.

All her estates were put in Chancery: her property was controlled by the
Court of Chancery until the legal dispute was resolved.

Canute: VSW had two elk-hounds, Cnut and Freya; the first name is the
Anglo-Saxon rendering of 'Canute'.

101 *Lord Keeper . . . Lord Chamberlain*: the Lord Keeper of the Great Seal
performed the duties of the Lord Chancellor of England (and from 1707,
of Great Britain), but without the Chancellor's dignities and emoluments.
None of VSW's ancestors served in the role, but Knole has a portrait of
Thomas Egerton, 1st Viscount Brackley (1540–1617), Lord Keeper from
1596 to 1603. The post of Lord Chamberlain was held by two of VSW's
ancestors: Edward Sackville, 4th Earl of Dorset (1590–1652), from 1644
to 1649; and Charles Sackville, 6th Earl of Dorset and 1st Earl of Mid-
dlesex (1643–1706), from 1689 to 1697. Knole has portraits of both.

the arras . . . huntsmen . . . Daphne: see note to p. 66.

102 *Mary Queen of Scots on the scaffold*: in VW's *Night and Day* (1919), Mrs Hilbery claims to own 'the very chair that Mary Queen of Scots sat in when she heard of Darnley's murder' (chapter 1).

103 *Thoughts are divine, etc.*: the phrase alluded to comes in various forms, placing divine thoughts (or 'truths') in antithesis to words, which are human. VW is most likely to have known the phrase from a note by Byron to 'The Vision of Judgement': 'The words are human; but the truths they express, and the doctrines they teach, are divine' (*The Works of Lord Byron*, with notes by Thomas Moore et al. (London: J. Murray, 1842), 525).

105 *She hastily hid her manuscript*: in this act, Orlando echoes (or anticipates) Jane Austen, described in a memoir as hiding her work when anyone was near (Austen-Leigh, *A Memoir of Jane Austen* (6th edn., London: R. Bentley, 1886), 96); VW had Katharine Hilbery, the heroine of *Night and Day* (1919), do the same, although Katharine's vice is mathematics.

106 *the gape*: more usually 'the gapes', a disease of poultry of which one symptom is a gaping mouth.

107 *Fly Loo*: a game that Leslie Stephen had played in France: 'every one puts down a piece of sugar and a 10 centime piece before him, and the one on whose sugar the first fly settles, gets the money' (F. W. Maitland, *Life and Letters of Leslie Stephen* (London: Duckworth & Co., 1906), 220). It was also played at Knole (Bowlby, 330).

   expense of spirit: a glance at Shakespeare's sonnet 129, which begins 'Th'expence of spirit in a waste of shame | Is lust in action.'

108 *£40,885:6:8*: i.e. £40,885, 6 shillings, and 8 pence. Until decimalization in 1971, there were twelve pence in every shilling, and twenty shillings to the pound. Six shillings and eight pence is one-third of a pound.

109 *the proper way of dipping sheep*: an allusion to VSW's *The Land*, 58–9, which includes a scene of sheep dipping.

   a siren in a cave: in Homer's *Odyssey*, the Sirens attempt to lure Odysseus and his crew onto the rocks. There is, however, no mention of their being in a cave.

   so dark, so bright, so hard, so soft, was she: an allusion to the fourth poem of Ben Jonson's 'A Celebration of Charis' (also known as 'The Triumph') (written *c*.1616) which ends 'O so white, O so soft, O so sweet is she!'

112 *the Mall*: a broad road in central London, leading from Trafalgar Square at its eastern end to Buckingham Palace at its western end.

   the celebrated lawsuit: in 1913 VSW's mother had been involved in a court case which attracted considerable attention. She had been left a considerable sum of money by Sir John Murray Scott, and his family had disputed the will. VSW gave evidence at the trial, and she gives a brief account of it in Nicolson, *Portrait*, 37–8, as does Nigel Nicolson in the same work on pp. 67–71.

113 *Lady Suffolk . . . Lady Tavistock*: the four names all derive from ennobled
families, but it is not clear that VW had specific women in mind. The like-
liest to have a real counterpart is Henrietta Howard, Countess of Suffolk
(*c*.1688–1767), who counted Alexander Pope and Jonathan Swift among
her circle.

routs: fashionable gatherings or evening parties.

Southwark: a district on the south bank of the Thames, opposite Blackfriars on the north side. If Orlando is in Blackfriars and the sun is 'blazing
over Southwark chimneys', it is late in the morning.

114 *the reign of Queen Anne*: Anne (1665–1714) reigned from 1702 to her death.

that black humour which ran in the veins of all her race: i.e., melancholy,
one of the four 'humours' of medieval physiology. Several times in *Knole*
(pp. 71, 176, 194), VSW notes the melancholic tendency of her ancestors.

Pippin: VSW owned a spaniel called Pippin in the 1920s.

Arlington House: an anachronism. In the seventeenth century Arlington
House stood on the present-day site of Buckingham Palace. It was completely rebuilt in 1702–5 for John Sheffield, 1st Duke of Buckingham,
after which it took the name Buckingham House.

117 *Old Madame du Deffand*: Marie de Vichy, Marquise du Deffand (1697–
1780), a French literary hostess.

The hostess is our modern Sibyl: a reference to the society hostess Sibyl Colefax (1874–1950), whose name appears frequently in the correspondence
between VW and VSW in 1927–8. VW was also familiar with the essay 'A
Discourse on Modern Sibyls' (1913) by her aunt, Anne Thackeray Ritchie
(1837–1919), which concerned itself with early Victorian female novelists,
and may also have had in mind Lytton Strachey's reference to Madame
du Deffand as 'an ancient Sibyl' (Strachey, *Books and Characters: French
and English* (London: Chatto & Windus, 1922), 90).

her famous 'mot de Saint Denis': Lytton Strachey had recorded the saying
and its context in his *Books and Characters: French and English*: Madame
de Deffand's 'famous "mot de Saint Denis," so dear to the heart of Voltaire, deserves to be once more recorded. A garrulous and credulous Cardinal was describing the martyrdom of Saint Denis the Areopagite: when
his head was cut off, he took it up and carried it in his hands. That, said
the Cardinal, was well known; what was not well known was the extraordinary fact that he walked with his head under his arm all the way from
Montmartre to the Church of Saint Denis—a distance of six miles. "Ah,
Monseigneur!" said Madame du Deffand, "dans une telle situation, il n'y
a que le premier pas qui coûte" ["in such a situation, it is only the first step
that is difficult"]' (p. 91).

118 *Link-boys*: boys employed to carry a flaming torch (a 'link') to light passengers along the streets.

South Audley Street: a street in Mayfair, in the west of central London, running from Curzon Street at its southern end to Grosvenor Square at its northern end.

some squat reptile set with a burning topaz in its forehead: an allusion to the 'toadstone', a precious stone with magical powers, supposedly secreted by toads.

119 *rash to stand on one foot on the top of St Paul's*: on the eve of Queen Mary's coronation in 1553, a man known as Peter the Dutchman had performed acrobatic feats on the spire of the old St Paul's. There is a version of the story in Froude's *History of England from the Fall of Wolsey to the Defeat of the Spanish Armada* (1856–70), which VW had read in July and August 1897.

It is marl . . . By the truth we are undone. Life is a dream. 'Tis waking that kills us: a medley of allusions: Satan walks 'over the burning Marle' in John Milton's *Paradise Lost*, i. 296; 'The truth shall make you free' (John 8:32); the title of Pedro Calderón de la Barca's play *La vida es sueño* (1635), or a reference to 'the dream of life' in Shelley's *Adonais*; 'We term sleep a death, and yet it is waking that kills us, and destroys those spirits that are the house of life' (Sir Thomas Browne, *Religio Medici* (1642)).

Park Lane . . . Tottenham Court Road: Park Lane is a major thoroughfare in central London, at the eastern edge of Hyde Park and the western side of the Mayfair district; Tottenham Court Road, also in central London, runs from the junction of Oxford Street and New Oxford Street at its southern end to the Euston Road at its northern end.

120 *Berkeley Square*: a square in Mayfair.

121 *Piccadilly Circus . . . degraded creatures*: in the late nineteenth and early twentieth centuries, Piccadilly Circus, a junction in central London, south of Soho, was well known for prostitution.

now . . . the late Lord Tennyson: the 'now' is the time of narration; Alfred, Lord Tennyson (1809–92) was Poet Laureate from 1850 to his death.

122 *Rape of the Lock . . . Spectator . . . Gulliver's Travels*: *The Rape of the Lock* (1712, revised and expanded 1714) is a mock-epic poem by Alexander Pope; *The Spectator* (1711–12) was a periodical founded by Joseph Addison; *Gulliver's Travels* (formally *Travels into Several Remote Nations of the World*, 1726) is a satirical novel by Jonathan Swift (1667–1745).

Whether the Nymph . . . at a Ball: from Pope's *The Rape of the Lock*, ii. 105–9.

congee: a bow made on departure.

passage from the Spectator: the passage by Joseph Addison had in fact first appeared in *The Tatler*; it was reprinted in Logan Pearsall Smith's *A Treasury of English Prose* (London: Constable, 1919), 111, immediately below one by Addison from *The Spectator*.

123 *marry a Countess*: in 1716, Joseph Addison married Charlotte Rich, née Myddleton, Countess of Warwick (bap. 1680, d. 1731).

'*I enjoyed perfect Health . . . splenetick tedious Talkers. . . .*': from Jonathan Swift's *Gulliver's Travels* (1726).

and will die . . . in a madhouse: from 1742 until his death in 1745 Swift suffered serious mental incapacity.

in the Round Parlour, which she had hung with their pictures: based on the Poets' Parlour at Knole, the portraits in which included one of Pope (*Knole*, 151).

124 *Lord Chesterfield whispered it to his son*: Philip Dormer Stanhope, 4th Earl of Chesterfield (1694–1773), had written a series of letters of advice to his illegitimate son Philip (b. 1732), published in 1774. VW was reading them in December 1927 (*Diary*, iii. 166) for an essay ('An English Aristocrat') published 8 March 1928, and later reprinted as 'Lord Chesterfield's Letters to his Son' (*Essays*, v. 410–17).

'*Women are . . . flatters them*': from Lord Chesterfield's letter of 5 September 1748.

125 '*Characters of Women*': VW alludes to Pope's 'Epistle II: To a Lady' (1735), the opening couplet of which is 'Nothing so true as what you once let fall, | "Most Women have no Characters at all"'.

she felt as if the little man had struck her: Bowlby (p. 333) suggests this alludes to an incident in April 1928 in which Clive Bell had 'smacked' VW 'in public' (*Diary*, iii. 179, and VW's letter to Bell, *Letters*, iii. 486–7).

the clothes she had worn as a young man of fashion: the female Orlando's cross-dressing is reminiscent of VSW's adventures dressed as 'Julian'.

126 *Leicester Square*: in the mid-eighteenth century, Leicester Square in central London was a residential square with formal gardens at its centre, dominated by Leicester House on its north side; many of the houses were occupied by aristocratic families. By 1928 it had ceased to be residential, and was dominated by entertainments, particularly theatres (*LE*, 479–80).

Gerrard Street: a street in Soho, central London, known in the 1920s for its nightclubs (*LE*, 323–4).

127 *the plain Dunstable of the matter*: the plain truth of the matter; the phrase derives from the Dunstable Road, parts of which follow the straight line of an old Roman Road. The *OED* cites an almost identical phrase from Samuel Richardson's novel *Clarissa* (1747), 'That's the plain Dunstable of the matter, Miss!'

the perruque maker of that name in Jermyn Street: in the late 1920s Jermyn Street was a thriving retail street, home to tailors, tobacconists, turf accountants, and jewellers; there were no wig-makers, nor anyone called Pope, but there was a hair specialist, Madame Iona Feriford, at no. 67.

Several were the natural daughters of earls: VSW's mother Victoria Sackville-West (1862–1936) was the illegitimate daughter of Sir Lionel Sackville Sackville-West, 2nd Baron Sackville (1827–1908).

128 *Mr S. W.*: 'Edward Sackville-West, Vita's cousin, made a great fuss about this, thinking it referred to him. VW assured him, mendaciously, that she meant Sydney Waterlow' (Nigel Nicolson, quoted in Bowlby, 333).

Drury Lane: a street in central London running from the Strand to Holborn; until a slum clearance programme at the start of the twentieth century, the area was notorious for poor housing and criminality.

129 *the lady's husband followed them*: in early 1920, VSW and her lover Violet Trefusis eloped together, not to the Netherlands, but to France. Their husbands, Harold Nicolson and Denys Trefusis, flew to Amiens, and VSW was persuaded to return to England. VSW gives an account of the episode in Nicolson, *Portrait*, 118–21.

Bolt Court: a small street in the City of London, off Fleet Street. Dr Johnson (see next note) lived at 8 Bolt Court from 1776 to his death.

Dr Johnson, Mr Boswell, and Mrs Williams: Dr Samuel Johnson (1709–84), author and lexicographer; James Boswell (1740–95), lawyer, diarist, and biographer of Johnson; Anna Williams (d. 1783), poet. Boswell and Williams shared Johnson's house from the 1750s onwards.

130 *Hampstead* (214): in the eighteenth century, a rural area to the north of London.

Highgate: to the east of Hampstead, in the eighteenth century Highgate was also rural in character.

132 *fitful gusts*: the distinctive quality of the weather owes something to that identified by the Victorian art-critic and writer John Ruskin (1819–1900) in his lecture 'The Storm Cloud of the Nineteenth Century' (1884): there, he complained of a modern 'plague wind' that 'always blows tremulously' 'with a peculiar fitfulness' (Ruskin, *Selected Writings*, ed. D. Birch (Oxford: Oxford World's Classics, 2004), 271).

the brothers Adam: the four Adam brothers, particularly Robert (1728–92) and James (1732–94), were pioneers in the adaptation of classical forms to domestic architecture throughout the British Isles in the eighteenth century.

133 *obfusc* (219): VW's own coinage, apparently meaning 'obfuscated', but also echoing 'subfusc', a word originally meaning 'Of a dark, dusky, or dull colour; sombre, subdued, gloomy' (*OED*), but most often used with reference to clothing worn in formal academic contexts at the University of Oxford. In July 1927 VW had used the word in relation to Lord Sackville, who had been at VSW's house while VW was visiting: 'I found him smooth & ambling as a blood horse, but obliterated, obfusc, with his great Sackville eyes drooping, & his face all clouded with red & brown' (*Diary*, iii. 145).

133 *Eusebius Chubb*: Chubb's first name may be borrowed from the pen name
     of Edmund Rack (*c.*1735–87), writer on agriculture, or that of Joseph
     Robertson (1726–1802), Church of England clergyman and writer.

     scrolloping: see note to p. 62.

134 *clouds . . . like whales*: the clouds' shapes recall Hamlet's quibbling with
     Polonius about a cloud shaped like a camel, or a weasel, or 'like a whale'
     (*Hamlet*, III.ii.366–72).

     St James's Park: a park in central London, to the east of Buckingham Pal-
     ace. Given the next location named, it seems that Orlando is driving along
     the Mall, to the north-west of the park.

     where the statue of Queen Victoria now stands: the Queen Victoria Memor-
     ial, to the west of St James's Park, in front of Buckingham Palace; it was
     unveiled in 1911 (*LE*, 673–4).

     crystal palaces: a reference to the Crystal Palace, a glass and steel structure
     erected in Hyde Park for the Great Exhibition of 1851, and afterwards
     removed to Sydenham Hill in south London; it was destroyed by fire
     in 1936.

     bassinettes: Wickerwork baskets, with a hood over one end, used as a cradle
     for babies.

135 *sponge-bag trousers*: men's checked trousers; the checked pattern was com-
     mon on bags used to carry bathroom sponges.

     Constitution Hill: a road running east–west from the Queen Victoria
     Memorial to Duke of Wellington Place.

136 *'A crinoline'*: a form of petticoat or underskirt common in the mid-
     nineteenth century. Made of stiff fabric and often reinforced with rigid
     hoops, it supported skirts of a large diameter. By the early twentieth cen-
     tury it had become emblematic of the difference of the Victorians from
     later generations.

     Lord Burghley: William Cecil, 1st Baron Burghley (1520/1–98), royal
     minister. He was father of Robert Cecil, 1st Earl of Salisbury (1563–1612),
     politician and courtier, referred to later.

     'Little man . . . to princes?': Orlando recalls an anecdote of Queen Eliza-
     beth's last days: 'When Robert Cecil declared that she "must" go to bed
     the word roused her like a trumpet. "Must!" she exclaimed; "is *must*
     a word to be addressed to princes? Little man, little man! thy father, if he
     had been alive, durst not have used that word"' (J. R. Green, *History of
     the English People*, 4 vols. (London: Macmillan, 1877–80), ii. 499).

     black bombazine: bombazine is a dress material with twilled or corded
     ridges; in black it was often worn for mourning.

137 *the spirit of the age*: a common translation of *Zeitgeist* (German), and the
     title of a collection of essays (1825) by William Hazlitt (1778–1830).

Queen Victoria is on the throne: Victoria (1819–1901) came to the throne in 1837.

138 *to . . . caracole*: to move in a zigzag.

I am myself . . . Murmur—: the stanzas from 'Lines of Life' by Letitia Elizabeth Landon (1802–38) had been reprinted in *L.E.L.*, *A Mystery of the Thirties*, by D. E. Enfield, 57–8, published by the Hogarth Press in March 1928, and advertised on the jacket of *Orlando*. The full poem is twenty-seven stanzas long. Woolf omits one stanza between the two quoted:

> My first, my last, my only wish,
> Say, will my charmed chords
> Wake to the morning light of fame,
> And breathes [*sic*] again my words?

The final truncated line in the quotation runs 'Murmur some song of mine?' (Enfield, *L.E.L.*, 58).

She was so changed . . . tomb: this passage is extracted from a longer poem by Landon, first published as 'Fragment' in the *Literary Gazette* in 1818; it also appears in Enfield's Hogarth Press book (*L.E.L.*, 60).

she became conscious, as she stood at the window . . . as if she were made of a thousand wires . . . playing scales: the passage suggests the Aeolian harp, a stringed instrument which produces musical tones when the wind blows across it. In Romantic poetry, it became an emblem of poetic inspiration, as in S. T. Coleridge's poem 'The Eolian Harp' (1795).

140 *pinchbeck*: an alloy of copper and zinc which resembles gold, and is used in cheap jewellery.

Lord Melbourne: William Lamb, 2nd Viscount Melbourne (1779–1848), prime minister from 1834 to 1841. That he is 'said to be fond of women' refers to his multiple romantic affairs: in 1836 he was cited in divorce proceedings.

141 *the lines of her character were fixed*: it was commonly believed that women's characters were fixed at or around the age of 30. The anti-feminist Mrs Archibald Colquhoun had written that 'After the age of thirty the average woman gets more "set" in her ways, is less adaptable, just as her body is less pliant' (*The Vocation of Woman* (London: Macmillan, 1913), 314). As Bowlby notes, Sigmund Freud made a similar estimate in his essay 'Femininity' (1933) (Bowlby, 335).

142 *till death them do part*: a phrase derived from the Solemnization of Matrimony from the Church of England's Book of Common Prayer.

the Archduke . . . had married a very great lady: in 1922, Henry George Charles Lascelles, 6th Earl of Harewood (1882–1947), formerly one of VSW's suitors, had married Princess Mary, the only daughter of King George V.

142 *made sacks in Botany Bay*: he had been transported to a penal colony in
Australia.

143 *Sir Bedivere . . . Arthur*: in Arthurian legend, when Sir Bedivere throws
King Arthur's sword Excalibur into a lake, an arm rises from the water,
catches the sword, and vanishes with it.

heather roots . . . the moor: the paragraph recalls several details from Emily
Brontë's *Wuthering Heights* (1847). The detail about the 'wild birds'
feathers' recalls the scene in chapter 12 where Catherine Earnshaw (Mrs
Linton) tears open a pillow and examines the feathers, finding a turkey's,
a wild duck's, and a pigeon's.

145 *Marmaduke Bonthrop Shelmerdine*: the name Marmaduke has never been
common except in a small area of North Yorkshire. The most prominent
person by this name in the period was the writer and translator Marmaduke Pickthall (1875–1936). 'Bonthrop' has no significant antecedents.
The surname Shelmerdine almost certainly derives from the heroine of
a series of novels and stories by Michael Arlen (born Dikran Kouyoumdjian, 1895–1956). Shelmerdene [*sic*] had first appeared in *The London
Venture* (London: Heinemann, 1920) (parts of which had appeared in the
periodical *The New Age* from 1918 onwards), where she is characterized
as a 'delightful adventuress' (*London Venture*, 28); she reappeared in *These
Charming People* (London: Collins, 1923) and in *May Fair* (London: Collins, 1925).

146 *a ship in full sail*: in her diary, VW often wrote of VSW in similar terms:
'her being so much in full sail on the high tides, where I am coasting down
backwaters' (21 December 1925, *Diary*, iii. 52); 'like some tall sailing ship'
(23 January 1927, *Diary*, iii. 125); 'giving me great pleasure to watch &
recalling some image of a ship breasting a sea' (4 July 1927, *Diary*, iii. 146).
In VW's *Night and Day* (1919), Ralph Denham uses the phrase 'like a ship
in full sail' in relation to Katharine Hilbery (*Night and Day*, ed. Suzanne
Raitt (Oxford: Oxford World's Classics, 1992), 346).

He had a castle in the Hebrides, but it was ruined: as well as referring to
Harold Nicolson's Scottish ancestry, the lines also suggest *To the Lighthouse*, in which the Ramsay family's holiday home in the Hebrides falls
into delapidation.

'For the Horn': Cape Horn, the southernmost tip of the Tierra Del Fuego
peninsula of South America, and a notoriously dangerous stretch of
water.

147 *we leave a great blank here*: while visually the blank lines recall Woolf's
Jacob's Room (1922), which made creative use of blank space, the self-
consciousness with which the space is introduced recalls Laurence
Sterne's *Tristram Shandy* (1759–67).

Peelers: policemen, named informally after Sir Robert Peel (1788–1850),
British politician and prime minister (1834–5, 1841–6), who established
police forces in Ireland and in London.

148 *taking up . . . a stand with his hands behind him in front of the fireplace*: the
image may recall Harold Nicolson, whom VW recorded in July 1924 'sitting on the iron bar before the great burning logs' (*Diary*, ii. 307).

'*The lawsuits are settled*': as well as the 1913 lawsuit referred to earlier (note
to p. 112), in 1909–10, following the death of Lord Sackville in 1908, Vita's
mother had been involved in a legal battle over the inheritance of Knole.
See Nicolson, *Portrait*, 64–7.

Lord Palmerston: Henry John Temple, 3rd Viscount Palmerston (1784–
1865), prime minister 1855–8 and 1858–65.

barouches and landaus: a barouche is 'A four-wheeled carriage with a half-
head behind which can be raised or let down at pleasure, having a seat
in front for the driver, and seats inside for two couples to sit facing each
other', and a landau 'A four-wheeled carriage, the top of which, being
made in two parts, may be closed or thrown open' (*OED*).

Rat and Sparrow clubs: clubs for the extermination of pests.

149 *Mrs W. E. Gladstone*: Catherine Gladstone (née Glynne) (1812–1900),
philanthropist and wife of William Ewert Gladstone (1809–98), politician
and prime minister.

Mar: VSW's pet name, used by her mother and her husband.

150 *read Pascal*: the French mathematician, physicist, and moralist Blaise Pascal (1623–62). VW's library contained several editions of his *Pensées*, and
a multi-volume edition of his works.

Bishop Berkeley's philosophy: George Berkeley (1685–1753), Church of
Ireland bishop of Cloyne and philosopher, held that objects of perception
had no existence independent of their being perceived. VW had read some
of his works in 1920 (*Diary*, ii. 33, 36).

Lady Palmerston or Lady Derby: the wives of politicians: Emily Mary Tem-
ple (née Lamb), Viscountess Palmerston (1787–1869), who married Lord
Palmerston in 1839; and Mary Catherine Stanley (née Sackville-West),
Countess of Derby (1824–1900), who married Edward Henry Stanley,
15th Earl of Derby (1826–93), following the death of her first husband,
James Gascoyne-Cecil, 2nd Marquess of Salisbury (1791–1868).

151 *Shelley*: Percy Bysshe Shelley (1795–1822), English Romantic poet.

154 *And then . . . like Egyptian Girls—*: the lines are from the 'Spring' section
of VSW's *The Land* (1927), 44.

Wordsworth . . . sanctions it: William Wordsworth (1770–1850), English
Romantic poet. In October 1926, introducing VSW's talk 'Tradition in
English Poetry' at the Royal Society of Literature, Edmund Gosse had
described *The Land* as 'A poem of which neither Tennyson nor Wordsworth
need have been ashamed' (VSW to Harold Nicolson, 26 October 1926,
Vita and Harold: The Letters of Vita Sackville-West and Harold Nicolson,
ed. Nigel Nicolson (London: Weidenfeld and Nicolson, 1992), 166–7).

154 *to compare great things with small*: a phrase that may have been familiar
    from translations of Virgil's *Georgics* (iv. 176) or Milton's *Paradise Lost*
    (ii. 921–2).

155 *the Hogarth Press*: the publishers of the first trade edition of *Orlando*; the
    Press had been established by Leonard and Virginia Woolf in 1917, and
    had published all her novels from *Jacob's Room* (1922) onwards.

    wool-gathering: 'indulging in wandering thoughts or idle fancies' (*OED*).
    On 18 February 1928, while writing the last chapter of *Orlando*, VW wrote
    in her diary that 'My mind is woolgathering about Women & Fiction,
    which I am to read at Newnham [College, Cambridge] in May' (*Diary*,
    iii. 175). Mrs Ramsay also uses the phrase in *To the Lighthouse* (1927), ed.
    D. Bradshaw (Oxford: Oxford World's Classics, 2006), 57.

157 *Love . . . is woman's whole existence*: VW alludes to Lord Byron's lines from
    Don Juan (1819): 'Man's love is of man's life a thing apart | 'Tis woman's
    whole existence' (canto i, stanza 194).

    gamekeeper: the passage that follows suggests that Woolf may have been
    familiar, at least in outline, with D. H. Lawrence's *Lady Chatterley's Lover*,
    in which Constance Chatterley has an affair with Mellors, the gamekeeper
    on her husband's estate. However, as *Lady Chatterley* was not published
    until July 1928, and Woolf had completed her revisions of *Orlando* by
    mid-June 1928, it is highly improbable that she had read the text itself.
    A more probable source is E. M. Forster's *Maurice*, which VW had read in
    manuscript in 1915; it was published posthumously in 1971.

158 *wine-blue purple-dark hill*: the phrase incorporates the well-known
    Homeric epithet for the sea, 'wine-dark'.

159 *Blackfriars . . . Salvation Army*: the Salvation Army was (and is) a revival-
    ist Christian missionary organization, founded in the 1860s by William
    Booth (1829–1912). Since the 1890s it had run a shelter for homeless men
    at 115a Blackfriars Road, on the south side of the Thames in Southwark.
    In 1926 its next-door neighbour was a boot repair shop, but there were no
    fewer than two umbrella handle manufacturers on the road.

161 *penny-a-liner*: a phrase (first recorded in the 1830s) for writers who were
    not salaried but paid by the line, and who thus had little incentive to
    brevity.

    Litt.D.: Doctor of Literature, a title awarded as an honorary degree by
    many British universities.

    sprucely dressed: in May 1919 VW described Logan Pearsall Smith as
    'a very spruce man' (*Letters*, ii. 358), and the epithet stuck: in early June
    1927, she described him as 'pink & spruce' (*Diary*, iii. 137).

162 *Tennyson, Browing, Carlyle*: in the late nineteenth century, all three were
    numbered among the leading literary figures of the age. For Tennyson, see
    note to p. 121; Robert Browning (1812–89), poet; Thomas Carlyle (1795–
    1881), author, biographer, and historian.

he had lived long in America: of the two principal models for Greene, Logan Pearsall Smith was American-born, while Edmund Gosse had lectured there in the 1880s.

163 *Addison's Cato*: a tragic drama in blank verse by Joseph Addison, first performed in 1713.

Thomson's Seasons: a series of four poems concerned with nature and farming published 1726–30 by James Thomson (1700–48). As an English georgic poem, it influenced VSW's *The Land*.

164 *hansom cabs . . . barouche landau*: horse-drawn carriages. A hansom is a two-wheeled carriage intended to carry two passengers; a barouche landau is a four-wheeled carriage intended to carry four passengers with two facing double seats inside.

a cypher language: VSW and Harold Nicolson used private codewords when communicating by telegram.

165 *Spenser*: Edmund Spenser (1552?–1599), poet and administrator in Ireland.

Duke of Hamilton . . . Lord Mohun: James Hamilton, 4th Duke of Hamilton and 1st Duke of Brandon (1658–1712), died on 15 November 1712 following a duel in Hyde Park with Charles Mohun, 4th Baron Mohun (1675–1712), who also died of his injuries.

166 *John Donne*: Donne was an interest shared by two of the possible models for Sir Nicholas Greene, Edmund Gosse and Logan Pearsall Smith. Gosse had written *The Life and Letters of John Donne, Dean of St Paul's* (1889), while Smith had edited *Donne's Sermons: Selected Passages* (1919).

the Serpentine: a lake in Hyde Park, central London. The account of the sinking boat in the following paragraph may derive from a childhood memory later recounted by VW in 'Sketch of the Past' (*Moments of Being*, 89).

two dogs dancing on their hind legs: a glance at Dr Johnson's notorious misogynistic remark 'Sir, a woman's preaching is like a dog's walking on his hinder legs. It is not done well; but you are surprized to find it done at all' (James Boswell, *The Life of Samuel Johnson, LLD* (1791), ed. G. B. Hill (Oxford: Clarendon Press, 1887), i. 463).

Lamb: Charles Lamb (1775–1834), essayist; Lamb was among Woolf's favourite nineteenth-century essayists.

Tupper . . . Smiles: the names suggest two nineteenth-century writers, Martin Farquhar Tupper (1810–89), best known for *Proverbial Philosophy* (1838), and Samuel Smiles (1812–1904), best known for *Self-Help* (1859).

167 *eight-hour bills . . . covenants . . . factory acts*: references to Victorian legislation that aimed to regulate working conditions.

it's ecstasy that matters. Thus she spoke aloud: Orlando echoes Katharine Hilbery, heroine of VW's *Night and Day*, who distractedly quotes Dostoevsky as she walks through central London, saying 'It's life that matters, nothing but life' (*Night and Day*, chapters 10 and 11).

167 *Stanhope Gate*: a short street in Mayfair, leading from Park Lane to South Audley Street; it was formerly known as Great Stanhope Street. In John Galsworthy's *The Man of Property* (1906) (the first volume of *The Forsyte Saga*), it is the address of the old patriarch of the Forsyte family, old Jolyon.

168 *four-in-hand, victoria*: a four-in-hand is a horse-drawn carriage with four horses driven by one person; a victoria is a 'light, low, four-wheeled carriage having a collapsible hood, with seats (usually) for two persons and an elevated seat in front for the driver' (*OED*).

Curzon Street: a street in Mayfair, running from Park Lane in the west, running eastwards and curving northwards to Fitzmaurice Place at its other end.

Alexander Smiths . . . Jamesons: names of eminent Victorian writers: Alexander Smith (1829–67), poet and essayist; Richard Watson Dixon (1833–1900), ecclesiastical historian and poet; Adam Black (1784–1874), publisher and politician, or William Black (1841–98), journalist and novelist; Henry Hart Milman (1791–1868), historian and dean of St Paul's; Henry Thomas Buckle (1821–62), historian, whose *History of Civilisation* is also alluded to in *Mrs Dalloway* (p. 72); Hippolyte Adolphe Taine (1828–93), philosopher, critic, and historian; Edward John Payne (1844–1904), historian, or Leslie Stephen's friend James Payne (1830–98); Tupper (see note to p. 166); Anna Brownell Jameson (née Murphy) (1794–1860), writer and art historian.

169 *octavo*: a format of book smaller than the folio or quarto formats, and often considered a cheaper or more popular format; the page size was determined by the size of a sheet folded thrice to form eight leaves.

Miss Christina Rossetti: Christina Rossetti (1830–94), poet.

the Influence of this upon that: in VW's *To the Lighthouse*, Mrs Ramsay's approximate understanding of Charles Tansley's dissertation is that it concerns 'the influence of something upon somebody' (p. 14).

Carlyle's sound-proof room in Chelsea: in 1853–4 Thomas Carlyle had a study built on the top floor of his house at 5 (now 24) Cheyne Row, Chelsea, with double walls to provide soundproofing.

Chesterfield House: a Palladian-style mansion in Mayfair, central London, built 1748–9 for Philip, 4th Earl of Chesterfield (for whom see note to p. 124); it was bordered by Curzon Street to the south, South Audley Street to the west, and Chesterfield Street to the east. It was demolished in 1937.

170 *Kew*: the Royal Botanic Gardens at Kew, to the south-west of London.

outrigger: Kew Gardens are by the River Thames; the outrigger is a rowing boat ('outrigger' (noun), *OED*, 3b.).

171 *half-crown tickets*: in the pre-decimal system, half a crown was two shillings and sixpence.

dark flows the stream: possibly a recollection of 'Songs of the Winter Days' by George MacDonald (1824–1905), Scottish poet and novelist. The relevant stanza runs:

> Dark flows the stream as if it mourned
> The winter in the land;
> By frosty idleness adorned
> That mill-wheel soon will stand.
>
> (MacDonald, *The Disciple*
> (London: Strahan, 1867), 69)

172 *King Edward*: Edward VII (1841–1910), reigned 1901–10.

brougham: a carriage drawn by a single horse, for two or four passengers.

a certain lady opposite: Alice Frederica Keppel (née Edmonstone) (1868–1947), King Edward VII's mistress from 1898 to his death. One of her daughters was VSW's lover Violet Trefusis (1894–1972). Trefusis claimed in later life that King Edward was her biological father, but this is unlikely.

men's faces were as bare as the palm of one's hand: the popularity of beards as a sign of masculinity had begun to wane in the 1890s (Christopher Oldstone-Moore, 'The Beard Movement in Victorian Britain', *Victorian Studies*, 48/1 (2005), 7–34), and suffered a further decline as a generational reaction against the perception of the Victorians and the First World War generals as bewhiskered.

173 *It was the eleventh of October. It was 1928. It was the present moment*: *Orlando* was published on 11 October 1928.

174 *Marshall & Snelgrove's*: a department store at 334–8 Oxford Street.

The Cumberlands had a house in Portland Place: Portland Place is a broad street in central London, running from Regent Street in the south to the Marylebone Road in the north. Though many titled families lived there, the Cumberlands could not have done so in 1928: the title of Duke of Cumberland had belonged to Prince Ernest Augustus of Hanover (1845–1923), but he was stripped of it in 1919 under the Titles Deprivation Act (1917), for having sided with Germany during the 1914–18 war.

175 *Louise then*: the name comes from Louise Genoux, VSW's maid at her house, Long Barn.

the Prince Consort. 'Sale bosch!' ... another war: Prince Albert (1819–61), Queen Victoria's husband, was German. Louise calls him a 'filthy hun'; the war was the First World War (1914–18).

she was now thirty-six: VSW's thirty-sixth birthday was on 9 March 1928.

177 *the Dictionary of National Biography*: a multi-volume reference work containing brief biographies of great men and women of British history,

founded by the publisher George Smith in 1882, with VW's father Leslie
Stephen as its first editor. The first volume appeared in 1885; Stephen
stepped down as editor in 1891.

177 *The Old Kent Road*: a road in south-east London running from Southwark
to New Cross, serving as one of the major routes out of the city in the
direction of Kent.

'*Ra—Un*': Gilbert suggests the banners may say 'Rally of the Unem-
ployed' or 'Rally Against Unemployment' (*Orlando*, ed. Sandra Gilbert
(Harmondsworth: Penguin, 1992), 262–3).

Amor Vin: almost certainly a fragment of 'Amor Vincit Omnia' (Latin,
'love conquers all').

180 *that don't count*: 'don't' was a common contraction of 'does not' among the
upper classes at the time. See, e.g., VW to VSW, 24 June 1926: 'you sell,
and she dont' (*Letters*, iii. 394).

Seven editions. A prize: VSW's *The Land* did not reach its seventh reprint
until December 1929. Putting 'The Oak Tree' into seven editions may be
a play on the name of the town Sevenoaks, adjacent to Knole. *The Land*
had won the Hawthornden Prize in 1927.

'*The Burdett Coutts' Memorial Prize*': the name of this fictitious literary
prize recalls Angela Georgina Burdett-Coutts (1814–1906), a philanthropist and keen collector of antiquarian books and paintings.

the accent never falls where it does with a man: VW echoes her own
description of modern fiction: 'the accent falls differently from of old;
the moment of importance came not here but there' ('Modern Fiction'
(1925), in *Essays*, iv. 158).

A porpoise in a fishmonger's shop: the image recalls a time that VW had met
VSW in a shop in Sevenoaks. In her diary in December 1925 the shop was
a grocer's: 'she shines in the grocers shop in Sevenoaks with a candle lit
radiance, stalking on legs like beech trees, pink glowing, grape clustered,
pearl hung' (*Diary*, iii. 52), and on the following day uses the same imagery
in a letter to VSW (*Letters*, iii. 224). In later letters the shop becomes
a fishmonger's: 'I don't find much of that festal light, though, which
stands in the door of the Sevenoaks fishmonger' (25 December 1926, *Letters*, iii. 309); 'I do miss you. There's no fishmonger and porpoise in my
life without you' (6 March 1928, *Letters*, iii. 468).

181 *flowering trees*: Nicolson notes that VSW used her prize money to plant nut
trees at her home, Long Barn (Bowlby, 339).

182 *enclosed them completely*: in September 1928 VW wrote in an essay on
Laurence Sterne that 'No writing seems to flow more exactly into the very
folds and creases of the individual mind, to express its changing moods, to
answer its lightest whim and impulse, and yet the result is perfectly precise
and composed. The utmost fluidity exists with the utmost permanence'
(VW, 'A Sentimental Journey', in *Essays*, v. 403).

red Spanish wine: in October 1926, VSW had asked a wine merchant to send VW a dozen bottles of Spanish wine (*Letters of VSW to VW*, 160), and VW had later mentioned getting 'tipsy' on Spanish wine (16 February 1927, *Letters*, iii. 330). Nigel Nicolson notes that VSW's favourite Spanish wine was Allella (Bowlby, 339).

183 *She fancied that the rooms . . . opened their eyes*: VW's personification of Orlando's house may owe something to the opening pages of VSW's *Knole*: 'It has the deep inward gaiety of some very old woman who has always been beautiful, who has had many lovers and seen many generations come and go, smiled wisely over their sorrows and their joys, and learnt an imperishable secret of tolerance and humour' (*Knole*, 2).

the Ambassador's bedroom: the Venetian ambassador's bedroom at Knole merits a lyrical description in VSW's *Knole* (pp. 15–16).

184 *Cecil*: beginning with the royal minister William Cecil, 1st Baron Burghley (1520/1–98), the Cecil family were powerful and influential in sixteenth- and seventeenth-century political life.

Lady Betty's table: VSW gives several pages of *Knole* to descriptions of Lady Betty Germain (Germaine in VSW's spelling) (1680–1769) and her rooms (*Knole*, 12–13, 167–72).

a tunnel bored deep into the past: in 1927, after she had been taken on a tour of Knole by VSW, VW recorded that 'All the centuries seemed lit up, the past expressive, articulate; not dumb & forgotten; but a crowd of people stood behind, not dead at all; not remarkable; fair faced, long limbed; affable; & so we reach the days of Elizabeth quite easily' (23 January 1927, *Diary*, iii. 125).

Poitiers: Poitiers, in central France, was the scene of a major battle in the Hundred Years War on 19 September 1356. One of VSW's ancestors Sir Thomas Sackville (*c*.1336–1406) was active in the wars in France.

188 *a cheque for two hundred guineas*: in 1927 VSW was awarded the Hawthornden Prize for her long poem *The Land*; VW and Leonard Woolf attended the presentation of the prize on 16 June, and VW's diary refers to the literary 'gentry' 'on the platform'. At £100, the prize was less than Orlando's two hundred guineas (£210). There is no record that John Drinkwater, who presented the prize, compared VSW to Milton, but he discussed it as a long poem, and it is possible that he invoked Milton's *Paradise Lost* (1667).

189 *Nelson*: Horatio Nelson (1758–1805), naval officer and hero of many naval battles; he lost his life at the Battle of Trafalgar.

190 *baring her breast to the moon*: Orlando's actions echo those of Ursula Brangwen in D. H. Lawrence's *The Rainbow* (1915): 'She turned, and saw a great white moon looking at her over the hill. And her breast opened to it, she was cleaved like a transparent jewel to its light' (*The Rainbow*, ed. Kate Flint (Oxford: Oxford University Press, 1997), 317).

LIST OF NAMES

Bell, Angelica (1918–2012). VW's niece, whose 'service' was to pose for the plate 'The Russian Princess as a Child'.

Bell, Clive (1881–1964). Art critic and writer; husband of VW's sister, Vanessa.

Bell, Colonel Cory (1875–1961). Lieutenant-Colonel William Cory Bell; Clive Bell's brother.

Bell, Julian (1908–37). Elder son of Vanessa and Clive Bell.

Bell, Quentin (1910–96). Younger son of Vanessa and Clive Bell.

Bell, Vanessa (1879–1961). Artist; sister of VW.

Berners, Lord (1883–1950). Gerald Hugh Tyrwhitt-Wilson, 14th Baron Berners. Composer, and acquaintance of VW.

Birrell, Francis (1889–1935). Literary journalist.

Boxall, Nelly (1890–1965). Leonard Woolf and VW's live-in servant from 1916.

Brontë, Emily (1818–48). Novelist.

Browne, Sir Thomas (1605–82). Writer and doctor.

Cartwright, Mrs. Worked at the Hogarth Press from 1925 to 1930.

Case, Janet (1862–1937). Classical scholar who taught VW Greek.

Cecil, Viscountess (1868–1959). Lady Eleanor (Nelly) Cecil, a friend of VW.

Colefax, Lady (1874–1950). Society hostess.

Davidson, Angus (1898–1980). An assistant at the Hogarth Press, 1924–7.

Defoe, Daniel (1660–1731). Novelist.

De Quincey, Thomas (1785–1859). Essayist.

Dickinson, Violet (1865–1948). One of VW's longest-standing friends.

Eliot, T. S. (1888–1965). Poet and critic.

Eliot, Vivien (1888–1947). Writer; wife of T. S. Eliot.

Forster, E. M. (1879–1970). Novelist; friend of VW.

Grant, Duncan (1885–1978). Painter and decorative artist; Vanessa Bell's lover; father of Angelica Bell.

Hudson, Nan (1896–1957). Anna Hope Hudson, painter.

Hutchinson, St John (1884–1942). Barrister; friend of VW.

Keynes, J. M. (1883–1946). Economist; husband of Lydia Lopokova; friend of VW.

Lopokova, Lydia (1892–1981). Ballet dancer; wife of J. M. Keynes.

Macaulay, Lord (1800–59). Thomas Babington Macaulay, historian, essayist, and poet.

MacCarthy, Desmond (1877–1952). Literary reviewer; husband of Molly MacCarthy; friend of VW.

MacCarthy, Molly (1882–1953). Writer; wife of Desmond MacCarthy; friend of VW.

Mirrlees, Hope (1887–1978). Writer and poet; acquaintance of VW.

Morrell, Ottoline (1873–1938). Literary hostess.

Mortimer, Raymond (1895–1980). Writer on literature and art critic.

Nicolson, Harold (1886–1968). Diplomat and writer; husband of Vita Sackville-West.

Pater, Walter (1839–94). Author and aesthete.

Raverat, Gwen (1885–1957). Artist and friend of VW.

Rylands, G. H. (1902–99). 'Dadie' Rylands; worked briefly at the Hogarth Press in 1924; fellow of King's College, Cambridge.

Sackville West, Edward (1901–65). Novelist and music critic; Vita Sackville-West's cousin.

Sands, Ethel (1873–1962). Painter and hostess.

Sanger, C. P. (1871–1930). Barrister; friend of VW.

Scott, Sir Walter (1771–1832). Poet and novelist.

Sheppard, John T. (1881–1968). Classical scholar; friend of VW.

Sitwell, Osbert (1892–1969). Writer.

Snowdon, M. K. (1878–1966?). Friend of VW and of Vanessa Bell.

Stephen, Adrian (1883–1948). VW's brother.

Sterne, Laurence (1713–68), author of *The Life and Opinions of Tristram Shandy* (1759–67).

Strachey, Lytton (1880–1932). Biography and literary reviewer; friend of VW.

Sydney-Turner, Saxon (1880–1962). Civil servant; close friend of VW, Leonard Woolf, and Lytton Strachey.

Taylor, Valerie (b. 1902). Actress; briefly Clive Bell's lover in 1927.

Tomlin, Stephen (1901–37). Sculptor.

Waley, Arthur (1889–1966). Translator of Chinese and Japanese literature.

Walpole, Hugh (1884–1941). Novelist.

Wellesley, Dorothy (1889–1956). Poet; dedicatee of Vita Sackville-West's *The Land*.

Woolf, Bella (1877–1960). Bella Southorn; Leonard Woolf's sister.

American Literature

British and Irish Literature

Children's Literature

Classics and Ancient Literature

Colonial Literature

Eastern Literature

European Literature

Gothic Literature

History

Medieval Literature

Oxford English Drama

Philosophy

Poetry

Politics

Religion

The Oxford Shakespeare

A complete list of Oxford World's Classics, including Authors in Context, Oxford English Drama, and the Oxford Shakespeare, is available in the UK from the Marketing Services Department, Oxford University Press, Great Clarendon Street, Oxford OX2 6DP, or visit the website at www.oup.com/uk/worldsclassics.

In the USA, visit www.oup.com/us/owc for a complete title list.

Oxford World's Classics are available from all good bookshops. In case of difficulty, customers in the UK should contact Oxford University Press Bookshop, 116 High Street, Oxford OX1 4BR.